Scottish Migration Since 1750

Reasons and Results

James C. Docherty

Hamilton Books

An Imprint of
Rowman & Littlefield
Lanham • Boulder • New York • Toronto • Plymouth, UK

Copyright © 2016 by James C. Docherty

Hamilton Books
4501 Forbes Boulevard, Suite 200, Lanham, Maryland 20706
Hamilton Books Acquisitions Department (301) 459-3366

Unit A, Whitacre Mews, 26-34 Stannary Street,
London SE11 4AB, United Kingdom

All rights reserved
Printed in the United States of America
British Library Cataloguing in Publication Information Available

Library of Congress Control Number: 2016937662
ISBN: 978-0-7618-6794-4 (pbk : alk. paper)—ISBN: 978-0-7618-6795-1 (electronic)

∞™ The paper used in this publication meets the minimum requirements of American National Standard for Information Sciences Permanence of Paper for Printed Library Materials, ANSI/NISO Z39.48-1992.

For the motherless children

Contents

List of Tables	ix
Preface	xi
Acknowledgments	xiii
Introduction	1
Confronting Caledonia	1
Historians and Population History	4
Family and Population History	5
Unlocking Migration	7
What This Book Offers	9
Highlands, Lowlands, and Clearances	11
1 Discovering the People	13
Scenery and Scarcity	13
A Blended People	15
Robert Wallace and the Population Debate	16
Alexander Webster's Scotland, c. 1751	19
Sir John Sinclair's Scotland, c. 1791	21
John Rickman and Scotland	23
Rev. Thomas Malthus and Scotland	24
How Many People?	27
Why Did the Population Grow after 1650?	30
A Mainly Female People?	32
James Cleland's Glasgow, 1820s	33
Enlightenment Indeed	34
What Were Their Names?	35
What Were Their Faiths?	37

	Were They Married?	38
	Household and Family Size	40
	Only Slow Improvement, 1750–1900	41
2	Scotland Made and Unmade	43
	Not the Land of Opportunity	44
	A Conscripted Urban People	45
	The Victorian Economy: Mixed Results	47
	Enter the Irish	49
	The Slow Death of Labor Demand, 1901–1971	51
3	No Simple Story	55
	Destination Ulster, 1608–c. 1720	55
	Scotland Revisited, c. 1720–1776	56
	Destination North America, c. 1720–1776	58
	The Expatriates Return, c. 1800–1820	61
	The Two Sides of Scottish Migration, 1840–1930	62
	How Many Left?	63
	Not All It Seemed	65
	Deciding to Go	66
	Helping the Poor and Getting Land, c. 1820–1880	67
	Looking for Work That Paid, c. 1870–1930	68
	Where Did They Come From?	69
	The Scottish Presence, c. 1930	69
	What Future?	70
	No Easy Answers	72
4	England	73
	The Manchester Scots, 1837	74
	Henry Mayhew's London Scots, 1856	75
	Important and Distinctive, 1820–1930	75
	North England and London, 1841–1931	76
	Presbyterianism	76
	Where Did They Come From?	77
	What Did They Do?	77
	Were They Married?	78
	Few Surprises	78
5	North America	79
	Making the Sources Speak	80
	Did They Stay?	82
	Where Did They Go?	84
	What Did They Do?	85
	What Were Their Names?	87
	What Did They Believe In?	88
	Were They Married?	88

	A World of Kith and Kin	89
	The 1900s	90
	Moving On	92
	John Kenneth Galbraith's *The Scotch*	92
	Reluctant Americans?	93
	How Well Did They Do?	93
	Southward Bound?	94
6	South Africa and Australasia	97
	A Variable Presence	97
	South Africa: Failure to Thrive	98
	Success in the Antipodes: Australia and New Zealand	99
	Gold and Distance	100
	Did They Stay?	101
	Governments Lend a Hand	102
	Where Did They Go?	103
	What Did They Do?	104
	Were They Married?	106
	Children	107
	What Did They Believe In?	108
	How Healthy Were They?	109
	Only If Necessary	109
7	A Changed World	111
	Still Distressed: Scotland c. 1930–1970	112
	First Choice: England	113
	Less Popular: Canada	114
	Not Really Wanted: United States	115
	Still Welcome: Australia and New Zealand	116
	Putting It Together	117
	The Man on the Bridge	120

Appendix A: Population Timeline	123
Appendix B: Scotland: The People's Names	137
Part 1: Scotland: Principal Family Names by Region and County, c. 1650	137
Appendix C: Some Vital Data	139
List of Tables	140
Bibliography	143
Introduction	143
Outline of the Bibliography	144
1. Bibliographies and Genealogical Research Guides	144
2. Scotland: General Surveys and Reference	145

3. Scotland: Population History and Related Studies	145
4. Immigration Encyclopedias and Population Histories	147
5. Robert Wallace and the Population Debate	147
6. Selected Pre-1830 Scottish Sources	148
7. Scottish Nationalism and Scotland's Future	148
8. Economic History	149
9. British Emigration	149
10. Scotland: Emigration and Immigration	150
11. Scottish-Born in Australia and New Zealand	152
12. Scottish-Born in Canada	152
13. Scottish-Born in the United States	153
14. Scottish-Born in Other Countries	153
15. Statistical Sources: Scotland	153
16. Statistical Sources: Scottish-Born Outside Scotland	154
17. Life Tables	157
18. Population and Related Works	160
Index	161
About the Author	165

List of Tables

All tables follow page 141.

Table 1. Scotland, Estimated Population, c. 1000–1821
Table 2. Scotland, Irish-Born, 1841–1931
Table 3. Scots-Born, Net Migration by Birth Region, 1871–1911
Table 4. Scots-Born Migration, England and Wales, 1820–1930
Table 5. Scots-Born, England and Wales by Region, 1841–1931
Table 6. Scots-Born, England and Wales by Birth Region, 1911
Table 7. Scots-Born Migration to Canada, 1820–1930
Table 8. Scots-Born Migration to the United States, 1820–1930
Table 9. Scots-Born Marital Status, Scotland, Canada, and the United States, c. 1880
Table 10. Scots-Born Birthplace of Spouses, Canada and United States, c. 1880
Table 11. Scots-Born Profile, Canada and United States, c. 1900
Table 12. Scots-Born Profile, Canada and United States, 1900s arrivals
Table 13. Scots-Born, South Africa, Australia and New Zealand, 1831–1931
Table 14. Scots-Born, Migration to Australia, 1830–1930
Table 15. Scots-Born, Migration to New Zealand, 1850–1930
Table 16. Scots-born, Migration to England and Wales, 1931–1991
Table 17. Scots-Born, Migration to Canada, 1931–1991
Table 18. Scots-Born, Migration to United States, 1930–1990
Table 19. Scots-Born, Migration to Australia, 1931–1991
Table 20. Scots-born, Migration to New Zealand, 1931–1991
Table 21. Scotland: The Most Common Family Names, 1858, 1935, and 1958

Table 22. Scotland: The Most Common Male First Names, 1858, 1935, and 1958
Table 23. Scotland: The Most Common Female First Names, 1858, 1935, and 1958
Table 24. Scotland, Population, Selected Features, c. 1000–2011
Table 25. Scotland, Births and Deaths, per thousand males, c. 1651–2012
Table 26. Scotland, Births and Deaths, per thousand females, c. 1651–2012
Table 27. Scotland, Life Expectancy at Birth and 20 Years by Sex, c. 1651–2012
Table 28. Scotland, Marital Status, Age 20 and Older by Sex, c. 1791–1971
Table 29. Scotland, Land Ownership by Large Owners and County, 1882
Table 30. Scotland, Labor Force, by Sex and Type 1841–1971
Table 31. Scotland, Urban-Rural Population, c. 1701–1971
Table 32. Scotland, Urban Population by Size of Center, percentage, c. 1751–1971
Table 33. Scots-Born Migration, thousands, 1820–1990
Table 34. Scots-Born Migration, by Sex, thousands, 1820–1930
Table 35. Scots-Born by Age and Sex, Scotland and outside Scotland, thousands, 1881
Table 36. Scots-Born by Age and Sex, Scotland and outside Scotland, thousands, 1931

Preface

Emotion, ignorance, and frustration prompted me to write this book. Researching my family origins made me realize how little I knew about either Scotland's population past or its migration history. Frustrated at not finding the book that I wanted, I thought that maybe others have had the same experience.

This may seem strange, as those wanting to investigate their Scottish roots are spoiled for choice of excellent guides. Two obvious examples are Adolph Anthony, *Collins' Tracing Your Scottish Family History* (2008), and Graham S. Holton and Jack Winch, *Discover Your Scottish Ancestry: Internet and Traditional Sources* (2004); and there are many others. But where do you go after you have put your findings together and want to know how they fit into the main historical trends? The answer is: nowhere. In my case I just wanted to know the circumstances behind my father coming to Australia in the late 1930s. It may seem that the subject had been well covered already, but this is not the case. Scotland since 1750 still tends to be treated as a lift-out supplement to British History Proper, and one that, some may consider, should be lifted out. Even worse, those familiar with Scotland's population and migration history might also consider that there is nothing new to say.

My response is that this subject, far from being finalized, is in need of substantial revision and not just for the Scots. So this book is designed to help those who have completed their Scottish family history and want to make historical sense of their findings. It links family history and historical demography by examining long-term economic and social trends, ignoring the froth of current events and the doings of the well documented. I hope that others will ask the questions of other nationalities that I have asked of the Scots.

Acknowledgments

The resources of the National Library of Australia and the Australian National University provided the main materials for this study. For assistance from outside Australia, I thank Andrew White, Population and Migration Statistics Branch, General Register Office for Scotland, and Adrian Gallop, Government Actuary's Department, London, for the supply of life tables for Scotland from 1891 to 1932. David Shelton at the Demography Division of National Records of Scotland saved me from gaffes in my lists of common Scottish names and Lynn Weber saved me from gaffes in general when she proofread my work. For the supply of Scottish census statistics for 1961, 1981, and 1991, I thank Linda Taylor, Customer Services, General Register Office for Scotland. Arvind Saharan at Statistics New Zealand supplied me with some census figures I did not have. For the information from the South African censuses for 1921, 1926, and 1936, I thank Ms. Naomi Billinghurst of the State Library of South Australia. I thank Alyson Hazlett of Statistics Canada for confirming the unavailability of unpublished data on Scots-born from the post-1961 population census. For advice regarding model life tables, I thank Dr. Rebecca Kippen of the Australian National University.

For advice, encouragement, and moral support, it is my pleasure to thank Professor Kris Inwood at Guelph University, Ontario. Without Professor Inwood, I would not have known about the North Atlantic Population Project. For extracting unpublished census tables for Scotland, England and Wales, Canada, and the United States from the Project, it truly is my pleasure to thank Brandon Tampe in Minneapolis, Minnesota, and Amy West, the Project's government documents librarian, for getting me information from the 1980 U.S. census. The obligations are entirely mine as are errors and misleading statements. The work is a tribute to all those who have gone before me, and in different ways they are remembered in the pages that follow.

James C. Docherty
Canberra

Introduction

The Scots have a mixed reputation. Dour, hardworking, brave in war, but tight-fisted, they have long had more than their fair share of ethnic stereotyping, a stereotyping fed by their own mythmaking. Clans, tartans, and bagpipes may be always associated with Scotland, but all came from Ireland. Scottish migrants were welcomed migrants and never subjected to discrimination. With their high level of literacy before the 1870s, they could be expected to succeed in their receiving countries in the nineteenth century and many did so. Celebrated for their achievements, they made a pleasing change from the underachieving Irish. Before the 1870s, Scots played their part in taking land from the indigenous peoples of North America and Australasia, a pioneering activity lauded in the nineteenth century but now considered distasteful as well as ironic for a people usually viewed as having been dispossessed of land in their own country. In more recent times, the rise of Scottish nationalism with its calls for independence from the rest of the United Kingdom has been greeted with a mixture of disbelief and denials of its financial practicality. Whatever may be said about the Scots, it would seem that they have lost none of their ability to inspire, irritate, and, above all, to remain interesting.

CONFRONTING CALEDONIA

For 400 years, the Scots have been famous for being in lands other than their own, whether as soldiers or settlers. Between 1820 and 1930 they left their country on a scale that has remained extraordinary, accounting for 2 million of the 50 million Europeans who made new lives primarily in North America and Australasia. Scottish emigration is important not just because of its scale but also because most of its migrants came from an urbanized, industrialized society, unlike Ireland or Norway. For most of the past 250 years, Scotland has been the textbook example of a Western country gripped by an ongoing demographic crisis, with emigration continuing until the late 1980s. This is the past that is confronted in this book. It is not about the Scotland of romantic myth, picturesque scenery, medieval battles, royal intrigues, or antiquarian curiosities; those wanting these topics should shut this book now. Instead it offers an analysis of how the Scottish population changed and why and how Scottish migration happened the way it did.

Scottish history was introduced into Scottish university teaching nearly a century ago by John D. Mackie (1887–1978) during his time as lecturer at the University of St Andrews. He became professor of Scottish history and literature at the University of Glasgow in 1930, a post he held for twenty-seven years. In keeping with the times, Scottish history was distant history. When Mackie published his popular Penguin *History of Scotland* in 1963, only a quarter of his text was devoted to the "modern" period, that is, after 1700. And it is only in relatively recent times that the historical study of Scotland has attracted detailed research. Scottish emigration received even less attention; it was an embarrassing, painful topic, a national affront. Apart from government officials, geographers at Edinburgh University were almost alone among academics from the 1920s in investigating Scotland's population directly, although economic historians dealt with it occasionally. The outstanding exception among historians was Donald F. Macdonald, whose Oxford doctoral thesis was published as *Scotland's Shifting Population, 1770–1850* in 1937. Using the insights of Arthur Redford's *Labour Migration in England, 1800–1850* (1926), he was the first to draw attention to the importance of Irish immigration and seasonal migration as well as emigration. In 1947 the distinguished Scottish constitutional lawyer Lord Thomas M. Cooper investigated the population of medieval Scotland in the *Scottish Historical Review*.

Scotland's geographers were mainly concerned with the changes in its population growth and distribution, publishing their work in the *Scottish Geographical Magazine*. In 1927, P. R. Crowe mapped the changes in the population of the Lowlands in detail between 1801 and 1921, and Andrew O'Dell surveyed population changes from 1755 to 1931 in 1932. They were followed by Catherine P. Snodgrass's survey of the 1920s and 1930s (1944) and a study of population and migration for the parish of North Uist by G. L. Davies in 1956. In 1958, another geographer, Richard H. Osborne, published the first general account of internal migration in Scotland between 1851 and 1951 in *Scottish Studies*.

The 1950s were notable also for the contribution made by James G. Kyd, the registrar general for Scotland, who published Alexander Webster's census of 1755 in 1952, and his successor, Edmund A. Hogan, who included a detailed survey of Scotland's population trends from 1861 to 1951 in his annual report for 1953. In 1954 the noted economist Sir Alec Cairncross edited *The Scottish Economy,* a wide-ranging study of Scottish society and economy contributed by the staff of Glasgow University and covering population, the economy, housing, health, and religion. In 1953 N. H. Carrier and J. R. Jeffery performed a valuable service with their *External Migration: A Study of the Available Statistics, 1815–1950* on behalf of the United Kingdom General Register Office and published as No. 6 in a series on medical and population topics. Prepared on a typewriter, it summarized the published British migration statistics up to 1950 for the United States, Canada, South Africa, and Australasia. It gave separate figures for the Scots and the Irish, and combined figures for the English and the Welsh. It is still an essential source but difficult to find.

Historians began to study Scottish migration in the 1960s, led by Charlotte J. Erickson who investigated the ages and occupations of English and Scottish immigrants to New York in the 19th century, onerous research based on microfilmed records. In 1966 Gordon Donaldson published a survey, *The Scots Overseas*. Migration studies generally were boosted in 1980 with the publication of the *Harvard Encyclopedia of American Ethnic Groups*. It contained two large entries on the Scots and the Scotch-Irish, entries that brought together a wealth of US scholarship, inspiring similar encyclopedias for Australia and Canada. The entries summarized the conditions in the country of emigration and reviewed the activities and achievements of each immigrant group in the United States.

Scottish population history languished until 1977 when Michael Flinn, a distinguished economic historian, led a research team of Judith Gillespie, Nancy Hill, Ailsa Maxwell, Rosalind Mitchison, Christopher Smout, Duncan Adamson, and Robin Lobban that produced their landmark work, *Scottish Population History* (1977). In keeping with the population studies at the time, its main concerns were fertility and mortality but it included a chapter on migration, which the authors admitted to be "cursory." Seven years in the making, Flinn's book was a significant advance for its day, but it only went up to 1938 and it gave most attention to the period before 1900. Although it did made good use of the computers of its day, these were primitive, unfriendly devices and the team lacked what it really needed—spreadsheets—denying them the opportunity to easily check whether population models fitted the Scottish population and to carry out modeling. There was no follow-up to Flinn's large-scale, long-time-period approach. Duncan Macniven, the registrar general for Scotland, offered a general survey of Scottish population history from 1855 in his annual report for 2004 to mark the 150th anniversary of the work of the Office of the Registrar General and this was followed by a brief history of the Scottish census by Ian White in the Office's annual report for 2009.

Before the 1980s, the academic study of Scottish migration tended to treat it more as a subset of British migration rather than a topic in its own right. The correction was started by David Dobson and Thomas M. Devine, who investigated Scottish migration to the Americas. In 1994, T. C. Smout, Ned C. Landsman, and Thomas M. Devine published their general study of Scottish migration that grew out of an international conference on European migration before 1800, which had not originally planned to include Scotland. The research was joined by Marjory Harper from 1988. She carried out the first scholarly investigation of Scottish migration in the 1920s and 1930s and was one of the few researchers to recognize the importance of return migration. In 2011, Thomas M. Devine published the culmination of his many years of research in his *To the Ends of the Earth: Scotland's Global Diaspora, 1750–2010*.

Despite the efforts of these and other scholars, there is still a sense in which emigration remains the spoiler of Scottish History Proper, the unwanted guest at the party, spreading gloom all around. It seemed to be the negative, inexplicable chapter in modern Scottish history, in contrast to Scotland's outstanding contribution to the European Enlightenment in the eighteenth century. Within Scotland itself, official attention since the 1960s turned from external to internal migration, a byproduct of administrative planning and tacit recognition of the growth of Scottish nationalism. Moreover, because migrant Scots were overrepresented among the achievers in their receiving countries before 1900, it has been almost unconsciously assumed that most Scottish migrants were successful or rich, as typified by Andrew Carnegie, who was hardly typical. This belief has seeped into their historical treatment and has threatened to give rise to a new version of the "great man" view of history—popularized ironically by the Scottish author Thomas Carlyle (1795–1881)—which pushes the collective experience of Scottish migrants aside and descends into a series of ripping yarns about well-known or successful Scots, ignoring the majority and distorting its history. Readers should be aware that this book differs from all previous works in its methods and concerns.

HISTORIANS AND POPULATION HISTORY

One of the prime differences between European history before and after 1800 is the rising supply of population statistics. Before 1800 such information is rare. Surprisingly, general historians have made only superficial use of this primary material (or even avoided it altogether) to graze in the more familiar pastures of politics and war. There seem to be three main excuses for this neglect and negativity. The first excuse is "the data are not available." This is often true in the sense that no one has previously collected it and published it, but it does not mean that the data cannot be made available with some effort. The second, and more common, excuse is that "there are data available but they are unreliable." Again, this is often true but it is also true that poor data can often be corrected or least improved. The third excuse is implied: "this is technical work best left to experts." It is true that population history can be pursued in a highly mathematical way, but its methods and tools can still be readily used by non-mathematicians (like myself) to illuminate the past. As for the experts, they are usually not historians, lack the breadth of historical knowledge to tackle this work, and have far better-paid prospects elsewhere.

General historians need to learn some demography. If Scottish history sources had, for some bizarre reason, been written in Portuguese before 1940, there would be no question that a reading knowledge of Portuguese would be required. Historians would have to learn that language to proceed. Population sources are written in the language of demography, and the need to understand that language is no different. Colin McEvedy and Richard Jones showed what could be achieved by generalists in 1978 in their *Atlas of World Population History,* a work that foreshadowed some of the complaints made here. The population census and other demographic sources are indispensable *primary* sources that should demand the first attention of historians, not the last. Although he was writing about the history of the Roman empire in 1957, the views of Harold Mattingly have a wider truth about writing any kind of history. He said that the primary materials must always be considered first and that the works of even the best historians must be taken as "comment, and comment only." Mindful of these tendencies, I have used the primary sources first, the secondary ones later.

FAMILY AND POPULATION HISTORY

In the Scotland of their day, William Hill and Janet Young were of no importance. Married in 1855, the first year when Scottish marriages were officially recorded, they could, like most bridal couples, sign their names in the marriage register. Thereafter, their blameless lives were marked by debilitating poverty in and around Forfar, in southeast Scotland. Forfar has two main claims to fame: John Jamison (1759–1838), the author of *Etymological Dictionary of the Scottish Language* (1808), was an unwilling resident there from 1781 to 1797; and in the property boom of the early twenty-first century it had some of the cheapest housing in Britain, just another poor town in a poor land. William Hill worked in a series of unskilled outdoor jobs—quarryman (1855), general laborer (1874–1881), and cattle driver (1891). In nineteen years of married life, the Hills produced six sons and four daughters. Neither of their deaths was registered, so it is likely that they were buried as paupers. But their lives have some claim to longer-term significance because without them, you would not be reading this book: they were my paternal great-grandparents.

The Hills also show some of the traps of writing population history. Because their deaths were not registered, they were not counted as part of the natural increase—births minus deaths—and they are assumed to have migrated; but the Hills never left Forfar. Janet Young almost certainly died after the birth of their last child in 1874 as William Hill declared he was a widower at the 1881 census. His last address was a former brewery stable and he was probably being cared for by his youngest daughter, Jessie (1874–1918), a domestic servant. Unable to give his correct age at the 1891 census—presumably because of ill health—the census collector estimated his age at about 65; most likely he was 60 but he could also have been only 59. This means that instead of being recorded in the 55–59 or 60–64 age groups, he would have been wrongly recorded in the 65–69 age group. He must have died not long afterwards, and by 1901 Jessie had moved to St Andrews. This is an instance of how published figures can be incomplete even from a time where their accuracy is taken for granted and a reminder too that any results or reconstructions based upon them, no matter how clever, will always have an element of error.

For many people researching their family histories, findings like these are commonplace. Unless your forebears were illustrious or did something unusual or criminal to be recorded, the chances are that they left little if any trace in the written records. So what more can be done? One way is to turn to the science of population—demography—which is essentially built from births and deaths; family history is often demography written small. Few fields are more generous and practical than demography. It provides the theoretical framework for understanding the information collected by most family historians and placing it in perspective. It even provides a toolbox of techniques to analyze and test information. Demography has only one weakness for historical analysis; it is much better at telling what and how something happened than why. That said, it still has the most to offer for the study of family history; but most family historians do not know this and usually go to the work of general historians to get their historical perspective. Unfortunately, general historians typically have only a limited acquaintance with, or interest in, population history, theory, and issues. Yet these topics are fundamental to understanding much of world history since 1700. Population for many historians is a dull, technical topic, perhaps discussed in a superficial way or even omitted. For their part, historical demographers as a group have done little to make their work interesting and accessible to the general reader. This is a great pity because not only has knowledge of population history increased enormously over the past forty years but much of it is of value to family historians.

Family history is a paradox: fascinating to those engaged in it but devoid of interest to anyone else. No one cares about your family tree except you. It is the triumph of the particular over the general. For many people, myself included, researching their family history can a depressing and disheartening experience. Yet it does have its compensations, no matter how grim. At the very least it provides an answer, if an entirely personal one, to one of the questions Paul Gauguin asked in one of his paintings of 1897: where do we come from? Genealogy—a pariah in academic circles—has not helped as much as it could in showing how individuals fit into the broader picture. True, it has been responsible for creating large databases on individuals based on births, deaths, marriages, the population census, and wartime service. Unfortunately, these databases typically lack any means for extracting general information. For example, it is often an easy matter to find out an individual's war service, but quite another to know the ages of those killed in World War I. Since the 1960s, the popularity of family history has grown. It used to be largely something that was done outside Britain, but that has changed with television programs such as *Who Do You Think You Are?* and the US series *Faces of America*. Not only that, the Internet has made it possible to conduct family history research no matter where you live.

Alas, it is not all good news. Historical research of any kind is not as easy as presented on television, and family history is no exception. First, you have to find your records and then try to make sense of them. Even when records are available they may be neither complete nor accurate or may have other problems. For example, the original enumerators' sheets can be accessed online for the 1911 Canadian census, but the originals were destroyed and many of surviving sheets are so blurry that they are difficult to read. Tracing migration is often assumed to be a simply a matter of checking the shipping records and finding your ancestor. It is not. Shipping records are often incomplete before 1850. You may be lucky, you may not, especially if your forebear had a common family name such as Smith. Fortunately, the Internet and other advances have transformed what can now be done in this field, most critically by providing a wealth of unpublished information from the population censuses for the United States (1880), Canada, England, Wales, and Scotland itself (1881), enabling new topics to be explored that were previously impossible.

UNLOCKING MIGRATION

Contrary to popular belief, migration in free societies is a difficult topic to study. Commonly presented as a largely one-way event, it is actually the hardest aspect of population change to measure and none of the historical sources—whether censuses, departures and arrival counts from ports, or registration of births, deaths, and marriages—are perfect. All have their limitations, but they have their opportunities too, provided the nature of migration is understood from the outset. Intuition, like patriotism, is not enough to analyze these kinds of sources; they require demographic theory and methods if they are to be understood. Previous research has been largely inductive, attempting to build a picture from fragments of evidence, the traditional approach of general historians. Such anecdotal or narrative evidence may be representative of the general picture, but it might not be; there is no way of telling. Anecdotes may be useful as examples when statistics are lacking, but they can also be misleading or simply wrong as they are inclined to record the exceptional ahead of the usual.

Text-based research works well for many historical subjects, but population history is not like other forms of history because it is amenable to a deductive approach where fragments of evidence can be fitted to known models. This work takes the deductive path; it is not about adding numbers to the accepted story but creating a new story from the numbers. It does not play safe. It tackles large topics and returns to the broad sweep of the older migration works. Much of it is likely to be controversial or disputed, and its findings are not what I or anyone else expected. It attempts to bridge the gap between guides to family history and population history to expose of the main features and trends of Scottish migration since 1750. It is *not* a history of Scotland. It takes a global view of a global subject in defiance of the aggressively nationalist approach of most other studies; in this field, comparative history is not just interesting, it is essential. This also means that much of it is about making connections rather than corrections. More than most subjects, too, the path to perdition in this field rests on assumptions; therefore, in this work assumptions have been kept to the barest minimum. Obvious problems and gaps in the historical record are not ignored and are addressed with new information and explanations that may be contentious.

The history of Western European migration before the 1930s has been neglected in recent years. The field has become comfortable with what has been done, seeing little need to revisit, let alone use or analyze, the rich statistical sources available. Repetition has grown in attractiveness, being safe, predictable, and unlikely to upset anyone. Asking new questions, let alone undertaking any comparative cross-country research, seems to have become unfashionable or just too much work. Historical demography, the discipline that has most to contribute to it, has largely failed to do so; far from filling the gap, it has retreated into the safe caves of small case studies, technicalities, and equations. These tendencies rob migration of its historical understanding and often its humanity too. By its nature, migration is a multidisciplinary field. And yet in Scotland, at least, the various disciplines that can contribute to its understanding—general history, economic history, historical demography, and population geography—mostly ignore each other's work and are dug in behind walls of their own making, waiting for foes that may not come or even exist.

Because British historical demography is normally seen through an English lens, the immense value of the Scottish records have been not been appreciated. The statistical sunshine is certainly stronger from 1855 when the national registration of births, deaths, and marriages was introduced, but the outlines of the earlier period can be recovered using models, even though few Scottish parish registers have survived. Ironically, this general lack of parish registers has saved Scottish population history from "family reconstruction," an inductive method invented in France by Louis Henry in 1956 and applied to English population history by E. A. Wrigley and R. S. Schofield, who published their findings in *The Population History of England, 1541–1871* (1981). Hugely labor intensive, this method has produced limited results that are hard to verify; in contrast, the Princeton population models that are used in this work fit the Scottish evidence tightly, enabling its population history from 1650 to 1860 to be reconstructed with confidence, detail, and clarity. Having said that, I repeat: this work is *not* a history of Scotland and it largely ignores the doings of its elites and well-documented minorities such as explorers or missionaries because they have been covered by others. It brings to the forefront the years from 1900 to 1930 when nearly a million Scots left never to return, redressing the balance in favor of these unimportant Scots. It was their going that in many ways defined twentieth-century Scotland, the result of its switch from a low-wage economy to a low-wage, no-new-jobs economy.

WHAT THIS BOOK OFFERS

Considering all that has been written, it may seem that that there is no need for yet another book on Scottish migration. But this work is truly different. It is not another Celtic sob story but a work that exploits all the statistical sources both for Scotland and the countries they settled in. The opening chapters are devoted to Scotland as the source of migrants. They examine Scotland's population history, how the economy shaped the history of its migration, and the main features of Scottish migration up to about 1930. The remaining chapters examine Scottish settlement in England, North America, South Africa, and Australasia, again up to about 1930. The last chapter briefly surveys Scottish migration from the 1930s to the 1980s.

The book is made from numbers, a lot of numbers. I have also made extensive use of standard demographic methods to analyze Scottish population and migration, particularly life tables and model populations; this is usually what is meant by my repeated references to "modeling." These models are powerful and proven techniques for making seemingly impossible source materials give up their secrets and filling what is otherwise a void. They expose previously hidden patterns by comparing what should have been with what was recorded, and without models the original data remain opaque.

Whether anyone likes it or not, much population history has to be reconstructed from later, frequently much later, information. This is not just because direct information about earlier periods is lacking but because historical demography is usually about survivors whose past numbers can be estimated from death rates. To document these procedures in detail would require a second, lengthy, and unbelievably tedious book. That said, my concentration on results at the expense of method often makes me sound unintentionally dogmatic about topics where contemporary primary evidence is scanty or just not there; but this, broadly speaking, is what I have done. First, for the pre-1860 period, I have used the model North populations developed at Princeton University by Ansley J. Coale and Paul Demeny with the age information for Scotland for 1751, 1791, 1811, 1821, 1841, and 1851 to produce birth and death rates. These particular models were based mainly on Sweden and Norway, nations with known high incidences of tuberculosis, and their close fit to Scotland means it was the main killer of its people too.

Second, I have made extensive use of length of residence data by age and sex from the censuses for North America, South Africa, and Australasia from 1901 to 1926 to reconstruct the number of Scots who became permanent settlers, an approach that does not seem to have been used previously. For North America, I drew samples based on common family names among the Scots-born from various publicly available genealogical sites for Canada and the United States to estimate how many of those who came in a particular decade after 1820 stayed as settlers. Third, I have pillaged all the population censuses, both published and unpublished, for the British Isles, North America, South Africa, and Australasia for what they tell us about the Scots, plus any other statistical sources I could find. Readers might be surprised to learn that this has not been done before. My findings are set out in this book and many of them contradict what are given in other works; but this is incidental and not how they were made. They are the outcome of an extensive process of trial and error, mainly error, littered with cunning ideas that still failed testing; only those that passed testing with high marks are presented. I have tried to keep the number of tables down, but there are probably still too many for most readers and not enough for those who doubt my findings. There are no footnotes but I have indicated the main sources in the text. The bibliography lists all the sources I have used and sometimes gives information on how I have used them.

My objective has been to set out—as best as the current evidence will allow—a comprehensive view of Scottish migration. It uncovers a considered, variable process, not a lemming-like rush defying explanation by nameless, disconnected units of production. A good deal of the information I have used is difficult to obtain as well as being confusing and intimidating to the occasional user even if they have access to it. I have tried my best to make it tell its story, and the techniques I have used could be applied to other migrant groups. I make no claim for it being the final word on the topic; in due course it too will be revised—such is the nature of history—but would-be correctors had better be prepared to work as long and hard as I have done. This subject is neither closed nor completed. There is much to be done.

HIGHLANDS, LOWLANDS, AND CLEARANCES

Most histories of Scotland—and certainly the entries for the Scots in the migration encyclopedias for Australia, Canada, and the United States—give much attention to the traditional division of Highlands and Lowlands. This work does not because there is no agreed boundary between them. There are numerous historical maps purporting to show the "Highland Line" as their boundary, but its position varies according to the whim of the map maker. It is agreed that the former counties of Sutherland and Ross and Cromarty and the city of Inverness were the heart of the Highlands. But on its eastern side there was a messy transition zone made up of the former counties of Aberdeen and Perth where the demarcation is anything but clear. It became even less clear after 1790 with economic growth and the reach of the Glasgow conurbation into traditional Highland countries such as Bute and Argyll. The recruitment of Highlanders by the Glaswegian economy seems to have begun accidentally in 1791 when a ship carrying 400 immigrants from the Isle of Skye bound for Carolina was forced to berth at the mouth of the Clyde. Once ashore, the entrepreneur David Dale (1739–1806) offered them work at his factory at New Lanark, which many of them accepted. Thereafter, the Clyde basin attracted increasing numbers of Highlanders, either as settlers or as seasonal workers.

Over time the Highlands tended to become a place of the mind as well as a location, valid if viewed like this but of uncertain value for analysis. The 1861 census, the first to be conducted by the Scots, made no use at all of a Highland–Lowland division. Instead, it grouped the counties into eight regions, and the traditional Highland counties of Argyll and Bute were included with Stirling and Dumbarton to create its West Midland region, and these eight regions remained in use until 1901. At the 1911 Scottish census the Highland Line made a brief reappearance; this time it was shown as a straight line drawn from Aberdeen to the southern end of the Mull of Kintyre but it was never used again. In 1953, when Edmund A. Hogan, the registrar general for Scotland, conducted his review of Scottish population history between 1861 and 1951, he avoided any reference to the Highlands and

Lowlands. Instead, he used a four-part geographical division of Central, North-East, Southern, and "crofting counties" by which he meant the former counties of Argyll, Caithness, Inverness, Ross and Cromarty, and Sutherland and the islands of Orkney and Zetland (the former Shetland), a description that emphasized a traditional way of life more than location. All this casts the standard Highlands and Lowlands division of Scotland as simplistic and anachronistic. It ignores how the distinction between them was increasingly blurred by urbanization, internal migration, and economic change; therefore, the terms Highlands and Lowlands are used sparingly in this work.

Finally, readers should know that I refuse to use the traditional Scottish term "clearances" where it refers to the forced evictions of traditional land occupiers as opposed to cleaning out a desk. It is one of those ugly political euphemisms that George Orwell rightly railed against in 1946, comparable with "pacification" (bombing defenseless villages followed by machine gunning) or "transfer of population" (robbing peasants of their farms and evicting them) and more recent additions such as "ethnic cleansing" (the organized murder or violent eviction of ethnic groups). "Clearances" should join Orwell's other offensive political euphemisms and be called what it was: forced evictions.

Chapter One

Discovering the People

Modern humans came late to Scotland, reaching what is now outer Edinburgh about twenty-seven centuries ago or about twenty-three centuries after the Aborigines entered northern Australia. By 3000 BCE Celtic tribes controlled Scotland, later known as Caledonia by the Romans. Human rights as understood today did not exist and there is no reason to believe that ancient Scottish society was any better than other Celtic societies of the time. In their accounts of Celtic Gaul (modern France) from about 50 BCE, both Julius Caesar and the Greek author Diodorus of Sicily noted that most of the people were little more than slaves; Diodorus added that it was common for tribal members to be sold as slaves by their chieftains for wine. The world of the tribe cared only for chiefs, and their bards extolled their greatness and martial valor; they did not waste words or song on ordinary folk.

SCENERY AND SCARCITY

Much of Scotland is almost an island. At its narrowest, between the estuaries of the Clyde on the west and the Forth on the east, the mainland is only about half the width of the Panama Canal; above this isthmus lies three-quarters of modern Scotland. The Romans were the first to recognize the strategic importance of this neck of land when they built the Antonine Wall by about CE 165 to keep out the Caledonian tribes. Fifteen centuries later, others wanted to use the isthmus to join the North and Irish seas for commerce. The idea was promoted by Daniel Defoe in 1726 and a canal linking the headwaters of the two rivers was eventually finished in 1790. It was of limited capacity and it never became the driver of Scotland's economic prosperity that Defoe hoped it would. At various times to the mid-1920s a much larger canal was proposed; it was never built, but if it had been, it would have made much of the mainland of Scotland an island.

Scotland's offshore islands are a conspicuous part of its physical geography. Its northern most islands, the Shetlands, are about the same distance from Norway—of which they were a part until 1472—as they are from southern mainland Scotland. The 1861 Scottish census counted 787 islands—of which 521 were in the Hebrides, a rugged archipelago off the west coast—but only 186 of them were inhabited. Some of the uninhabited islands were able to support 400 sheep in 1861, others only one. It was through its offshore islands that English readers were introduced to Scotland. In 1703 Martin Martin published his *Description of the Western Islands of Scotland*, a work that inspired Dr. Samuel Johnson to make his famous visit seventy years later. Most of the islands were insignificant, but others like the Scapa Flow naval base in the Orkney Islands were of strategic importance to the British Isles; it was there on October 14, 1939, that the *Royal Oak* was torpedoed, the first German attack on British territory in World War II.

The hostile topography of the islands was mirrored by much of the western mainland that was made by volcanoes and then shaped by glaciers. Scotland's scenic grandeur may have inspired geologists and poets, but it did not make for an abundant food supply. In the words of Sir John Sinclair in 1831, much of Scotland was "barren, rocky, and irregular" and, as my father was fond of saying, "you can't eat scenery." The Highlands and the islands accounted for about half of Scotland. In a landscape dominated by mountains and valleys, it was understandable that its society would be tribal. The Highlands and the islands also protected Scotland, providing a redoubt from the Romans and impeding the journey of Samuel Johnson and James Boswell in 1773.

Much of Scotland's geology and geography is diagonal. The Highlands themselves are split northeast by southwest along a rift valley known as the Great Glen that includes Loch Ness. The military value of the Great Glen in controlling the Highlands was shown by Oliver Cromwell's forces in the mid-seventeenth century in the building of what became Fort William at its southern end to complement Inverness in the north. It again showed its usefulness a century later in controlling the defeated Highlands after the Duke of Cumberland's victory at Culloden in 1746. In the south, the stripe of coalfields that made Scotland's Industrial Revolution possible also run roughly northeast by southwest from Fife to Ayr.

Geography encouraged the emergence of two Scottish cultures, the Highlands and the Lowlands, a division first described by the chronicler John of Fordun in 1380. English was the language of the towns and the Lowlands, which looked south to England or France for their culture, in contrast to the Gaelic-speaking, feudal society of the Highlands with its poor, harsh landscape and warrior world. For much of Scottish history, the Highlands and the

English border lands were a British version of Afghanistan with real political power in the hands of clan chiefs, not kings; and as in other mountainous lands, like the Balkans and Japan, it encouraged ongoing tribal violence. Before they were romanticized by Sir Walter Scott, the Lowlanders seem to have regarded Highlanders as second-class Scots. In the 1750s Robert Wallace, the population scholar, described the Highlanders as needing to be "civilized" without which they would continue to be in a "state of barbarity and of idleness."

Much of Scotland was, and is, economically unproductive. Mountains, lakes, and heath make up about 75 percent of the land, grasslands about 8 percent, and only about 17 percent is arable, largely in the Lowlands in the central-south and along the east coast. The land was not only inherently poor, it was very much private property; in 1882, about 630 individuals owned 80 percent of Scotland but they earned on average only £0.35 per acre. Their incomes were lowest in the Highlands and highest in the Edinburgh region and the east coast.

The heavily indented coastline meant that for most Scots the sea was never far away. The climate was, and is, cold, and, although moderated by the Gulf Stream, it shortened the growing season compared with England. These inescapable facts of physical geography underpin Scottish history. They did not determine that history but they restricted the kind and scale of economic development that could take place. Nature denied Scotland the large agricultural base that gave England its economic power, and its northern location placed it on the edge of the main trading routes, adding to its other disadvantages.

A BLENDED PEOPLE

Scotland's people were formed from an assortment of different peoples. The early history of the two largest groups is unclear, but from about CE 500 the *Scoti* (Scots), an Irish Gaelic people, begin to colonize parts of southwestern Scotland, then occupied by the Picts, and for centuries they fought each other. From CE 760 to 800, another uninvited group, the Vikings, arrived from Norway and settled in northern and northwestern offshore islands and attacked the mainland. Over time, the conflict between the Picts and the Scots eased, and in 889 Donald II became the first king to rule over both peoples. By this time, the Scots had become the dominant political and cultural group and the former "Pictland" became Scotland. The other group that contributed to the Scottish people were the descendants of the Britons in the south who had been part of the Roman occupation.

From 1100 Scotland began to take shape as a nation, especially during the rule of David I (1124–1153) who kickstarted Scotland as a medieval kingdom. He introduced feudalism, organized shires, and founded fourteen burghs or townships surrounding castles; they included Aberdeen, Dundee, Edinburgh, and Perth, and so began Scottish urbanization. He also minted the first Scottish silver coins, an act that signaled the beginnings of a money-based economy. Like other medieval monarchs, he wanted towns in order to provide markets and generate trade that could be taxed. David was fortunate in that his reign coincided with the Medieval Warm Period (c. CE 900–1300) that brought higher temperatures and less rainfall to Western Europe, trends that boosted food production, reduced the likelihood of famines, and enabled the population to double. From about 1250, average temperatures began to fall until about 1650 when they began to rise again, even if slowly and erratically.

ROBERT WALLACE AND THE POPULATION DEBATE

Despite the financial disaster of the Darien scheme, epidemics, and famines at the end of the seventeenth century, Scotland entered the eighteenth century intellectually strong. The decision by the Presbyterian Church in 1696 to found schools in every parish made Scotland over time one of the most literate societies in Western Europe, rivaled only by Switzerland and Sweden. Reading in itself was not enough; the people also had to understand texts and discussions based on them. This emphasis on first principles gave rise to a generation of Scottish intellectuals who made Edinburgh the center of the Enlightenment in Britain. Their contributions to modern philosophy, geology, and economics are well known, but their contribution to population thought has been overlooked. At its heart was one of the main Western European debates of the time, the nature of humankind. Were humans inherently good but made bad by social and economic conditions, or were they, as the Bible said and Christianity preached, inherently sinful?

In the Western Europe in this era, reliable knowledge about population was scanty. The Bible was the unquestioned source of knowledge about population, not just morals. It was the literal truth. It told the people how to live their lives and what to expect. It told them to go forth and breed, fulfilling God's commandment to Noah after the Flood (Genesis 1:28). It also told them that they could expect to live to seventy, eighty if they were strong (Psalms 90:10), but it offered conflicting advice about other population matters, notably census taking. At the start of the Book of Numbers, God commands Moses to take a census, but in the Second Book of Samuel, King David commits a grave sin by holding a census against God's wishes for which God punishes his people in the form of the plague (2 Samuel 24). These texts were taken seriously; in at least one Scottish parish in the 1790s the parishioners objected to being counted on the grounds that it was a repeat of David's sin. Then there was the inconvenience of Mary having to give birth to Jesus in a manger because the demands of the Roman census meant that there was no room at the inn. Census taking was theologically sensitive because it seemed to trespass on knowledge about who would live and who would die, knowledge only God could possess. Western European governments, though, were less concerned about committing David's sin in their quest for taxation, and a number of them held censuses before 1800. Theological objections certainly did not stop the Scots from conducting two counts of their people in 1751 and in 1791, although religious opposition to census taking, based on David's sin, seems to have been stronger in England.

From the Renaissance until about the middle of the twentieth century, to be considered educated meant knowing Latin, preferably Greek as well, and having a thorough knowledge of classical culture as well as the Bible. Leaving behind an enormous intellectual legacy and impressive ruins, it was easy for educated opinion before 1800 to believe that the population of the ancient world must have been larger than the present. The idea seems to have originated with the Belgian humanist Justus Lipsius (1547–1607) who published exaggerated estimates of the populations of the cities of the Roman empire. It was taken up and promoted by the Dutch scholar Isaac Vossius (1618–1689) in 1685. He estimated that the population of Western Europe, including Russia, was about 30 million (it is currently thought that population of Western Europe was about 100 million at this time) but believed it had been higher in the past. Others who promoted the idea were two English Biblical scholars, William Whiston in 1696 and Richard Cumberland in 1724. It was given much more coherence by the Scottish scholar Robert Wallace (1697–1771), a leading Presbyterian. Wallace was an anomaly for his time. For him at least, Presbyterianism was no bleak faith, but a bright and shining one, born of intolerance but magnanimous and open. He held advanced opinions about other matters too, believing that the sexual drives of men and women were similar.

In 1753, Wallace published his *Dissertation on the Numbers of Mankind in Ancient and Modern Times* He followed this with his *Various Prospects of Mankind, Nature and Providence* in 1761, the same year that his works were translated into French making them available to educated opinion in Western Europe. Wallace considered that the population estimates of Vossius for Europe were too low and doubted his claims that the population in antiquity had been higher that at the present. Starting with Adam and Eve as the "original couple" from whom everyone was descended—again, it must be stressed that his age accepted the literal truth and authority of Genesis and rest of the Bible—he argued, like Whiston, that the world's population should have grown geometrically; but he went further and produced a table showing how it would have grown if had doubled every thirty-three years. With the benefit of current knowledge, Wallace had made a promising start, as genetics has since revealed that modern humans really are descended from a very small group and that there actually was an ancient biological "Adam" and a small number of biological "Eves." Logically, his model, which seems to be the first of its kind, pointed to there being more people in the present than in the past, but he presented various reasons why this was not so; these included historical reasons (such as the suppression of independent states by the Roman empire); religious and social customs; legal issues (particularly primogeniture), the maintenance of large armies, and government policies.

He was concerned about the lack of encouragement for marriage and especially the neglect of agriculture, complaining that "men live not on money, but on food." He made imaginative use of every available classical writer but his arguments were cloudy and speculative, and his main conclusion—"that there was a point of time, when at least Europe was better peopled than it has ever been since, or shall ever be hereafter"—elusive and prone to misinterpretation, particularly when he admitted that the evidence was insufficient to say just when this had been. A better-known Scot, his friend, the philosopher David Hume (1711–1776), criticized Wallace's case that the population of the past was higher than the present; but the two agreed to disagree and Wallace made the extraordinary gesture of including Hume's critique in his work. It has been forgotten that Wallace was Hume's protector as well as his friend in a Scotland that regarded atheism as a serious crime and would have surely have hanged him a generation earlier. It has been forgotten too that Wallace's works were the orthodox view of population within Britain for the next forty years. Between them, Wallace and Hume made important contributions to the population debate of the eighteenth century: Wallace by exploring the link between population and the food supply and Hume by casting doubts on the accuracy of population figures in Greek and Roman sources. The debate was revived by a Welsh dissenting minister, the Rev. Richard Price (1723–1791), in his *Essay on the Population of England from the Revolution to the Present Time* (1780) in which he used excise and window tax returns to argue that the population of England had fallen by about 250,000 between 1761 and 1777. He blamed the decline on military recruitment, emigration, the enclosure of farms, high prices, and, "above all, the increase in luxury and of public taxes and debts."

Today, we all expect to be counted by someone at some time and become a statistic somewhere, but 200 years ago this seldom happened. Not only that, blessed as we are with an abundance of population information, this debate about whether the population was higher or lower than in the past seems absurd, but at the time there were no reliable statistics to settle the issue. Some European countries had held censuses but their results were treated as state secrets and remained unpublished, so that educated Europeans had access to better knowledge about the solar system than they did about the size of the populations around them. With the benefit of considerable research, the mid-eighteenth century is now seen as one of the great turning points in world history, the time when the population began to grow faster than in previous ages and kept growing with momentous results that shaped much of subsequent history.

ALEXANDER WEBSTER'S SCOTLAND, C. 1751

Unlike Hume, Wallace was not just a theorist and he was able to apply himself to one of the pressing problems of the time, the protection from destitution of the widows and orphans of Presbyterian ministers and university staff. Before the presentation of his *Dissertation* in 1750, he had assisted the General Assembly of the Church of Scotland with analyzing responses to questionnaires for setting up a pension scheme for their benefit in 1743–1744. The idea was hardly new—it had been envisaged by John Knox and Andrew Melville, the founders of Presbyterianism, nearly 200 years before—but its implementation was delayed not just by wars and political instability but by a lack of the necessary information; to make it work, it was essential to know the ages of the clergy and the population generally. Not only that, the ages of the people needed to be known by single year in order to calculate their chances of living from year to another so that contribution and benefits rates could be set fairly.

To get this information, the Church took one of its greatest executive decisions: under the leadership of Dr. Alexander Webster (1708–1784), it resolved to conduct a complete count of the people—a census—a decision based on the knowledge that many parishes did not have registers of births, deaths, and marriages. Webster began his work in the late 1740s and completed it in 1755. He did not just rely on his well-known personal charm to have the work done; he made it clear to the clergy that their schools would have their status (and funding) withdrawn for noncompliance. His questionnaire to the clergy has not survived, but it is clear from his published results that it must have included the following:

- The area of their parishes
- The population of their parish
- Their ages (and most likely those of their wives and children too)
- The ages of their parishioners
- The number of Roman Catholics

Webster's census covered 906 parishes. His original total population was 1,265,000—the figure used in every book about Scotland; but in his footnotes, he updated the figures to take account of the growth of Paisley, Perth, Dundee, and Aberdeen, adding about 53,000 people to raise the total to

1,319,000 or by 4 percent. As the census was undertaken over a number of years, it must refer to a time much earlier than its completion date of 1755—at least one of the parish returns was dated 1749 and another 1750. Even better evidence for the date of most of Webster's census comes from the population reports received by Sir John Sinclair by the Scottish clergy in the 1790s. Nearly all of these reports were compiled in late 1790 or early 1791 and when they compared their population counts to Webster's, they almost always said that his had been made forty years before, indicating that most of Webster's census was finalized by around 1751. The novelty of the enquiry and the need to collect figures from all 906 parishes, many of them remote, would have taken much time, not to mention the time needed for their checking and collation. Webster was justified in saying that his census was "the result of long and deliberate enquiry."

As the first census conducted in the British Isles, it was an astounding achievement. In the early 1790s, some clergy claimed that Webster's figures for their parishes were undercounts, but there is no good reason to doubt his claim that his census was "very near the Truth." The recently conquered Highlands contained about 363,000 or about 27 percent of the people, defining them as the total of the former counties of Argyll, Bute, Inverness, Orkney, Ross and Cromarty, Shetland, and Sutherland plus half the populations of Aberdeen and Perth counties. The towns were small but growing, home to about one in five Scots compared with about one in ten in 1700. Edinburgh, which had replaced Perth as the capital in 1436, had 67,000 residents if St Cuthbert's parish was included. Glasgow was Scotland's second largest town with 23,500. After Glasgow, the next largest towns were Aberdeen (22,000) and Dundee (18,000). The census estimated that the number of men of military age—generously defined as men ages 18 to 56, or "fighting men"—was one-fifth of the total population. It also asked about the number of Catholics but only 16,488 admitted their faith to the prying Presbyterian clergy. Surprisingly, Webster did not ask about gender and seems to have assumed the number of both sexes was the same. Modeling of the expected ages based on estimated births from 1650 to 1750 agrees with Webster's revised total population of 1.3 million and his broad age estimates, which explains why they could be used to accurately predict deaths among the 948 Presbyterian minsters of his day. Contemporaries were impressed.

Webster's census was remarkable for including estimates for single year of age for persons, something that was not published until the 1871 Scottish censuses and again from 1911. No other European country produced this information for the eighteenth century, not even Sweden. Webster's figures showed that half the Scots were ages 23 or younger, which was about three years higher than the Scottish population in the first half of the nineteenth century but comparable with what has been estimated for England in 1751. It was the first time that the ages of the population were available for any part of Britain, and it inspired the Rev. David Wilkie, the minister of Cults parish, Fife County, to produce a life table for Scotland in 1792. Based on the work of the astronomer Edmond Halley (1656–1742) and lacking information on deaths, his table was naturally inaccurate by modern standards—he only estimated life expectancy at birth at 31 whereas Webster's age structure indicated it was about 35—but it was one of the earliest attempts to produce a life table anywhere in Britain covering a large number of people.

Webster's census was also one of the earliest censuses in Europe; only a few places in Europe were earlier: the Habsburg Empire (1695), Iceland (1703), Prussia (1725), Hesse-Darmstadt (1742), Hesse-Cassel (1747), and Sweden-Finland (1749). The general accuracy of his census was made possible by its being held under the auspices of the national religion and having a clear and direct benefit to the clergy required to collect the figures—the support of their widows and orphans. Without an obvious need for continuing the work, it was understandable that this pioneering initiative was not continued. So far from marking the beginning of a pioneering statistical era, it remained a one-off exercise, often quoted, but not published until 1952. Webster's census was the benchmark for all later investigations of Scotland's population. It was the earliest attempt at a general population count anywhere in the British Isles and a torch in the demographic darkness of its time. But it was much more than this: by accurately estimating the ages of the people, it created a pathway to Scotland's population past back to 1650. It showed that the age structure was the product not of one but of three different levels of mortality applying at different times, in the same way that changes in climate can be recorded in rock layers. It proved that Scottish mortality was mainly stable from about 1650 to 1705, fell slightly in around 1706, and fell again from about 1740.

SIR JOHN SINCLAIR'S SCOTLAND, C. 1791

There were proposals for other Scottish censuses after 1755 but they failed to attract support. Frustrated by the lack of information, Sir John Sinclair (1754–1835), a Scottish landowner in Caithness at the northernmost end of the British Isles, tackled the problem with characteristic vigor. Agricultural reformer, politician, and pioneering social and economic investigator, he undertook his own survey in the 1790s, which he published in twenty-one volumes between 1791 and 1799 as *The Statistical Account of Scotland*; it included a count of the population for the early 1790s, which he found to be 1.5 million. In 1831 he published an updated summary of his work as *Analysis of the Statistical Account of Scotland* and he introduced "statistics" into the English language in its modern sense. Sir John was a paternalist whose goal was to raise the productivity of Scottish agriculture and his role model seems to have been Prussia's Frederick the Great. Today, *paternalist* has the pejorative meaning of condescending, but Sir John was a benevolent paternalist who wanted to protect a people threatened with famine in the 1780s; and to do that he needed a lot of timely and useful information. The Presbyterian clergy in every parish were the shock troops of his investigation and he asked much of them. His wide-ranging questionnaire of 100 items included these questions on population:

- The size of the "ancient" (that is, before the present) population
- The number of males and females
- The number in towns or the countryside
- The average number of births and deaths
- The reasons for its increase or decrease
- The number of families
- The current size of the population
- Marriages and marital status
- Birthplaces
- Ages
- Religion
- Occupations

It was a far-reaching undertaking for the early 1790s, and it was not surprising that most of the parishes were unable to supply all the information he requested. Clergy who did not respond were harassed by Sir John's employees, for he knew his cause was just: the welfare of the people. What was surprising was how much information Sir John received on these and the many other topics in his questionnaire. It was clear from their responses that most clergy did not have the population registers necessary to give a complete picture of Scotland's population, but they provided enough critical information to overcome these deficiencies. Most of the population reports Sir John received were from late 1790 or early 1791. Some of the reports contained records of births, marriages, and deaths for the previous decade, and others presented all the figures that they could find going back a century or more; for instance, Alloa parish in Clackmannan County included baptisms from 1668. This information was truly exceptional. Nothing like it had been collected, let alone published, for any other part of Britain, and Sir John's tireless efforts over four decades can only be described as heroic. He created a body of information for Scotland that was not available for England and he inspired a follow-up multivolume *Statistical Accounts* series for 1834–1845 and even a third series in the 1950s. But it was his 1790s series that was the most important because he preserved so much ephemeral information on Scotland and its people that would otherwise have been lost.

JOHN RICKMAN AND SCOTLAND

Even by the 1790s the debate about whether the British population was higher or lower than in the past remained unresolved and began to cause official concern. In response to these fears, the Pitt government considered enacting a Poor Law that would have given a shilling a week to laborers who had three children to have more to promote population growth. In 1796, the English government statistician John Rickman (1771–1840) realized that the only way to settle the debate was to find out the current size of the population by a complete count and to collect figures on births and deaths from the parish registers for the past century. He also believed that this information would assist government planning in the war with Revolutionary France. His proposal was adopted, and the first national British census was held in 1801. As part of the census, local authorities in England, Wales, and Scotland were also asked to lend their surviving parish registers back to 1700.

In Scotland, the census was largely conducted by school masters, and its results compared well with the parish returns collected by Sir John Sinclair ten years earlier. The results for the parish registers were less impressive. Rickman received registers for only 96 Scottish parishes; in contrast, Wales, with only 40 percent of Scotland's population, supplied 790, confirming the wisdom of Webster's assessment of fifty years earlier that the only way to get national Scottish population figures was to conduct a census. Rickman was also concerned that the geographical spread of the registers he received was biased and considered that "a large proportion" of them were from "the Manufacturing parts." From the limited information provided he estimated that the population of Scotland in 1700 was 1,048,000—about 600,000 less than in 1801. There was no longer any doubt from these figures, and those for England and Wales, that the British population in 1801 was indeed higher than in 1700. The population debate was finally resolved.

Rickman's summary was the first attempt to produce a national series of Scottish birth and death figures for the eighteenth century, and it has since been regarded as an unreliable collection, a view reinforced by the odd and inconsistent population totals he derived from them. He declined to present a marriage series, citing their highly incomplete registration, a surprising omission given its religious importance. Rickman was disappointed by the low number of registers he received and judged that it would be "useless" to collect any more Scottish data at the 1811 and 1821 censuses. There is no doubt that in their original condition Rickman's figures are an inaccurate guide, but were they valueless? Despite his view that most of the registers came from manufacturing districts, it is hard to see that they were severely biased. They included two of the largest urban centers, Glasgow and Aberdeen, and various Lowland parishes. The Highlands were absent simply because few maintained registers of any kind before about 1750.

The surviving registers may not have been a random sample in the modern sense but they are a passable representation of the Lowland parishes where most Scots lived even in the eighteenth century. In all, the registers he used covered 218,000 people, or 14 percent of the population in 1801, compared with 157,000, or 12 percent of the population in those same parishes when Webster conducted his census. And his results can be used to estimate a national series of births and deaths. First, his birth figures can be adjusted so that the sex ratio—the number of males per 100 females—is 105, the expected biological number. Second, mortality models can be used to adjust the figures for under-registration that can be scaled up to the total population. A similar procedure can be used for deaths. The results are indicative only but the variations in them are comparable to England from 1700 to 1800 but without the spike in English deaths in the late 1720s. So despite his disappointment with the Scottish data, Rickman still made a significant contribution to its population history.

REV. THOMAS MALTHUS AND SCOTLAND

Like other parts of the world, Scotland's population grew faster after about 1750 than before it. This growth was based on milder climatic conditions and the spread of the potato and turnip. The result was that in the brief lifetime of Scotland's most famous poet, Robbie Burns (1759–1796), the residential population grew by 200,000. The increase would have been twice as big but for out-migration to North America, England, the West Indies, and India. It was a classic case of a country poor in natural resources undergoing a population explosion that threatened its food supply, precisely the conditions of interest to an ambitious and intellectually frustrated English clergyman from Guilford, Thomas R. Malthus (1766–1834). Such clergy were common in pre-1914 European society because apart from teaching, law, and later, medicine, religion was usually the only career available to the educated; the presence of talented clergy was shown in many of the reports made to Sir John Sinclair in the 1790s.

Malthus published his influential *An Essay on the Principle of Population, as it affects the Future Improvement of Society with Remarks on the Speculations of Mr. Godwin, M. Condorcet, and other Writers* in 1798 in which he argued that the human population grew geometrically but that the food supply grew only arithmetically. This meant that the population grew faster than the food supply and that it was only held in check by starvation and other calamities such as wars and epidemics. Malthus is routinely hailed as the originator of these ideas, as a solitary genius, and the outstanding visionary and prophet of later global population problems, but closer examination of his work unmasks him as the black knight of population studies.

As mentioned, the idea that the population tended to grow geometrically predated Malthus by over a century and Malthus learned it from Robert Wallace who had published it nearly fifty years before.

The original *Essay* was a polemical reply to one of the foundation works of English anarchism, the the third edition of *Enquiry Concerning Political Justice, and Its Influence on Morals and Happiness* by William Godwin (1756–1836), which had been published earlier in 1798. It addressed in particular Godwin's optimistic view of the perfectibility of humans and society. His fundamental objection to Godwin was his claim that people were "perfectible," by which he meant that they had the potential of "being continually made better and receiving perpetual improvement" (not that they were capable of "being brought to perfection"). Despite this qualification, Malthus saw the danger in this argument if left unchallenged and the threat to him and his way of life, for if people were capable of "perpetual improvement," it could lead people to eventually become perfect and to replace God and clergymen like himself. But only God was perfect. Human beings were inherently sinful and their lustfulness would lead to God's punishment; their numbers would increase and exceed the food supply, and they would starve to death. Emigration did not solve the problem of population growth; it merely shifted it elsewhere because human beings took their sinfulness with them. Toward the end of his life, Godwin replied to Malthus in *Of Population* (1820), in which he lamented the lack of charity in Malthus's Christianity.

Both Godwin and Malthus were well acquainted with the work of Robert Wallace; he was, after all, the leading British author on population and his *Dissertation* was reprinted in 1809, by which time it now looked obsolete and irrelevant. Godwin cited his book, identified him as "Wallace," and discussed his ideas generally; but Malthus unfairly suggested that "Mr Wallace" wanted to turn the whole Earth into a garden. Both complained about Wallace's discussion of social equality: Godwin for his abandonment of it because it would lead to "excessive population" and Malthus for his support of it. Nowhere in his *Essay* did Malthus acknowledge that it was Wallace who had first prepared a theoretical table showing how the human population could have been expected to grow geometrically from the "original couple," Adam and Eve. Neither did Malthus acknowledge the close attention Wallace had given to the importance of the food supply in sustaining population growth.

For all his enormous influence, Malthus was a derivative, mendacious author lucky enough to write at a time receptive to his views. He wrote to promote himself, and in this he was singularly successful. The original version of the *Essay* was a highly conservative political tract. Stripped of its selective use of population statistics, it was essentially sermon denouncing the sin and lust of humankind. Neither did he want governments to add to the problem by paying people to have children, and he criticized as misguided the Pitt government's proposal to pay laborers with three children to have more children. Malthus was always a clergyman and a morals crusader. He may have been Britain's first professor of political economy from 1805 to 1834, but he always signed himself as the Rev. T. R. Malthus and his real achievement was to shift the population debate from data to morals.

The first edition of his *Essay* was a response to the war with Revolutionary France and its supporters. It was a war fought in books as well as in battles and it was the ideas nursery of the modern Western political "right" and "left." The later Malthus, the collector of global demographic information, has been remembered, but the original Malthus, the ideological warrior who plundered the ideas of authors safely dead, notably Robert Wallace, has been conveniently forgotten. Worse still, at the start of his career, Malthus discovered disturbing evidence that undermined his fertility thesis. In 1802 he undertook his second study tour, beginning in France and ending in Switzerland where he must have seen a report on the population in the Vaud region of Switzerland written by another clergyman, Jean-Louis Muret, in 1766. Based on original research, Muret analysed mortality, traced epidemics in Switzerland from 1313 to 1668, considered the effects of migration, and interpreted his findings using the international literature available. It must have dismayed Malthus that total baptisms in Vaud from 1630 to 1760, although incomplete, were virtually flat, devoid of the continued growth that he had led his readers to expect. Muret's message was clear: fertility was stable and that the causes of population change needed to be sought in mortality and migration.

Confronted with Muret's pioneering research and scientific methods, Malthus had the chance to reconsider his views, but he obscured their significance in his later works. Henceforth, he approached the study of population with a mind that refused to open; he collected information to support his ideas, not to change them. Fixated with fertility and its association with sin, vice, and unrestrained sexual pleasure, he could not admit that the reasons for population growth must lie elsewhere. This was why, unlike Muret or Richard Price, Malthus never carried out or commissioned original research—it would have proved him wrong—and why he only used published population figures, often selectively, to confuse rather than inform his readers. Neither did he use his mathematical ability to make any contribution to population theory. The defense of the sociopolitical order was always his prime concern, and his population writings, masquerading as science, proved to be an ideal vehicle for doing this. His aim was not to advance the scientific study of population but to kill it off, which he managed to do for a generation in Britain. But his persistent insinuation that population growth was caused by an unexplained surge in sexual activity was not only widely accepted but also seeped into modern historical writing. For example, Ian Morris in *Why the*

West Rules—For Now (2011) asserted that in England between 1780 and 1830 "rich landlords did not drive country folk off the land; sex did."

Unable to accept falling mortality as the cause of population growth, Malthus in his *Summary View of the Principle of Population* (1830) was also unable to offer any constructive suggestions about how to slow it down, and he was reduced to repeating himself and the use of code language dressed as philosophy. As birth control was a vice, he could only urge "moral restraint," by he meant sexual abstinence. Malthus succeeded because he told those in positions of power what they wanted to hear: that the reason for the increase in population was the lack of sexual restraint by their social inferiors who had no one to blame but themselves for having large families. Moreover, there was nothing that could be done to prevent the inevitable mass starvation that this would cause; it was just nature taking it course. With these sentiments, Malthus elevated Lust as the greatest of the deadly sins and in so doing succumbed to another deadly sin, Pride.

His original *Essay* was published anonymously and made few references to Scotland beyond noting the poverty of the Scottish peasants and the overpopulation of the Highlands. Only when criticized did he explicitly acknowledge his debt to four authors in shaping his ideas: the Welshman Richard Price and three Scots, the philosopher and historian David Hume, Robert Wallace, and the founder of modern economics, Adam Smith. All four were the subject of spiteful, unfounded, or condescending criticisms by Malthus in his original *Essay,* presumably to disguise his theft of their ideas, but he succeeded in taking the population debate away from the Scots and the Welsh and placing it firmly in English hands. Nevertheless, the origins of his core ideas in the Scottish Enlightenment are undeniable. In the sixth edition of his *Essay* (1826), a calmer Malthus dealt at length with the demographic evidence for Scotland, drawn from the *Statistical Account* of Sir John Sinclair published nearly thirty years earlier. In his view, emigration, the spread of the potato, and manufacturing had improved the condition of those who had remained behind. He considered that Scotland was still "overpeopled" but judged that the Scots were better off than they were in 1750 or 1700.

HOW MANY PEOPLE?

No one knows for certain how many Scots there were before 1750, nor will they ever know. Yet in order to make sense of migration, it is essential to have some idea about the likely size of Scotland's population before 1750. Like everywhere else Scottish governments only counted their people if they wanted to tax them. Money, not people, justified the trouble of counting. Thus the first indication of the size of Scotland's population is from church revenues for 1291, which showed that the population in Scotland was roughly 19 percent that of England. In 1947, the distinguished lawyer Lord Thomas Cooper (1892–1955) used this information to estimate the Scottish population at about 400,000, and this figure is accepted here in the absence of a better-argued estimate based on his evidence for the relative prosperity of Scotland at this time. Contemporary estimates mainly start from 1700. At the Act of Union in 1707, it was estimated that Scotland had a population of about one million. The source of this figure is not known and it is usually dismissed as a lucky guess. But it may well have come from the Presbyterian Church, the only national Scottish organization with an interest in and knowledge of the topic, and, if so, it may have been accurate. Administering an education program in every parish from 1696 would have required the Church to have had some idea of the number of children in each parish in order to provide the resources they needed. It is possible too that it may have undertaken a quick count of the people for this purpose fifty years before Webster's count. When the first church was opened in Gladsmuir parish, Haddington County in 1697 a count was made of the people, and this may have been a common practice for a church then establishing itself as the new national religion. Modeling also points to a total Scottish population of about 994,000 in 1700, a result that seems too close to be coincidental. Other published estimates of the time were less accurate; for example, in his *New Survey of the Globe* (1729), Thomas Templeman gave the Scottish population as 1.5 million.

Scottish population records before 1750 were few in their day and become fewer thereafter. Parish birth registers were used from 1538 and were in general use by 1640 but most perished, either through wars, civil unrest, or neglect. Not only were there far fewer registers in Scotland than for either Wales or England, but there were serious deficiencies in those that survived. For instance, the Presbyterian clergy were more inclined to record baptisms than burials or even marriages. It is unclear why this was done but it may have been that the creation of the soul was considered more important to record than its departure to heaven where it would be in God's hands. It could have also been the administrative burden and cost of recording deaths in a society where they were so frequent. Many parishes were small and poor and to record births, deaths, and marriages required ledgers; today, such an item is taken for granted, but it was a luxury item before about 1750 that many of them may not have been able to afford.

The coverage and survival of parish registers also suffered from religious divisions. In Glasgow in 1733 the "Secession" Presbyterian group started a baptism register separate from the main church. The Episcopalians began their own baptism register in 1751 and the Roman Catholics in 1793. There were often large gaps in the surviving registers; for example, baptisms were first recorded in Glasgow in 1611 and maintained up to 1617, resumed in 1656 but halted in 1663, and then started again in 1700. A burial register was begun in 1694 but neither the names of the deceased or any details about them were added until 1783. The general registration of births was also discouraged by a national tax that was imposed in 1783 and not repealed until 1794. There is uncertainty about how the tax was enforced but none about its effect. The Rev. Mr. Findlater of Linton parish, Peebles County, reported in the 1791 that "There is no register of burials or marriages. The register of baptisms is not very accurate; a shilling is paid for registering, and poor people have an interest in omission." Bills of mortality—summaries of statistics for births, deaths, and marriages—were compiled by some parishes, but there was no effort to consolidate them or to ensure their survival.

The early history of smallpox gives a clue to the minimum size of Scotland's population before 1700. This horrifying and disfiguring disease had entered England by 1562 and infected its first recorded Scottish victim, Lord Henry Darnley, in Glasgow in 1567. In 1610, there was a second outbreak at Aberdeen, which seems to have come from within Scotland. To have a second outbreak of smallpox requires a pool of 250,000 people who are not immune to the disease, according to medical modeling. The Aberdeen outbreak implies that it had reached a second group of 250,000 people in northern Scotland who had no exposure to the disease. To have this happen points to a total population of at least 500,000 by about 1600. Something like this also seems to have happened to the Aborigines of southeastern Australia where smallpox claimed its first victims among coastal dwellers in the 1790s following contact with Europeans. This first outbreak was followed by a second large-scale outbreak among those in the interior in the 1830s before the arrival of European explorers, indicating that the Aboriginal population was at least 500,000, according to the economic historian Noel G. Butlin in *Economics and the Dreamtime*. A hearth tax for about 1691 is the first national source of Scotland's pre-1700 population. Its results were examined by Michael Flinn and his team in the 1970s, and they estimated that the population was about 862,000, assuming that each house contained 4.5 people. If they had assumed 5 people in each house, as Alexander Webster did fifty years later, it would have raised their estimate to about 960,000, providing additional evidence that the Scottish population really was about 1 million by 1700. Without the work of Alexander Webster, Robert Wallace, Sir John Sinclair, and John Rickman the reconstruction of Scotland's population before the first official national British census of 1801 would be a daunting and desperate enterprise. But by combining their results with what is known about other Western European populations before 1700, it becomes possible to make realistic estimates of the size of the Scottish population up to 1821 (refer to table 1).

WHY DID THE POPULATION GROW AFTER 1650?

Population history is dismal science. The new social history that emerged in the 1960s looked back at the mid-nineteenth century when many official statistics became available and found it wanting. Life seemed so short and bad that it was hard to believe that this time was an improvement on what it had been previously, yet it was. Going back to the mid-fourteenth century is a journey to hell. The bubonic plague—the Black Death—devastated the people of Western Europe between 1347 and 1353. It reached Scotland in 1349 and made repeated visitations up to 1649. The three surviving Scottish chronicles all claimed that its first visitation killed one in three. It did not simply kill large numbers of people; it weakened those who survived their infection, severely disrupted trade, and made economic recovery harder and slower. The Scottish population seems to have taken about 150 years to recover from the plague, hampered too by repeated famines that were recorded from 1449, when the Scottish parliament first prohibited the export of food. By this time the population was probably only about 300,000—a quarter less than it may have been in 1300. The scale and generality of death in the past is barely comprehensible to the present, even by Third World standards. Between about 1550 and 1650, probably about a third of Scottish baby boys and a quarter of baby girls died before they were one year old. Life expectancy at birth was about 30 for females but only 27 for males. The population grew slowly because so many died young, narrowing the gap between births and deaths. Today, dying is mainly done by older people and the deaths of the young are regarded as tragic, but for most of history it was the other way round; in Scotland, nearly half of deaths between 1740 and 1820 occurred among those under 20 years of age.

It has long been known that from about 1750 world population growth was faster than before it, but how this came about has remained obscure. Matching the ages of the Scottish population between 1751 and 1821 with population models, it is possible to find out when and how these changes happened. They reveal that Scottish mortality declined in three distinct steps (rather than gradually) and that it occurred mostly among those under 5 years of age. The first of these falls began around 1650, the second around 1706, and the third around 1740. Their effects were small at first but over time they reshaped the Scottish population. Why did they happen?

These falls in mortality are certainly consistent with the general warming trend in southeast Scotland from around 1650 first identified by the geographer M. L. Parry in 1975, but this was likely to have been slow and unsteady. In his assessment of this period, Michael Flinn pointed out that although there was no agricultural revolution, there was an increase in country markets and fairs, of which 246 new ones were licensed between 1660 and 1707, suggesting than an improvement in food distribution may have been more important than climate change. More likely, these falls in Scottish mortality were caused simply by the lack of new epidemics and the absence of the large-scale violence and wars that had characterized the period from 1550 to 1650. They were well under way before the widespread cultivation of the potato, and it seems unlikely that they were confined to Scotland, as mortality in Scandinavia and Switzerland is also known to have declined at about this time.

From about 1706 to 1740, life expectancy at birth for both sexes rose, even though this improvement came from a low base—30 years for males and 33 years for females—but the improvement was real nevertheless. It happened because of a fall in the number of deaths among infants and toddlers; in a population of a million that meant that there were 6,000 more young children surviving each year. These changes would not have been evident to contemporaries, as the death rate of those ages 5 and older hardly changed. They might seem trivial compared to later periods, but they were permanent; and as the additional survivors went on to have children of their own, they caused a sustained rise in the population that strained the capacity of Scotland to provide for its people. Understanding this hidden demographic revolution casts a new light on eighteenth-century Scottish history. By 1750 it would have added about 60,000 to the population. It meant too that there would have been about 12,000 more males of military age (between 15 and 34) available for the 1745 Jacobite Rebellion than would have been available forty years before, a small figure in itself until it is remembered that the army that Charles Edward Stewart used to invade England was only 5,000 strong. With fewer people dying and more surviving to have children, the rate of population growth was higher starting in 1740. The reason for these changes was the same: falling mortality from 1650. Between 1740 and 1860, the infant mortality rate fell from 200 to 167 per 1,000 births for baby boys and from 271 to 142 for baby girls, very high levels compared with later years but a definite improvement on the rates before 1740.

Fertility—the number of births per 1,000—changed less before the 1880s when artificial contraception become gradually more available; between 1740 and 1860 it was mostly between 34 and 39 for males and 31 to 32 for females. The only exception was a spike in the birth rate in the 1810s caused by the return of soldiers from the Napoleonic wars. There was no doubt that population growth came from lower mortality, not higher fertility, and its cumulative effect doubled the Scottish population between 1700 and 1820 to 2.1 million. When the age distribution figures for counties at the 1821 census are grouped into regions, they show that these changes were generally applicable across Scotland and not confined to particular areas. Their effects of were not only pervasive; they gave Scotland what it needed least: more Scots. With the suppression of the 1745 Jacobite Rebellion, the demand for soldiers within Scotland vanished and the economic value of the additional people fell. No longer needed, they were indeed surplus to requirements and this grim fact underpinned the conversion of farming land to sheep grazing from 1762. The Presbyterian clergy repeatedly told Sir John Sinclair in the 1790s that the replacement of farming by sheep grazing had reduced the population of their rural parishes. When the clergy did report increases in their congregations because of fewer deaths, they mostly credited it to smallpox inoculations. although the Rev. Mr. William Bethune in Duirinish parish on the Isle of Skye, added the interesting observation that "a more judicious and rational treatment of children and women in child-bed, than was formerly observed" had also helped increase his parishioners. There was no question that population growth long proceeded the advent of the Industrial Revolution in Scotland.

A MAINLY FEMALE PEOPLE?

Recorded Scottish history is history with a hairy chest, dominated by warriors and kings. After 1750, the actors of Scottish history change from kings and warriors to politicians and business leaders but they remain male, as do its writers of renown. Females, apart from queens, are very much in the distance, yet even by 1650 most of the Scottish people were female. Sir John Sinclair was the first to ask about the numbers of males and females in Scotland in the early 1790s. Less than half the parish clergy bothered to count the sexes and their reports only covered 45 percent of the people. Nonetheless they included Glasgow, Edinburgh, Aberdeen, and Inverness, and they revealed that about 53 percent of Scots were female. Modeling confirms this finding, estimating that 54 percent were female, and every census since 1801 has shown that Scotland has had more females than males.

The long-standing female majority of Scotland is not a new finding: Michael Flinn judged in 1977 that a majority of Scots were females even by 1690 and definitely so in 1790 based on the parish reports to Sir John Sinclair. He also noted the female majorities among those living on estates forfeited to the Crown after the Jacobite Rebellion of 1745. The female majorities on these estates could, of course, have come about simply from the loss of men on military service, but it may well have been that they would have had female majorities regardless. With no other evidence for guidance, it has been assumed that emigration has been the main reason for the female majority. Emigration certainly reduced the male population, but it was not the underlying cause.

Modeling shows that even without emigration most Scots would still have been female because the same falls in mortality after 1650 that were responsible for increased population growth generally were more pronounced among females than males. As more females survived from infancy to adulthood, they slowly became the majority from as early as about 1680—but more likely from 1650—making up about 51 percent of the population by 1751, giving them a margin of about 34,000, mainly for those over 30. Thereafter, the female majority was maintained not just by their lesser mortality compared with males but also by the withdrawal of large numbers of Scottish men into the British army; of the 200,000 who left Scotland permanently between 1751 and 1776, probably about 120,000 were males and 70,000 of these were soldiers. This loss over a relatively short time considerably lowered the number of Scottish males and it was never quite recovered. In all, this loss amounted to about 15 percent of the population counted by Webster, wiping out all the population growth in the twenty-five years after his census. It left fewer women able to get married, and by staying single they avoided childbirth, the leading cause of female deaths apart from diseases; single women may have stayed poor but at least they survived. There was a second round of military participation during the wars with Revolutionary France and Napoleon when the number of Scots in the British army was again about 70,000; and although many returned by 1815, it was still not sufficient to produce a male majority. It was this combination of lower mortality among females and military participation that was primarily responsible for the female majority. Females would have outnumbered males by 150,000 by 1860 and by 120,000 in 1870, according to modeling without any allowance for emigration. And even through the mortality gap between the sexes narrowed after 1880, it remained and females still continued to have longer lives.

There is no question that emigration between 1840 and 1900 lowered the number of Scottish males, but its impact on their share of the population was nowhere near as great as commonly assumed then and later. In all, 1.14 million Scots left in these sixty years but 500,000 females left too, making the net loss of males only 140,000. The effect of migration on the sexes was even less between 1900 and 1930 when 940,000 left but net loss of males compared with females was only 38,000. What emigration did was to maintain the cumulative effect of previous military losses on the male population and the mortality advantage of females over males, ensuring that the Scottish people continued to be mainly female.

JAMES CLELAND'S GLASGOW, 1820S

Glasgow was the upstart of urban-industrial Scotland from about 1780, and by 1791 its city and suburbs had reached 107,000, overtaking Edinburgh with 89,000. The emergence of Glasgow as Scotland's most populous city fascinated James Cleland (1770–1840), its supervisor of public works from 1814 to 1834, and he monitored his city with a skill, devotion, and enthusiasm unmatched by another Scottish administrator of his age. He was a pioneering social and demographic investigator who deserves to be better known. In the 1820s and 1830s he critically examined, reformed, and published population statistics for Glasgow both past and present. His bills of mortality for Glasgow even included statistics on stillbirths, figures that were not published nationally until 1939, and his efforts must be among the first attempts anywhere to collect figures on this sad subject.

If Cleland saw something missing in a statistical collection, he put it in, at least for Glasgow. He added a question about birthplaces for the 1821 census, twenty years before it was asked of all Scots. For the 1831 census, he asked about religious affiliation, again twenty years before anyone else did in Britain.

He published most of his findings in two landmark works: *Statistical Tables Relative to the City of Glasgow* (1823) and *Enumeration of the Inhabitants of the City of Glasgow and County of Lanark* (1832). Cleland's achievements enable a portrait to be given of the population of Scotland's largest city for the 1820s, a decade marked by severe depression at its start; in 1821–1822, 3,000 Glaswegians were assisted to emigrate. He found that infant mortality was 262 per 1,000 births for 1821–1822 but that it halved to 137 by 1830. It was city with job opportunities too, gaining 36,000 migrants in the 1820s, of whom about half came from Ireland, raising its population from 147,000 to 202,000. Cleland was a generation ahead of his time. He began charting the long, messy shift to an urbanized society based on manufacturing, trends that characterized Scotland for the next 150 years. He can also be seen as the last in a line of investigators of Scottish society that began with Alexander Webster and Robert Wallace in the 1750s, a tradition was continued by Sir John Sinclair in the 1790s, men of great humanity who tried to improve the condition of the Scottish people. The Scottish Enlightenment may have died with him but his spirit of enquiry lived on.

ENLIGHTENMENT INDEED

This premise of this chapter—that the Scots were a people who needed to be discovered—may now seem to be less odd than at the beginning. Scotland's population history before 1860 has a richness matched by few other nations, and when the contributions made by its investigators—Robert Wallace, Alexander Webster, Sir John Sinclair, John Rickman, and James Cleland—are examined, their contribution to Western European population history can be given its long overdue recognition. Together, they provided the first hard evidence that there were three small but lasting falls in mortality in about 1650, 1706, and 1740, falls that brought faster population growth from 1750 than before it. Those who have rightly pointed to 1750 as the starting point for the acceleration of world population growth can take comfort from the Scottish evidence and thank its investigators who made this knowledge possible.

The pre-1830s investigations, particularly by Sir John Sinclair, established a benchmark not just for Scotland but for the study of the populations of Northern Europe in general. In the 1850s there was a renewal of interest in the Scottish people by its leaders. These investigations took various forms, not just through the population census, which the Scots conducted themselves from 1861, but also through the annual reports of the registrar general for Scotland, which were published from 1855. Some of this information is not available for any other country and some of it seems to be the first of its kind in the world. What kind of people did the investigators discover? Much of it records the transformation of their economic world to an urbanized, industrialized society with topics such as occupations and housing taking prominence, but other topics were explored too. Their works show that despite the scale of these changes, the pillars of the Scots' domestic world—family, marriage, and religion—changed only slowly, even though they too had to adapt to this transformation. Scotland remained very much a land of kith and kin, something especially evident later in its migrants to North America.

WHAT WERE THEIR NAMES?

One of the many benefits of the introduction of a national system for recording births, deaths, and marriages in 1855 was the collection of the names of the Scottish people for the first time. It made possible the conducting of Scotland's first onomastic survey by William P. Dundas, the first registrar general for Scotland to discover the fifty most frequent family and first names recorded for 1858. He published his results in 1860 and estimated that the most common family names covered about 30 percent of the people. The results were expected in most respects, but less so in others. Smith was easily the most frequent family name (as it was in England in 1853) and remained so in the subsequent Scottish name surveys conducted in 1935 and 1958. There have been several notable Smiths in Scottish history: the great economist Adam Smith (1723–1790) and John Smith (1938–1994) the leader of the Labour Party. More predictably, John, James, and William were the most popular male names and Margaret, Mary, and Elizabeth were most popular female names. Appendix 2 contains the ranking of the most numerous family and first names in 1858, 1935, and 1958.

The 1858 survey distinguished four main indigenous groups among the family names. The first group were names belonging to clans. These included all names beginning with Mac ("son of")—MacDonald, MacGregor,

MacKay, MacKenzie, MacLean, and MacLeod were all in the top fifty—as well as names such as Fraser, Douglas, Cameron, Kerr, and Grant.

The second group of names were also clan-related, recording their descent from the head of an important family, such as Robertson, Thomson, Johnston, Watson, and Morrison. This second group of names were often taken from occupations, notably Smith, Miller, Clark, Taylor, Walker, and Hunter.

Family names based on places made up a third group. Counties provided names such as Fife, Nairn, Stirling, Ross, Lothian, Sutherland, Berwick, and Roxburgh. Cities and towns gave rise to names like Glasgow, Leith, Aberdeen, Forfar, Montrose, Biggar, Lander, Melrose, and Hamilton. Some parishes also contributed to the mix with names such as Abbey, Fordyce, Alves, Peebles, Farr, Bathgate, Callander, Traquair, Campsie, Cullen, Kirkpatrick, and Bothwell.

Personal appearance or attributes provided a mixed fourth group. Some names came from colors, such as Black, White, Green, Gray, and Brown. Others, less kindly, recalled a resemblance to an animal such as Lyon, Bull, Bullock, Lamb, Hogg (meaning a one-year old lamb), Collie, and Tod (meaning a fox). Fish also inspired family names like Haddock, Salmon, Swan, Heron, and Fish on its own. Size provided family names such as Meikle (meaning large), Little, Long, Littlejohn, and Meiklejohn, as did personal attributes such as Strong, Stark, Swift, Bold, Good, and Noble.

Irish immigrants were said to have added a thousand family names to Scotland from 1820, but the survey may have overstated their long-term effect as many Irish did not stay in Scotland for long. The largest Irish family name, Kelly, for instance, was not in the top fifty family names in 1858, but was ranked forty-second in 1935 and forty-fifth in 1958. Gallacher, Murphy, McLaughlin, and Boyle were ranked between fifty and a hundred in 1935 and 1958. My family name, Docherty, was ranked sixty-first in 1935 and fifty-fifth in 1958, but I know my forebears were assimilated Scots long before 1820.

The naming tradition for first names of sons and daughters was limited and unimaginative with John and James being most common for boys and Margaret and Mary for girls. It was also common for the first born in families to be given the first names of their parents and it was a custom continued by Scottish emigrants. The 1881 Canadian census schedules point to about 40 percent of first born among the Scots-born being named after their parents. This was a common practice of the time and not confined to Scotland; a survey of East Londoners by Michael Young and Peter Willmott between 1953 and 1955 found that of those born before 1896, 58 percent of fathers and 38 percent of mothers had named their first born after themselves.

WHAT WERE THEIR FAITHS?

Religious fundamentalism in the form of Presbyterianism remade Scottish religion and society after its introduction by John Knox in 1559. A religion for violent and difficult times, Presbyterianism was a faith to fight and die for. It won its battle, eventually, in 1690 when it was established as the state religion. Now secure, it set about founding Presbyterian schools in every parish from 1696 and in 1709 launched a second program to take Presbyterianism and education to the Highlands and western islands. It also fed the Scottish Enlightenment. Literacy was central to Protestantism because it was through reading the Bible that Christians were brought closer to the word of God and made better Christians. Widespread literacy was to have another and unintended consequence; it meant that Scottish migrants were to have a useful advantage over other emigrant groups, such as the Irish, particularly before the 1870s.

If Presbyterianism was the church triumphant, Catholicism, Scotland's religion for most of the previous thousand years, was the church defeated. Purged from official life and the educational system, it collapsed. In his census of about 1751, Webster asked ministers to report the number of Catholics—everyone else was assumed to be Protestant—but only 16,488 were uncovered, nearly all of them in Argyll, Aberdeen, Banff, or Inverness and only five for all of Glasgow. The results must be an undercount, but even so it seems unlikely that Catholics were more than 2 percent of Scots or about 25,000 in all. Presbyterianism may have been the church triumphant, but it was not a united faith, undergoing a series of splits from 1733 before being eventually reunited in 1929. But these did nothing to reduce its political and social power, and Scotland retained many of the features of a theocratic state before 1940.

Within Protestantism, Scotland had some diversity of religions. In the parish reports for about 1791 in Sir John Sinclair's *Statistical Account*, some clergy went to the trouble of counting those of different faiths. As expected, they found that the great majority were Presbyterian of one sort of another, but they also found a sprinkling of Episcopalians, Methodists, a few Catholics, and even some Cameronians, a sect dating from the 1680s. Otherwise, Scotland's religious mix seems to have changed little until about 1820 when Irish immigration slowly raised the number of Catholics. In 1831 James Cleland included religion in the census for Glasgow and found that 86 percent were Presbyterians of some kind, 4 percent were Episcopalians, and 10 percent were Catholics. There were too few Jews to give a percentage. No other administrator followed his example, and it was not until 1851 that there was a general count of the religions of the people based on those who attended church services on Sunday, March 30. The results were detailed but they were a considerable undercount of Catholics (61,000) who were placed only just ahead of the Congregationalists (57,000). Yet at the time the census was taken, there were 207,000 Irish-born in Scotland and about half of them were probably Catholics, not including their children born in Scotland. It also falls well short of the percentage of Scots who married in the Roman Catholic Church, which was steady at 9 percent between 1855 and 1860. A possible reason for the disparity may have been the high mobility of the Irish-born in and out of Scotland.

In contrast to the Catholics, the figures for Presbyterians of all kinds were similar to those who married during the last half of the 1850s, 85 percent compared with 83 percent. For other faiths, the results were distinctly odd; for instance, only 35 Jews were identified compared with 3,237 Mormons. Clearly, the religious census of 1851 was an interesting, if only a partly representative profile of the Scottish people and, in the absence of any later census figures on religious beliefs for Scotland until 2001, the marriage figures must be given priority over this one-off count. Actual religious practice was far more difficult to measure because urbanization after 1851 weakened the hold of the Presbyterian Church in the big cities. Church attendances were low compared with what they had been in the rural areas, and its schisms seem to have been largely ignored by the laity and by Scottish emigrants after 1880. Nevertheless, the churches retained their power over marriage until 1939 when civil marriages were finally permitted. Divorce was effectively forbidden by the Church and they took thirty years to summon sufficient Christian charity to grant a divorce to my mother for her marriage in the 1930s, despite repeated appeals. It was not until 1921 that divorce was first recognized in the Scottish census as a marital status, and only 3,418 persons admitted that they were divorced.

WERE THEY MARRIED?

Was there a distinct Scottish marriage pattern? Much of the previous literature has seen marriage through the eyes of the Presbyterian Church, which concerned itself unduly with "irregular" marriages and illegitimacy as sin. What actually took place received little attention until 1993 when Michael Anderson and Donald J. Morse examined the Scottish marriage pattern from 1861 to 1914 and concluded that that it differed from England in a number of ways. They found that although the Scottish marriage rate was lower, the birth rate was comparable and that the number of children produced by marriages was much higher, differences they attributed to emigration. Their work raised two questions: Was this pattern evident before 1861, and was it caused by emigration?

Marriage was not a topic in Webster's census, but it was included in the parish reports demanded by Sir John Sinclair from all parishes for about

1791. The joy of this information was that it included counts of the population that make it possible to find out how prevalent marriage was and how many eventually married. Sir John received marriage figures for fifty-eight parishes of which nine included figures for about 1751 that can be linked with Webster's census. Few clergy responded to his request to collect information about the marital status of their people in the 1790s, but the figures they did supply, covering about 24,000, seem to have been reasonably representative of the whole population. Sir John also collected data from the parishes for 1821 that he published in 1831 and complained that the absence of marital status from the census was a "material omission." According to his reports the number of marriages averaged about 16 per 1,000 ages twenty or older between 1751 and 1791—almost the same as for the Scots-born in 1881 (17 per thousand), according to unpublished census data for 1881.

These results testify to the stability of the marital status of the Scots between 1791 and 1881 regardless of how they were considered by the Presbyterian Church. They demonstrate that there was certainly no aversion to marriage—about 58 percent over age twenty were married—but also that it was far from universal, with about 30 percent over twenty being unmarried at any one time. The proportion of widowers or widows increased from about 9 to 12 percent between 1821 and 1881. Most importantly, although it was legal to get married before twenty, it was socially taboo and very few did so. Of those who married between 1855 and 1901, half the men did so by twenty-six and by twenty-four for women, which was somewhat later that in England and Wales. The reason for this gap was noted in 1861 and attributed by William P. Dundas, the registrar general, to "the young men finding greater difficulty in procuring employment than in England." Another reason for the difference must also have been the high proportion of working Scottish women who were domestic servants, a socially isolated occupation that also lead to marriages later in life, or even not at all; in 1911, 92 percent of Scottish domestic servants over twenty were single. Between 1861 and 1864, Dundas also carried out the first investigation of the death rates for the married and widowed compared with the unmarried and found that the married and widowed generally had lower death rates, especially for men, figures that were not collected again in Scotland until 1911.

His suggestion that marriages in Scotland were limited by means finds support in the marriage patterns of the Scots in New South Wales, where their better prospects resulted in not only a higher level of marriage for Scottish women but also marriage at a slightly younger age. Regardless of cause, Dundas also noted that the later marriages in Scotland did nothing to lower the number of children born by Scottish wives and that indeed marital fertility was higher than in England as whole. This was true, but it was not unique to Scotland; for example, a similar pattern was also evident in South

Wales. Marital fertility was not only higher than in England but fell more slowly between 1861 and 1911.

In some ways those who never married reveal more about the Scottish marriage pattern than those who did. Of those who turned twenty between 1777 and 1811, about 9 percent of men never married—a fairly common proportion—but for it women it was about 20 percent according to the 1851 census. The causes of the disparity between the sexes lay not just in the social disruption caused by soldiers absent abroad but also, as discussed, in the underlying tendency of the Scottish population to produce more females than males from about 1650 to 1890, reducing the pool of eligible men. Unmarried women were not just lesser members of society, they were usually expected to care for elderly parents too ahead of their married siblings. The unmarried varied by region too. Strathclyde had the lowest proportion of unmarried for both sexes, and Grampian (Aberdeen and its hinterland) had the highest proportion of women who never married, 25 percent. As this was a period when there was limited Scottish emigration, it is likely that internal migration was more responsible for lowering the chances of women marrying in the north. Comparing the unmarried by age in 1851 with those in 1911, when there had been significant emigration in the previous decade, shows little difference for those ages forty-five or over but a somewhat higher level for those under forty-five—and shows that women were still less likely to marry than men. As mentioned, emigration reduced the number of males but it alone cannot explain these trends. Also, emigration varied greatly; it was high in the 1880s (249,000) but slumped in the 1890s (167,000). The grim truth was that marriage, like emigration, needed means, and the reason for the rising level of the unmarried from 1900 was the parlous state of the Scottish economy and the increased impoverishment it caused.

HOUSEHOLD AND FAMILY SIZE

Webster's census did not ask about either household or family size, but in his discussion of St Cuthbert's parish, Edinburgh, he estimated that there were 5 persons per house. In his census of about 1791, Sir John Sinclair asked the Presbyterian clergy to count the number of occupied houses and give the average number of their residents. Although many did not do this, the clergy in seven parishes (Cramond, Edinburgh; Kilrenny, Fife; Grange, Banff; Birse, Aberdeen; Erskine, Renfrew; Kilsyth, Stirling; and, Bendochy, Perth) not only counted the number of households, but also classified them by size. Covering 8,550 people, their returns showed that 57 percent of families had 1 to 5 occupants, which meant that the 68 percent recorded for Scottish households of this size in the 1860s was a distinct increase in overcrowding.

Information on family size in the population censuses of most Western countries before 1910 is scarce and even rarer before 1850. Scotland is most unusual in that some of this information was collected as part of Sir John Sinclair's work in the 1790s. In Kilsyth parish, Stirling County, the minister, Mr Robert Rennie, went to the trouble of counting the number of children in married couple families. This parish then had a total population of 2,450, a mixture of a township and surrounding countryside. He found that nearly half the couples had four children. Reports from five other parishes, although less detailed, suggest that these results were typical for Scottish families in the early 1790s and that 4–5 children per married couple at any one time was commonplace. In 1855, the newly appointed registrar general for Scotland, William P. Dundas, carried out what may have been the world's first retrospective investigation of the previous number of children born to married mothers. His published his results for Edinburgh, only covering 4,208 mothers, and found that wives who had completed their childbearing—those born in 1815 or earlier— had had an average of seven children. It was not until 1911 that the Scottish census directly investigated marital fertility; although its results were not directly comparable with Dundas's survey, it found a well-established trend toward fewer children compared with the 1850s. For those wives who had married at age twenty-four, it found that they had an average of 6.9 children before 1870 but fewer thereafter: 6.3 in the 1870s and 5.8 in the 1880s. This fall was not confined to Scotland but occurred throughout Western Europe to varying degrees.

ONLY SLOW IMPROVEMENT, 1750–1900

Between 1750 and 1900 the social institutions reviewed in this chapter grappled with the greatest structural changes in Scottish history. The forced evictions, together with considerable internal migration, meant that Scottish family names in the north and west were less geographically concentrated than they had been previously. Urbanization and manufacturing pulled, if not forced, rural people to the towns and cities, adding not only to the diffusion of family names but also diluting the influence of Presbyterian Church, even though its nominal strength remained strong and it retained its control over most marriages before 1940. Population growth underlay these trends, generated largely by falls in the death rate starting in 1650, but it was anything but continuous; between 1751 and 1776 it would have been flat because of large-scale military recruitment. Scotland should have had about 1.7 million people by 1791 but only 1.5 million were counted. Population growth resumed slowly from about 1775 to reach 1.6 million by 1801, after which time it was boosted by the return of about 144,000 expatriate Scots. In 1821 that the population was 2.1 million, double compared with what it had been in 1700.

Between 1821 and 1901, the Scottish population more than doubled from 2.1 to 4.4 million. The birth rate hardly changed between 1820 and 1880 (from 35 to 34 per 1,000) but the death rate fell, from 25 to 20 per thousand. Both birth and death rates fell and continued to fall after this time, marking the start of what is now known as demographic transition. Life expectancy at birth rose slowly, but it did rise; from having been stuck at 34 for males and 38 for females for a century from 1740 to 1820, it eventually reached 45 for males and 48 for females by 1901, mainly because of falls in infant and child mortality. That there were improvements in the condition of the people is unquestionable, but they were small and agonizingly slow, taking place in a highly inequitable society and within an economy that struggled to provide for them.

Chapter Two

Scotland Made and Unmade

Scotland was made and unmade by its economy. Before the eighteenth century the Scottish economy was largely confined to its eastern half, mainly between Aberdeen and Edinburgh. By about 1400, all but five of Scotland's twenty-one coin mints were in its eastern half, and the western half remained an economic backwater, well off the main trade routes of the North Sea, a wild west where life was even poorer and more violent than on the eastern side. From about 1725 this imbalance began to be redressed when England's trade in its second legal drug after alcohol—tobacco—was captured by Glasgow merchants. Over the next fifty years these merchants built a thriving trade with Virginia and Maryland until it was ended by the American War of Independence. In that time, they made Glasgow Scotland's largest city by 1791 and the heart of the new economy in the southwest. The money earned from tobacco was invested in manufacturing and infrastructure, and, despite Scotland being on the edge of Western Europe, it became one of the cradles of the Industrial Revolution. It was a revolution with an evil reputation—exploitation of child and women's labor, long hours and dangerous working conditions. But in Scotland, at least at first, at New Lanark under David Dale (1739–1806) and his son-in-law Robert Owen (1771–1858), it started with a concerted effort, through traditional paternalism, to improve the condition of the people. Their brave, humane beginning was ignored by most industrialists and condemned later by the Left as unscientific and irrelevant.

Scholarly interest in Scotland's economic history began in the 1920s and has been traditionally concerned with growth and production; it was not until the 1970s that the labor force received attention. In 1973, E. H. Hunt included Scotland in his analysis of British regional differences in wages between 1850 and 1913, and changes in the structure of the Scottish labor force were examined in *People and Society in Scotland, 1760–1990* (1988–1992) edited by Thomas M. Devine and Rosalind Mitchison. Clive Lee, an economic historian at Aberdeen University, used the regions created by the 1975 county amalgamations as the basis for his indispensable study, *British Regional Employment Statistics, 1841–1971* (1979). His work is the basis of much of this chapter, which surveys Scotland's economic history from the perspective of employment and migration up to 1930. Like elsewhere in Britain, Scottish economic history is regional history, but this is for others to investigate and this chapter sticks only to the broad trends. It considers the record of the economy starting with land ownership and urbanization, its mixed fortunes during the Victorian era, and Scotland's conversion into a "distressed region" after 1901.

NOT THE LAND OF OPPORTUNITY

Scotland consisted of land owned by only a few Scots. Figures published in the 1890 US census revealed that Scotland had the lowest level of land ownership in Britain, even lower than Ireland. There were only 19,225 Scots who owned one or more acres of land compared with 32,610 in Ireland. Larger land owners—those who owned ten acres or more—were even fewer: there were 25,700 in Ireland but only 9,720 in Scotland. In 1883, John Bateman published the last edition of his *Great Landowners of Great Britain and Ireland*, in which he gave a detailed listing of Scottish landowners by name, the acreage they owned, and their income from their lands at June 1882. His work revealed that about 630 individuals owned 80 percent of Scotland. This state of extreme inequality originated in Scotland's medieval past and was sustained by the poverty of the natural environment, much of it of volcanic origin. As in Wales, it aroused no popular resentment because most of the owners were Scots and so there was no "land question" (in contrast to Ireland where many owners were absentee English). On occasions, the Scottish landowners could unite to benefit Scotland too. For instance, in 1885 they successfully lobbied for the re-establishment of the cabinet post of secretary of state for Scotland after a gap of 139 years.

Scottish landowners have traditionally received terrible press for the forced evictions of thousands from their lands, dishonoring their implied but ancient obligations to care for their people. The worst case was the eviction of thousands from Sutherland County between 1807 and 1821, but the population of Sutherland County still grew to 25,500 in 1831 and only started falling after that. The forced evictions rightly aroused violence and animosity, but less well known were the very low returns landowners received from their lands. John Bateman's list of large landowners for Scotland in 1882 showed that the Sutherland County had the lowest income per acre of any part of Scotland at just £0.05, hardly a great result for decades of determined capitalist exploitation and only a third of the average income per acre for the Highlands as a whole. The brutal truth was that the land was simply too poor to support its rising population. It also needs to be remembered that not all large landowners behaved abominably toward their people. As discussed, Sir John Sinclair, a large landowner based in Thurso, Caithness County, cared passionately about the people and campaigned continually from the 1790s to his death in 1835 to boost agricultural productivity to ensure they had enough to eat. The Earl of Selkirk tried to found a settlement for Scots in what is now Manitoba, Canada, between 1811 and 1817. Moreover, the total income declared by the large landowners in 1882 was £5.4 million, an impressive sum for only 630 individuals, but on its own not such an impressive economic indicator; even the Scottish cooperative movement had sales of £3.8 million in 1882.

Despite urban and manufacturing growth, agriculture and rural dwellers continued to be prominent features of Scottish society. It was not until 1881 that most Scots lived in towns or cities. And although the rural share of the population fell, the number of rural dwellers continued to rise to reach a peak of 1.8 million in 1911, accounting for 38 percent of the total population, almost twice that of England and Wales. Even by 1931, a third of Scots were rural dwellers. Agricultural occupations remained important too. In 1881, the largest male occupation in Scotland was agricultural laborer (90,000) with farmers and their sons (68,000) holding equal second place with general laborers. Among women, agricultural laborer (27,000) was the third largest occupation behind domestic servant, dressmaker, and milliner. In all, 17 percent of the labor force worked in agricultural occupations in 1881 compared with 22 percent in 1871, and its share continued to fall. Dying demand for rural labor fed a sustained movement to Scottish towns and cities as a first resort rather than going to England or making an overseas journey to find work. Nevertheless many urban Scots retained their rural dreams to return to the land, and the goal of many Scottish migrants to North America and Australasia before 1880 was to acquire land.

A CONSCRIPTED URBAN PEOPLE

Robbie Burns's heart might have been in the Highlands at the close of the eighteenth century, but town life was an increasingly important fact of life for many Scots. Between 1700 and 1750, there was a substantial rise in Scottish urbanization from about one in ten to about one in five, defining "urban" as a town with at least 2,500 people. Between 1751 and 1791, the urban dwellers grew much faster than rural dwellers (185,000 compared with 25,000). By 1791 a quarter of Scots were urban dwellers, even if they had little desire to be so. This shift came about mainly because of the forced eviction of thousands of traditional occupiers from their land to make way for sheep grazing. They had no choice but to either go to the towns and cities or leave Scotland altogether, often with the army. It is common to blame the Industrial Revolution for the social problems of these times, but Scotland proved that accelerated population growth and forced urbanization long preceded significant industrialization.

Based on the towns' medieval origins as burghs and the physical geography, most Scottish town growth took place in a ragged triangle bounded by Aberdeen in the north to Edinburgh in the east and Glasgow in the west. The four largest cities in 1791—Edinburgh, Glasgow, Dundee, and Aberdeen—continued to be so, and by the mid-1870s half of Scots were urbanized, a level reached in England in 1851. The dominance of these cities was reinforced by the railroads, which linked Glasgow and Edinburgh in 1842 and were joined by Dundee and Aberdeen by 1875. Scottish urban growth came from the rural areas, the urban population already present, and immigrants, mainly from Ireland. But this growth was uneven and volatile before the 1880s, a mirror of the struggling Scottish economy. Although the emergence of Glasgow was the outstanding feature of Scottish urbanization from 1791 to 1931, small towns—those with 2,500–10,000 inhabitants—continued to hold a significant part of the urban population, home to about one in eight Scots between 1911 and 1971.

By 1931, 67 percent were urban dwellers compared with 62 percent in 1901, but growth did not mean improvement. Scottish urbanization was nasty, akin to that of a Third World country and Scotland became known for having, if not the most overcrowded housing in Western Europe, then among the very worst. There was nothing new about the overcrowding of Scotland's homes—Defoe noted it in 1726—and continued population growth magnified its many evils. Tuberculosis and other respiratory diseases flourished with devastating consequences for families. All too often young and middle-aged women were their victims, leaving a swathe of motherless children and widowers in their wake. On the other side of the North Sea, only the Norwegian artist Edvard Munch had the courage to sketch an all-too-common event in Scotland: the death of the mother from tuberculosis. His *The Dead Mother and the Child* (1899) captured the emotional catastrophe; the mother lies at peace, her little daughter holds her hands to her head unable to contain or comprehend her loss. Munch knew his subject well; tuberculosis killed his mother when he was five and his favorite sister when he was fifteen.

When Annie Cairns died at the age of thirty-seven in Glasgow of tuberculosis in 1884, her academically promising son James was forced to leave school at thirteen to get a job; he later added Cairns as his middle name in memory of his mother. He went to become the manager of the Oxford University Press in Glasgow in the 1900s and Cairns also became my middle name. Tuberculosis continued to be a prime killer of Scots well into the twentieth century. In 1911, for example, it killed 2,569 Scottish females of whom 71 percent were ages fifteen to forty-four, and of this group about 830 would have been married, leaving about 3,300 children motherless. In 1918, six women died of tuberculosis in St Andrews; one of them, Jessie Hill, a forty-four-year-old domestic servant, left behind an eleven-year-old daughter, Alma, and a four-year-old son, Tom, who used to sit on a low wall in Golf Place waiting for his mother. Later in life he adopted Hill as his middle name in remembrance of the mother he never had.

THE VICTORIAN ECONOMY: MIXED RESULTS

Scottish economic history has traditionally been about manufacturing and policy "problems." It has been seemingly untroubled by the lack of gross domestic product statistics for Scotland before the late 1980s and developing measures of the demand for labor, let alone migration or connection with other disciplines. Yet understanding Scottish migration requires an appreciation of these issues and the paradoxical record of the economy before and after 1901. By most output measures, the economy of Victorian Scotland grew strongly. Between 1841 and 1901, the labor force doubled from 1 to 2 million, a feat never achieved before or since. Coal production went up sixfold to 30 million. Shipbuilding on the Clyde—a touchstone Scottish measure—increased fivefold to 519,000 tons between 1867 and 1901. Railroad mileage more than trebled to 3,600 miles from 1854 to 1900, and the number of railroad journeys jumped tenfold to 122 million. Improved communication increased the flow of information. Between 1870 and 1900 the number of letters delivered in Scotland more than doubled to 197 million. True, there were periodic depressions, as happened elsewhere in Britain, North America, and Australia, but viewed only from growth indicators like these, it is hard to see what emigration should have been so high.

Alas, below the surface all was not well with the economy in the Victorian era. To begin with, industrial Glasgow, famous for its shipbuilding, faced increasing direct competition from neighboring Belfast. Second, there was cause for concern about some of the shifts in the sectors that made up the Scottish economy, notably agriculture, the third largest sector after manufacturing and services. Agricultural employment peaked in 1871 at 325,000 or 22 percent of the labor force but fell thereafter because of the general depression between 1875 and 1886 and because of cheaper imported food, mainly from North America. It continued to fall thereafter, and by 1901 agriculture employed only one in eight working Scots and less than one in ten by 1931 or about the same as in Wales.

Despite the scale of this change and the social disruption it caused, very little of it flowed directly into external migration, to the "land hunger" that characterized European migration to North America and Australasia before 1890. Some movement, undoubtedly, did occur but it was much less than might have been expected; for example, only about 2,400 of the 19,500 Scots who entered the United States between 1875 and 1880 gave their occupation as either farmer or agricultural laborer. There were two reasons why there seemed to be no obvious relationship between the decline in agricultural employment and external migration after 1870. The first was that rural society was deeply traditional, a world of close communities, poorer, more hesitant to go overseas, and less well-informed about the possible benefits of emigration. Rural Scots preferred to stay put, to go to other rural occupations, or to move to other parts of Scotland. This was evident too from the limited success of assisted migration schemes run by governments in Australia and New Zealand to recruit large numbers of rural workers for their farmers in the 1870s and 1880s.

The second reason was that the option of taking up cheap land was no longer readily available in either North America or Australasia by 1880, with the notable exception of central and western Canada. The frontier in both continents was effectively closed. Those Scots who wanted a life on the land overseas already had it. It was a far more prized possession then than later, carrying the promise of independence and status. In contrast, cities were crowded, unhealthy places with inadequate transport and facilities before the 1880s. In Canada, 54 percent of the Scots-born labor force worked in agriculture in 1881 compared with 21 percent in the United States. In North America and Australia about half of the Scots lived in rural areas or small cities. Canada was the most extreme case with 73 percent of Scots living in rural areas compared with 55 percent in the United States and 49 percent in Australia.

The other part of the primary sector, mining and quarrying, nearly doubled its share of the Scottish labor force to 6 percent between 1841 and 1901 with its numbers rising from 26,000 to 128,000. But as an occupation mining was not especially popular among Scottish emigrants. In the United States, 8 percent of working Scots were miners in 1880 compared with 5 percent in Scotland, 2 percent in England and Wales, and only 1 percent in Canada. No national figures are available for Australia but in New South Wales in 1901, 10 percent of the Scots-born labor force worked in mining, compared with 17 percent in agriculture, forestry, and fishing. This relatively high level of mining employment was the result of the severe depression caused by the financial crisis of the early 1890s and the intense drought that gripped eastern Australia from about 1895 to 1903. It is likely, though, that the distinction between mining and agricultural employment was not clear cut, as mining and agricultural regions often coexisted both in Australia and the northeastern United States.

Manufacturing employment dominated the Scottish labor force throughout the Victorian era, accounting for nearly 40 percent of jobs, but the fortunes of its various subgroups were mixed. Heavy industry and engineering enjoyed growth, but textiles, clothing, and footwear struggled. The service sector—the remainder of the labor force apart from agriculture and mining and manufacturing—also struggled and it only overtook manufacturing in 1901. Employment in wholesale and retail trade was low, as was public administration. Opportunities for advancement were poor. In 1901 only 11 percent of the Scottish labor force were employers or self-employed, half of what it was in Australia. Jobs for women were largely confined to domestic service and certain parts of manufacturing. More worrying was that employment growth simply followed population growth after 1861 or sometimes even lagged behind it.

Then there was the wages question. The link between migration and wages was well known; Adam Smith observed in *The Wealth of Nations* (1776) that emigration was more common from Scotland than England because demand for labor was lower in Scotland as were real wages. Regional wages in Victorian Scotland have been investigated separately by E. H. Hunt and Clive Lee, and although their conclusions differed, they agreed that Scottish wages were lower than wages in England. Scotland, like Northern Ireland, competed as a low-wage part of the British economy. The puzzle is why large-scale emigration—despite its effect of reducing the supply of labor—did not place upward pressure on wages. After all the bulk of the Scottish immigrants were of working age, but no one has suggested that their departure caused wages to rise. Instead, the evidence suggests that Scottish wage growth was slow and stayed in line with the British economy generally. The lack of wage growth was shown by the flatness of the expenditure per member of Scottish cooperative societies in the 1870s and 1880s at about £41 a year. This flatness and the lower level of wages could be attributed to structural weaknesses in the economy, such as undue dependence on metals manufacturing, distance from markets, and higher transportation costs. But there was another contributor to Scotland's economic problems that was outside its control: Irish immigration.

ENTER THE IRISH

Because so many Scots have left Scotland for so long, it is easy to read Scottish history and not realize that it had any kind of immigration at all, a tendency not helped by the rise of Scottish nationalism since the 1960s. Nationalism, by its very nature, looks inward, usually extolling the antiquity and achievements of the nation and, in the process, often distorting its history. These tendencies have been present in Scottish nationalism, which has, without realizing it, often tended to be more exclusive than inclusive until recent times. Yes, Scotland has a history of immigration, variable it is true, but it does exist. Immigrants were the "other" Scots, a reminder that not everyone who lived in Scotland were, or had been, born there. Scotland may have considered itself to be a nation, but it could not control who entered its borders from elsewhere in the United Kingdom. And from 1820 to 1914 most of the immigrants came from Ireland.

The Irish were not an isolated oddity of the 1840s but an integral part of Scotland's Victorian labor force, if not Scottish society, which regarded them as something Scotland could well do without. Typically, they were portrayed as taking jobs from Scots and prone to criminality, views that continued to be expressed up through to the late 1930s, consistent with the negative view of Irish immigrants in England. Cartoons in magazines like *Punch* in the 1870s had no qualms about presenting them as the missing link between apes and humans. They were certainly Christian, but about half were the wrong kind of Christian (Roman Catholic) and they were poorly educated, fit only for the lowest-paid jobs.

Unwelcome as the Irish were in Scotland, the Scots could do nothing to stop them coming. The 1871 census report for Scotland complained that they had "lowered greatly the moral tone of the lower classes," adding that where they had settled in large numbers it was necessary to enforce "sanitary and police precautions." Irish immigration was a continuous and large-scale fact of life in Victorian Scotland, no mere eddy in the great river of Scottish History Proper. There was no longer any distinction between "good" Irish (ethnic Scots descendants and Protestants) and the undesirable Irish (Catholics) as there had been century earlier, even though about two-thirds of the Irish-born in Scotland in 1881 came from what became Northern Ireland. Regardless of religion, the Irish were all packaged together as undesirable and continued to be so regarded. Certainly their size of their presence could not be denied, which was fairly stable at about 200,000 between 1851 and 1901. They made up about 5 percent of the Scottish population, but in the big cities this was much higher (Table 2).

Like Scottish emigration, Irish immigration was not always what it seemed. The Irish may have gone to Scotland but not necessarily stayed there; only 42 percent of those who were there in 1881 were still there in 1931 after taking expected deaths into account. The general absence of Catholics among Scots-born migrants to both Canada and Australasia before 1910 also suggests that many Irish Catholics did not stay in Scotland and may have gone back to Ireland. The Irish may have only accounted for 6 percent of the population, but their importance in the Victorian Scottish economy and labor force was far greater than this. In 1881, they made up nearly 9 percent of the labor force but they were very unevenly distributed throughout its various industries. They made up almost 10 percent of the male labor force, 16 percent of mining and quarrying employment, 11 percent of manufacturing, but, significantly, only 2 percent of agricultural workers. Their presence in certain occupations was much higher: no less than 32 percent of Scotland's male general laborers—the second largest occupation—were Irish-born, and they accounted for 27 percent of railroad laborers and construction workers. After the completion of most of the national rail system in the 1880s, they tended to leave Scotland; and those who stayed or entered Scotland over the next thirty years worked in metal manufacturing, in mining, or as general laborers.

Unpopular as they were, the Irish were well regarded by employers and considered more adaptable than the native Scots. They would take whatever work was available at the prevailing wage, which was bound to be higher than they what they could get in Ireland. They were the employers' and policy economists' dream, the go-anywhere, work-for-the-lowest-wage, flexible labor force. Did they take jobs away from the Scots-born? In many circumstances, they must have done so; but as so often happens to immigrants, they were scapegoats for conditions beyond their control. Just like the Scots, the Irish seemed to be everywhere looking for opportunities. There is no doubt that in the last half of the nineteenth century, Irish immigration to Scotland and overseas journeys from Scottish ports were directly linked and that the Irish, to some extent, replaced those who left. In the 1920s and 1930s they were not only blamed for taking jobs away from Scots but the Presbyterian Church even called for their deportation. All things considered, it would be fairer to say that the Irish immigration was both cause and symptom of the weakness of the economy of Victorian Scotland. Physically tough, they contributed mightily to building the infrastructure of Victorian Scotland, and through their desperation for work they helped maintain it as a low-wage economy, which was the underlying reason why so many Scots sought work outside Scotland. They were also an indicator of the demand for labor in Scotland and this became obvious after 1900. For most Scots the decision to emigrate before 1901 was a choice between remaining in a country with low wages and seeking out better opportunities elsewhere; after 1901, emigration was more about finding work, not just getting higher wages.

THE SLOW DEATH OF LABOR DEMAND, 1901–1971

In 1971, fewer men in Scotland had a job than in 1901, sad testimony to the failure of the economy to support its people adequately for most of the twentieth century. And although more women were employed, it was not enough to offset the long-term fall in men's employment. The conventional wisdom that Scotland became a distressed region after 1918 along with English Midlands, the North West, Northern Ireland, and Wales is wrong. Scotland led this grim descent into mass unemployment, poverty, malnutrition, and despair from 1901 with the others following later, and the 1900s, the decade when it began, has escaped the scrutiny it needs. It was the decade when the number of outward journeys from Scotland rose and kept on rising, interrupted by World War I and only halted by the Depression. The number of outward journeys from England and Wales rose too but at a lesser pace, and those from Ireland were steady at about 50,000 a year. Scottish migration was truly different. In 1903, 35,400 Scots left, exceeding the nineteenth-century peak of 34,000 in 1888 for the first time; and they kept on leaving, peaking at 83,000 in 1911. They left because there was no work. The great Scottish jobs drought had begun. Even the Irish were unable to find work: about 24,000 went to Scotland in the 1900s but about 26,000 left. Tellingly, about 11,000 Scots-born moved to Ireland in the same period, the highest number in 200 years.

Exactly why the Scottish economy lost its resilience from the 1900s is for others to investigate, but happen it did and it ended the ability of Scotland to compete as a low-wage economy within Britain. Comparing Scottish labor force performance in the 1900s with the whole of the Victorian era decades is revealing. Between 1840 and 1900, the labor force grew faster than the population in the 1840s, fell behind it during the 1850s despite the loss of 230,000 emigrants, matched it in the 1860s, fell behind again in the 1870s, and actually managed to stay head of it between 1880 and 1900. In the 1890s, the labor force exceeded population growth as many Scots who had left previously were forced back by the global depression and also because of the entry of about 30,000 Irish.

But in the 1900s the Scottish economy more or less stopped creating new jobs. There was a 4 percent rise in men's employment but none at all among women's. Mining, mechanical engineering, shipbuilding and transport, and communication grew as did wholesale and retail trade; but this may have been the result of a reclassification of this industry at the 1911 census, not because of real growth. The 1908 depression hampered growth too, but it was a symptom, not a cause of the drying up of the demand for labor, as it affected England too. Ominously, building and construction employment, a good indicator of underlying economic health, performed disastrously, falling by a fifth from 146,000 to 115,000; it continued to fall thereafter and it was not until 1951 that it again approached its 1901 level.

Other economic indicators tell the same story and uncover the 1900s as the fault line of modern Scottish economic history. For instance, only 46,000 new occupied dwellings were built in this decade, half the number of the 1890s and the lowest number since reliable housing figures began to be collected in the 1860s. Letter deliveries in Scotland also show that there had been a significant change in overseas migration. Between 1859 and 1900 there was no link between letter deliveries and overseas journeys from Scotland, but for the 1900s there was a positive link between the two. Whether those in authority admitted it or not, emigration assumed, understandably, a new urgency as many groups, especially construction workers, tried to escape the steady implosion of the Scottish economy.

During the 1900s, 270,000 Scots left permanently. Canada was the most attractive destination, drawing in 109,000, and it was no surprise that construction workers were the largest occupational group amongst them. Another indicator of the jobs crisis was the changing composition of Scottish migrants admitted to the United States. Between 1875 and 1900 less than 3 percent of these migrants claimed to have a professional occupation, but in the 1900s this nearly doubled. The 4 percent job growth in Scotland was not just the lowest recorded since the 1850s, it was even lower than that of comparable British regions; northeast England managed 14 percent and even Belfast managed 7 percent. Wales led the way with a gain of 22 percent, and it was little wonder that the 1900s came to be regarded there as something of a golden age.

The Scottish labor force rose more than the total population in the 1910s, but this was mainly because World War I killed 81,000 young men. Emigration resumed as soon as the war was over, spurred by depression between 1920 and 1923. Thereafter, the Scottish economy capitulated; in the last half of the 1920s the income tax paid in Scotland was only half of what it had been in the first half. The war boosted the Scottish economy temporarily by stimulating its heavy industries but it failed to cure its underlying weaknesses, many of which were also shared by Wales, Northern Ireland, the northeast, and the Midlands. The decline in shipbuilding was symptomatic of how these regions were bypassed by the "second" industrial revolution—based on new industries that were less dependent upon coal such as vehicle manufacturing—that was drawn to southeast England after 1918. Scotland suffered too, as did other outlying parts of Britain, from the closure of English-controlled companies, and much of its economy was more Third World than First World. For instance, Dundee, Scotland's third largest city, competed directly with Calcutta in jute production and emerged as the victor from this cruel contest. After his visit there in the 1930s my father told me, "I thought we were badly off in St Andrews until I saw Dundee." Scotland did not have to wait until the 1920s to become a "distressed" region; it had been one for twenty years.

It is sobering to compare Scotland's labor force trends with that of Wales, which, like Scotland, had a relatively poor natural environment in the north and an economic base in the south that was reliant on mining and manufacturing. Between 1841 and 1931, the Welsh labor force was about 40 percent that of Scotland's, and before 1881 their growth records were comparable; after that, however, they diverged. In the 1890s and 1900s employment growth in Wales was stronger than in Scotland. Both their peoples suffered greatly during the interwar years, but whereas there was a significant rise in Welsh employment after 1945, there was hardly any in Scotland and the economic benefits of industrialization after 1840 were not realized for most Scots. The housing crisis continued and was not begun to be addressed until the 1920s—and when it was, it was through socially segregated policies. There seemed to be an official unwillingness to admit, much less measure, the drift to disaster. Unemployment was not included in the Scottish census until 1931, and every effort was made to reduce their eligibility for assistance and to blame its victims for their plight. Most Scottish jobs continued to be low paid and of poor quality compared with England. White-collar jobs were scarce and poverty was widespread. Paid employment for girls and women was dominated by factory work and domestic service. Given all this, it was scarcely surprising that Scots seeking a better and longer life had to leave Scotland.

Chapter Three

No Simple Story

Migration, like crime, requires motivation, means, and opportunity. It is driven by hope, not just for a better job, but for a better future. But hope is not enough: it takes money to move. In a free society only a small proportion of the total population migrate, and those who do tend to be more enterprising and healthier. Migration can be viewed in many different ways, such as economic, geographic, or as a part of nation building. They all have advantages but probably the best way to view Scottish migration is to see it as a demographic process whose causes and scale have changed over time. Various theories have been proposed to explain migration, but they are of little use for historical analysis because they are usually reliant on statistics that are not available for earlier times. Neither is migration the simple subject that it may appear to be. It is not just about people moving from one place to another. It is the most difficult part of population change to measure because although a person can only be born or die once, they can move more than once, or they can go back to where they came from and stay there. The complexity of migration is demonstrated in this chapter, which reviews the history of Scottish migration from 1608 to 1930.

DESTINATION ULSTER, 1608–C. 1720

The first recorded Scottish migrants were mercenaries; possibly as many as 30,000 may have taken part in the Thirty Years War (1618–1648) at some time. Usually considered as a part of military history, these mercenaries could also be seen as temporary migrants, "guest workers" with swords, and their participation, together with the wars with England between 1644 and 1651, would have reduced the number of males in the population and made the population mainly female. The relative peace of the next hundred years and the reduced number of epidemics fed population growth by reducing mortality and encouraging migration. Some Scots went to the countries around the North Sea before 1650, but most went to the English "plantations" or settlements in Ulster. The purpose of these settlements was to control the Irish, and their scale was substantial. T. C. Smout, Ned. C. Landsman, and Thomas M. Devine estimated that about 40,000 Scots went to what became Ulster from 1608 to 1650 and a further 60,000–100,000 between 1650 and 1700. By 1701 Ulster had a population of at least 470,000 according to modeling, of whom possibly about 30 percent were ethnic Scots.

The first attempt at Scottish colonization in North America was made in 1622 at Nova Scotia ("New Scotland"), but the venture failed when the colonists were forced out by the French in 1632. Few went to the English colonies in North America, as it was illegal before 1707; but T. C. Smout, Ned. C. Landsman, and Thomas M. Devine estimated that about 7,000 did so nevertheless and about 33,000 went before 1760. Together with their estimates of Scottish migration to Ulster, this adds up to a net loss from Scotland of between 100,000 and 140,000 between 1650 and 1750.

SCOTLAND REVISITED, C. 1720–1776

Unlike Scotland, Ulster and the rest of Ireland was left out of the Act of Union of 1707 that made Scotland an integral part of the English economy. Ulster farmers faced steep increases in their rents, economic discrimination, bad harvests, and widespread impoverishment, conditions that triggered a stream of migration among their ethnic Scots to the American colonies—estimated as high as 250,000 between 1717 and 1776—where they became known as the Scotch-Irish. Ulster's population doubled during the eighteenth century to a million by 1801, according to modeling, more than sufficient to send thousands of emigrants both to North America and to Scotland. Above all, southcentral Scotland was experiencing, uncharacteristically, an economic boom in this period flowing from the tobacco trade that must have made it an irresistible destination to those in impoverished Ulster, if only for sufficient time to earn enough to go to North America. Ulster's population increased by about 100,000 in the 1750s, double that of the 1740s, and this would have added to the pressure to consider emigration and increased the number going to Scotland.

Some of the Scots-born Ulster immigrants may have stayed in Scotland but most would have left after they had earned enough money for their passage to North America. It always needs to be remembered that migrating costs money. Ship owners did not transport migrants from the goodness of their hearts; they had to be paid in one form or another. Those who did not have the money indentured themselves as servants. The US historian Arthur

Herman has estimated that about 100,000 of the Scots-born Ulster immigrants who went to North America did so as indentured servants; that is, they entered into contracts whereby their passage was paid for in return for working for four years for an employer in the American colonies. If this figure was right, it leaves the funding of the remaining 150,000 unexplained. A letter written in 1725 claimed that the passage between Ireland and Philadelphia cost £9, but this might have been for better-off migrants. The noted scholar of colonial America Bernard Bailyn found that the typical cost of passage was £3 or £4, a relatively large sum for wage earners. It had to be earned somehow to avoid the semi-slavery of indentured service, and a temporary work stint in Scotland would have provided that opportunity.

The evidence for the temporary presence of Ulster Scots in Scotland in the early 1750s is hidden in Webster's census; it is indirect, but it is there. Modeling confirms that Webster's count was fairly accurate, all things considered. His original count was 1,265,380, which he raised by 53,000 after receiving updates from the main cities. About 9,000 of this increase came from Aberdeen and Perth, but these people could have been refugees from the Highlands who had been included in the first round of counting. That said, the remaining 44,000 cannot be explained so easily, and they were not the victims of forced evictions because these did not start until 1762. Modeling also confirms the accuracy of Webster's age estimates too, indicating that they were carefully adjusted and not the original figures he would have been received. Taken at face value, these results were consistent with a stable population with no migration either in or out. There is no evidence for the loss of 100,000 to 140,000 emigrants in Webster's census whatsoever, a result in defiance of all the evidence to the contrary. There is only one way these results could have come about: immigrants must have replaced those Scots had had left previously and there was only one place that they could have come from: Ulster. In other words, the problem with Webster's census is not that it counted too few Scots but that it counted too many. If the estimates of the loss of 100,000 and 140,000 between 1650 and 1750 are correct, and there is no good reason to doubt them, Webster's total should have been at most about 1.2 million, not the 1.3 million he finally reported.

When he completed writing up his census in 1755 there must have at least about 65,000 people present who were not born in Scotland, maybe more. But if this was true why did Webster not mention them? The answer lies in the nature of his census, which was conducted by the Presbyterians for the Presbyterians. Webster was not interested in birthplaces, and the only other religion of concern was Catholicism. These Ulster immigrants would have been ethnic Scots and therefore not noteworthy, as they would have been Presbyterians. Neither was this movement a one-way affair. The US scholar James G. Leyburn found some documentary evidence of immigration to Ulster from Scotland in the mid-1750s although they could have just been

Ulster-born coming home. Much has been written about how different the Irish of Scottish descent were to the Scots-born in the American colonies, but it seems reasonable to suppose that those who went to Scotland in the mid-eighteenth century could have easily stepped back in Scottish society; they would have had Scottish names, had Scottish accents, been devout Presbyterians, and most been only a generation removed from their Scottish kin.

To summarize: between 1650 and 1750 the population of Scotland underwent three large-scale changes. The first two are well-known: emigration first to Ulster before 1720 and then to the American colonies. The movement to Ulster has been estimated by Thomas M. Devine and others as possibly as high as 100,000. The third migration, from Ulster to Scotland before going to the American colonies between 1725 and 1776, has been previously hidden from history but it was substantial; there were at least 65,000 migrants taking this route in the early 1750s. They did not come back to settle, only to stay long enough to earn their fare to leave, and this would also explain why there were so few immigrants in Scotland were reported to Sir John Sinclair in the early 1790s. For many Scotch-Irish the passage to the American colonies was, it seems, made possible by Scottish earnings.

DESTINATION NORTH AMERICA, C. 1720–1776

The Union with England in 1707 did not just open up trade between Scotland and the American colonies; it led to migration too. During his tour of Scotland in about 1726 Daniel Defoe was told that fifty ships a year left Glasgow and that there was continual migration of Scottish servants to Virginia. He was also told that English servants migrated too, but that the Scots were more likely to stay there. Defoe took a stern view of migration and in his list of improvements for Scotland he called for a "change in the disposition of the common people, from a desire of travelling abroad, and wandering from home, to an industrious and diligent application to labor at home." But he also conceded that they should receive more encouragement within Scotland and noted their diligence and labor outside Scotland. By the time of Defoe's visit, North America had replaced Ireland as the main destination of Scots migrants.

Considerable research into Scottish emigration to North America before 1800 on both sides of the Atlantic has produced varying estimates of how many migrated. The Scottish historian David Dobson has estimated that at least 150,000 Scots emigrated between 1612 and 1800. And, as mentioned, T. C. Smout, Ned. C. Landsman, and Thomas M. Devine estimated that 7,000 Scots went to North America before 1700 and another about 33,000 between 1700 and 1760. Sometimes soldiering and settling were combined, as for instance in 1736 when General James Oglethorpe founded New Inverness, now Darien, Georgia, with 177 Scottish Highlanders and their families. At the same time, about 500 Highlanders settled in New York.

The sources for estimating Scottish migration in the second half of the eighteenth century are better than for the first half, but far from ideal. As well as Webster's census, the returns submitted to Sir John Sinclair provided a second census for about 1791. From their work, Scotland's net loss from migration was about 200,000, most of whom left between 1751 and 1775. There is insufficient evidence to know how many of this group were male or female, although modeling suggests that about 60 percent were male. The only direct evidence comes from a register of British emigration compiled between December 1773 and March 1776, which has been analyzed by Bernard Bailyn; he found that 74 percent of the 8,329 Scots who went to North America were male.

Unlike the pre-1750 period, this migration was primarily military, and the bulk of it was to North America, although some went to England and India as required. The period was dominated by two important and related wars: the Seven Years War (1756–1763) and the American War of Independence (1775–1783). During his tour of Scotland in 1773, Samuel Johnson was told that 70,000 had been raised from the Highlands to fight in the British armies in North America, a figure he rightly doubted. He observed that to "count is a modern practice, the ancient [that is, before the present] method was to guess; and when numbers are guessed they are always magnified."

The 70,000 figure Johnson heard seems to have been based on a count of the number of soldiers recruited for both the Seven Years War *and* the American War of Independence for *all* of Scotland, according to the Rev. Dr. Alexander Duncan in his report to Sir John Sinclair for Smalholm parish, Roxburgh County. This is critical information and, if true, it implies that possibly as many as 40,000 of the 200,000 who left Scotland in this period were settlers, not soldiers. It is known that most of the Scottish settlers of this period went to North or South Carolina. They were most likely the better-off, with the less well-off opting for the army. It is possible too that some of those who joined the British army in Scotland during the Seven Years War were really Scotch-Irish.

Both of the North American wars seem to have been costly in Scottish life, and there is no evidence that large numbers of them came back; on the contrary, Johnson was told that those who fought in the American War of Independence "went to their destruction." Two of Alexander Webster's sons, John and James, fought on the British side in the American War of Independence; James was killed there in 1781. These losses made the remaining Scots far less willing to join the army in the following decades. Yet despite the dangers, the army offered the chance to make some steady money, as opposed to the uncertainties of the Scottish economy; and, unlike modern armies, the soldiers depended upon the wives who went with them for care if they were sick or wounded. The army also offered opportunities for the sons of soldiers to enter a manly occupation, as it was possible to join the army at age fourteen; the army even offered the possibility of a modest pension. The 70,000-strong Scottish part of the British army in 1801 was far too large to have been recruited directly from Scotland in the 1790s. It must have largely reproduced itself and it was the Scottish soldiers' sons who provided most of the Scottish forces that fought against Revolutionary France and Napoleon.

Sir John Sinclair's reports demonstrate that the military was regarded by the Scots as an occupation that paid—perhaps not much, but it did pay. And there is no evidence of large-scale recruiting in the early 1790s, let alone patriotic fervor, or even that the armed forces were well regarded. One minister, the Rev. Mr. James Scott, of Auchterhouse parish, Forfar County, took pride in his parishioners' lack of interest in the armed forces as "a sure proof of their not being addicted to idleness or vice," sentiments supported by other clergy. The general view was that apart from becoming swordsmen, the army had little appeal, the navy virtually none; even the persuasive Lachlan Macquarie had difficulty in recruiting the fifteen Scottish soldiers he needed to restart his military career in 1788. The report from Linton parish, Peebles County, added that "few enlist, as they have plenty of employment at home." Scottish women also participated in the Napoleonic wars. There is an oral tradition in my family that a direct ancestor fought with the Black Watch in the Peninsular War and at Waterloo and that his wife went with him to care for him if he was ill or wounded.

Even in the last half of the eighteenth century, Scottish migration was a carefully planned affair. Emigrants to North America from Aberdeen County and the Outer Hebrides are known to have written letters back home praising their new homes, and prospective migrants could get information about North America and the West Indies from publications. Then, as later, the emigrants' experiences were varied. Some sent money back to their elderly parents, which must be one of the earliest examples of transatlantic remittances. Others returned to Scotland from England and elsewhere much better off than before, to the irritation of those who had stayed poorer by staying at home. Others came back from North America destitute, the victims of fraud, tricked by false promises, shattering the idea that North America was "the fairy-land of wealth." Scottish emigrants were sometimes farewelled by a piper, which prompted the minister of Tyrie parish, Aberdeen, to complain that something should be done to stop the "progress" of emigration, something more than "giving premiums to pipers!" But no pipers welcomed Scots coming back.

Apart from the North American wars and their promise of payment, local economic conditions played an important part in encouraging emigration. The pioneering study by G. L. Davies in 1956 of North Uist parish in the Outer Hebrides offered an example, if an extreme one, of the economic and social forces that changed the population and gave rise to migration. In 1751 North Uist had a population of 1,900. Following an increase in rents of one-third by the chief of the MacDonald clan in the 1760s, some of his tenants set up a company that bought 100,000 acres in South Carolina and over 200 left between 1771 and 1775. The switch to kelp production in the 1770s not only enabled those left behind to stay—helped by a rise in the price of kelp caused by the American War of Independence—but allowed the population to grow to 3,200 by 1792. By 1821 the population had grown to 5,000, its highest level. In North Uist, at least, emigration was an option of last resort to be undertaken only if the local economy could not provide its people with a livelihood.

The period 1750 to 1775 was noteworthy because it was in these years that two Scots made a direct contribution to the emergence of the United States when they joined fifty-four others in signing the American Declaration of Independence: James Wilson (1742–1798) from Pennsylvania and John Witherspoon (1722–1794) from New Jersey. Wilson arrived in the American colonies in 1765 followed by Witherspoon three years later. Wilson and Witherspoon were honored exceptions; the great majority of Scots were loyal to England and paid for it. Arthur Herman has estimated that about 30,000 Scots left with the army or were expelled from the American colonies after the War of Independence, mainly to British America, later Canada. This must mean that the great majority of the 260,000 of apparent Scottish descent at the 1790 American census were Scotch-Irish, not Scots-born.

THE EXPATRIATES RETURN, C. 1800–1820

The Scottish population was far less stable between 1750 and 1820 than previously realized, according to modeling. As discussed, about nearly 200,000 left by 1776, of whom about 70,000 were recruited for the wars in North America. Between 1791 and 1821, Scotland's population rose from 1.5 to 2.1 million, which more than could have been expected from natural increase alone, the result of an inflow of about 144,000 from 1800. These people could only have been expatriates and their children. There is no other acceptable explanation as the only other suspects, the Irish, did not enter Scotland in significant numbers before 1820. So what were the likely reasons for this movement?

The French Revolutionary and Napoleonic wars stimulated manufacturing and urbanization, particularly after 1811, and provided some incentive to go back. But the emotional pull of the homeland should not be overlooked either. Those who were forced to leave the United States and go to what is now Canada were unimpressed; the Scottish settlers of Nova Scotia called it "New Scarcity." Those Scots who were in the army had no choice but to go, as they were on the losing side of the American War of Independence when it ended in 1783. The career of Lachlan Macquarie (1762–1824), who was governor of New South Wales from 1810 to 1821, offers an insight into the mobility of the Scots within the British empire in this era. Born on the island of Ulva in the Inner Hebrides, he joined the army in 1777 and served in North America. He returned to Scotland in 1784 and had a second military career in India between 1788 and 1803 with a break in Egypt in 1801. The expatriate Scots who returned would not have been seen as in any sense "foreign." They would have been easily reabsorbed into Scottish society without comment; they were Scots regardless of whether they had been born in Scotland or outside it. From 1815 to 1820 the bulk of returnees were ex-soldiers, and between 1811 and 1821 the number of Scots in the British army fell from its peak of 78,000 to 46,000. In-migration from Ireland and England was negligible.

If there had been a large influx of Irish immigrants in this period they would have been most evident in Glasgow, which benefitted most from the wartime demand for manufactured goods; but this was not the case. In 1821 Glasgow had only 17,200 Irish-born and less than 2,000 English-born. Sir John Sinclair estimated that the number of outside-born in Scotland in the 1820s was less than 30,000. The inescapable conclusion then is that the bulk of the in-migration to Scotland between 1800 and 1820 came from expatriate Scots and their children. Their return and the unwanted population increase they caused, particularly in the Highlands, would have underlain the forced evictions of the 1820s. With the end of the Napoleonic wars in 1815, the surviving Scottish military forces returned home; the oral tradition in my family is that they did so on foot from England. As in other parts of Europe, their return led to "baby boom" that reduced the median age from twenty-three to twenty years between 1811 and 1821. The return migration of the 1800–1820 era was only offset to a limited extent by emigration to Canada and England; by 1820 Canada had about 11,000 Scots and England about 35,000. Virtually no Scots settled outside these countries, but over the next 110 years this all changed.

THE TWO SIDES OF SCOTTISH MIGRATION, 1840–1930

Scottish migration, like charity, began at home but did not end there. It was never just about people leaving Scotland, and there was considerable movement *within* Scotland itself that changed both the distribution of population and the sources of regional emigrants to other lands. Indeed the number who moved from the county of their birth often rivaled those who left Scotland permanently. In 1901, 1.1 million Scots, one in four, had moved from the county where they were born while 1.3 million had emigrated. The direction of their movements was first investigated by Richard Osborne, a geographer at the University of Edinburgh, in 1958. Using county birthplaces for 1851, 1901, and 1951, he found that the main direction of movement was from the northwest and the inland areas to the coastal towns and cities, principally Aberdeen, Glasgow, and Edinburgh. Scotland continued to have a high level of internal migration after World War II. The 1961 census revealed that 35 percent of Scots had been at their present residence for less than five years, and a further 32 percent had moved since 1947.

Were internal and overseas migration linked? The question is not new: Donald Macdonald asked it in 1937 in his *Scotland's Shifting Population, 1770–1850* and considered that they were as they came from the same source. Unfortunately, the information needed for answering this question is not as good as it looks because only birthplace figures were collected at the census never length of residence until 1961. The net change in the numbers who moved from their birth county to another was steady and incremental between 1861 and 1901. It was the equivalent of about two-thirds of those who emigrated in the 1860s, 1870s, and 1890s, but only a third of those who emigrated in the 1880s and a fifth of those who left in the 1900s, indicating that there was no clear link between the two.

HOW MANY LEFT?

How many left Scotland between 1820 and 1930? The question is easy to ask but less easy to answer, despite the seeming abundance of sources. No less than four different measures are available:

1. The number of overseas journeys made from Scottish ports from 1825 to 1938. Originally published in British Parliamentary Papers, the figures for these journeys were assembled and published in 1953 by N. H. Carrier and J. R. Jeffery in their *External Migration: A Study of the Available Statistics, 1815–1950*. Hard to consult now, their results were summarized in Michael Flinn's *Scottish Population History* (1977) and more recently in Thomas M. Devine's *To the Ends of the Earth: Scotland's Global Diaspora, 1750–2010* (2011). Carrier and Jeffery were rightly concerned about the completeness of these figures but testing against census returns shows they are trustworthy, at least for the Scots. They included return migration figures from when they were first collected in 1895. That said, the destinations they show are *intended* destinations to Canada, the United States, Australasia, and South Africa (from 1877) and do not take into account that emigrants may have changed their destination after reporting it to emigration officials.

2. Port statistics on arrivals in Canada and the United States. In British America, later Canada, disembarkations were counted for the Scots from 1829 to 1880 and again from 1901. In the United States, the Scots were counted from 1820, and from 1908 the figures distinguished arrivals and departures. The figures before 1908 are so incomplete as to be of little value, although they are the only record of arrivals between 1820 and 1824. Scottish arrivals in New Zealand ports were published in detail from 1922 to 1932. In South Africa, arrivals and departures by the Scots were published from 1913 to 1956, but neither Scottish arrivals nor departures were ever published in Australia.
3. Estimating the net change in the number of Scots-born in a country for each decade, allowing for expected deaths after 1841. Using the censuses of Britain, North America, South Africa, and Australasia from 1841, this is a standard demographic method that has been used in this book for England and Wales. It works well when the age structure is known, but this information is usually not available before about 1910. It can also produce results that are technically correct but of limited value or interest; a zero result may simply disguise about the same number entering and leaving, and it can also give negative results, as for the depression decade of the 1890s.
4. Cohort analysis where a cohort means migrants who arrived in a country in a particular decade and became long-term settlers. This method has been almost unused for historical purposes mainly because the information it requires is usually not available. It depends upon knowing how long immigrants have lived in a country and, ideally, their age and sex. If this is known, then the number who arrived in an earlier time can be reconstructed taking account of likely deaths from when they arrived. When linked to departure and arrival statistics, this method offers the best measure of reconstructing settlement migration. It can be used for the main overseas countries the Scots went to and, strangely, for Scotland itself, which asked this question of the outside-born at its 1931 census. Like the other methods, it is not without its drawbacks, most notably that if many of a particular group left before their length of residence was recorded, it can underestimate of their original size when it is reconstructed.

These caveats aside, length of residence is indispensable for analyzing migration as it is enables those who settled in a country to be separated from those who just made an overseas journey. It has been published, to varying degrees of detail and frequency, in the censuses for North America, South Africa, and Australasia from 1901. This published information can be supplemented by searching the publicly available genealogical sites for the Canadian census for 1901 and the US census for 1910 for common family names such as Smith, Brown, Campbell, MacDonald, and Stewart to find out their ages and when they emigrated. These searches created samples of 10,000 for Canada and 7,200 for the United States that can be used to estimate not only the number of Scottish settlers for each decade but also the number who were there before they were counted by the census from 1842 in Canada and 1850 in the United States. This method has been used in this chapter for most of the Scottish destinations apart from those within Britain.

Taking findings from these sources together shows that about 2.2 million Scots left permanently between 1820 and 1930, of whom about 1.5 million settled overseas and the remaining 700,000 in England. Of the 1.5 million who settled overseas, 490,000 did so in Canada, 584,000 in the United States, 46,000 in South Africa, and 414,000 in Australasia.

NOT ALL IT SEEMED

As well as giving answers, these sources pose questions about how Scottish migration happened, notably by exposing the gap between overseas journeys and settlement and showing that all was not what it seemed to be. Between 1825 and 1900, 1.1 million people made an overseas journey from Scottish ports but only about 768,000 of them became settlers, demonstrating that return journeys at some time were a prominent feature of Scottish emigration. Comparing when wives and husbands arrived reveals that much of this gap did not exist and that most of the return journeys were made by husbands going ahead of their wives and children and going back to collect them later.

This is discussed in more detail in North America and Australasian chapters, but the broad pattern of return migration can be summed up here. There was little return migration to Scotland from overseas before about 1870 and those who went overseas before this largely stayed there. Second, before 1860 many changed their country of destination after they had left Scotland. Even the voyage to North America took weeks and there was ample opportunity for the passengers to get to know each other and share information about their prospects. In the 1830s and 1840s about 22,000 Scots who told the emigration authorities that they were going to Canada (then called British America) must have disembarked in the United States and stayed there. Similarly, in the 1850s about 12,000 Scots who originally declared that they were going to the United States must have changed their minds and gone to Australia instead to join the gold rushes.

After 1870 increased return migration became a feature of Scottish emigration, most of it from the United States in contrast to Australasia where it was negligible before 1890. Although the returnees were made up of different groups such as disappointed job seekers, in the main they were married men going ahead first because they lacked the money to establish all the family members in one trip. About 95 percent of Scottish married couples who migrated to Canada before 1900 came together, but only about 62 percent of those who went to the United States did so—and they took up to four years to get the money to finance the final journey of settlement. This pattern of many married men going first and then coming back to collect their families was repeated in the 1900s for both countries. In the 1910s return migration was largely caused by the outbreak of World War I as men returned to enlist. In the 1920s return migration fell but did not disappear, despite the severity of the Scottish depression. Just under 10 percent of those who went to the United States and New Zealand did not stay there; in New Zealand most of those who returned were tourists.

DECIDING TO GO

It was, and is, a huge decision for anyone to leave the land of their birth permanently, and in thousands of Scottish households the decision to emigrate must have been discussed at length. In a literate society, information flowed freely and emigration must have been an important topic. Between 1870 and 1900, the number of letters per head delivered in Scotland was 75 percent that for England, which seems high given that the English figures included London. There was no obvious link between letters deliveries and emigration before 1900 but there is a strong one between 1901 and 1913. In most cases it was economic, a desire or need to test the labor markets of other places; but it this was not always so, as these examples show.

One of those who arrived in the United States in 1848 was a thirteen-year-old damask weaver's son from Dunfermline, Fife, with his family: the future industrialist and philanthropist Andrew Carnegie (1835–1919). Faced with competition from steam-driven machinery, Carnegie's family wrote to his mother's two sisters in Pittsburgh, Pennsylvania, about their prospects. Receiving a favorable response, they sold their looms and furniture, but the sale failed to raise all of the £20 passage money and they had to borrow the rest. The Carnegies made the decision to emigrate for the future of their sons; Andrew Carnegie's father was then forty-three, his mother thirty-three, and his brother five. Alexander Graham Bell (1847–1922), the inventor of the telephone, left Scotland for health reasons. Born in Edinburgh, Bell contracted tuberculosis in 1867, the disease that killed his two brothers. After living in London, he moved with his family to Ontario in 1870 in the belief that the climate would help him recover; he moved again, this time to Boston, Massachusetts, in 1871.

HELPING THE POOR AND GETTING LAND, C. 1820–1880

Scottish migration varied by period, motivation, and region. Between 1820 and 1880, it had two main goals, depending upon the means of the migrants: helping specific groups of poor people and getting land, mainly in North America and Australasia. The return of so many expatriate Scots between 1790 and 1820, combined with the depression brought on by the end of the Napoleonic wars, placed enormous pressure on the Scottish economy. The introduction of the power loom threatened the livelihoods of handloom weavers, as did immigration by lower-paid Irish weavers. Conditions were worst in the Glasgow region, where about 3,000 Scots were assisted to migrate to Canada during 1820–1821. More would have been sent but the money ran out and the depression dragged on until 1827. The 1820s set the scene for what would become a common feature of Victorian Scotland, mass migration. The next occasion when the poor were assisted to emigrate was between 1837 and 1851 when about 10,000 Highlanders were sent to eastern Australia to escape famine. Mass emigration was hardly unique to Scotland—most of Europe had it too—but what set Scotland apart from Ireland and Norway was that from about 1875 it was from a largely urbanized, industrialized nation.

Scottish overseas migration was variable and not just because of downturns in the economic cycle, because these downturns also occurred in the economies that the Scots went to, even if there was a time lag between them. More generally, emigration was prompted from 1845 by the Scottish Poor Law Act, which denied unemployment assistance to anyone who had not been lived in their parish for five years. The grimness of this time throughout Europe was long remembered as the "hungry forties," although the Scottish cooperative leader James Deans said in his 1922 memoirs, that he had only "a dim and hazy recollection of them" but he had a "vivid recollection of the equally 'hungry fifties.'" He recalled widespread unemployment and that the most a man could earn was between about £32 and £42 pounds a year depending upon if he was unskilled or skilled. It was hardly surprising that in this decade 230,000 Scots emigrated, the equivalent of 9 percent of the Scots-born in Scotland, setting an ominous precedent for later decades.

The largest single group of poor—nearly 33,000—were assisted to migrate to Australasia between 1862 and 1891 or were nominated to do so by resident settlers. The better-off Scots migrants wanted land. As explained in chapter 2, 80 percent of Scotland's land was owned by only 680 individuals in 1882, so those who wanted land of their own had to find it somewhere else. The first wave of these Scottish migrants were part of the European appropriation of the lands of the indigenous inhabitants of North America and Australasia, an act now deemed to be ironic for a people who had suffered forced evictions themselves. Once they got their farms, they then had to find reliable labor to work the land. Usually these workers had to come from family or friends as Scotland's rural workers as a group were highly conservative and resisted emigration, largely ignoring persistent official efforts to woo them to Canada and Australasia.

After 1880, Scottish settlement in North America and Australia shifted to towns and cities. There were two exceptions to this shift: England and New Zealand. With no land available for settlement, there was no rural phase in Scottish migration to England. In New Zealand, the rural phase of Scottish settlement lasted longest simply because the Scots followed the rest of the population, which was mainly rural until 1911.

LOOKING FOR WORK THAT PAID, C. 1870–1930

Scottish migrants well demonstrated the truism that migrants follow economic opportunity, especially after 1870 as their priorities shifted from farming to becoming urban wage earners. Their preference for the United States over Canada was soundly based. Not only was the US economy larger and more diversified but its industrialization after 1870 made it wealthier too, whereas the Canadian economy remained largely agrarian before 1900 and relatively poorer. Between 1870 and 1900, Canada's gross domestic product per head was 60 percent that of the United States, although the gap narrowed after 1900 when it was about 70 percent up to 1930.

It was a different story in Australasia. Fueled by the gold discoveries of the 1850s, the Australian economy generally enjoyed buoyant conditions from about 1860 to about 1890. But the economy crashed badly in the 1890s when the effects of the 1893 global financial crisis were compounded by severe drought from 1895 until about 1903. Economic growth in New Zealand was comparatively slow until the 1890s when it was rescued by the expansion of dairy farming in the North Island, and this was why the number of Scottish settlers in the 1890s was about the same despite the larger size of the Australian economy. From 1901 to about 1930, it was again evident that economic performance played an important role in attracting Scottish settlers, especially in the 1900s when Canada had an economic growth rate of double that of the United States and was the preferred destination of Scottish settlers. Canada retained its lead during the 1910s but was overtaken by the United States in the 1920s. In Australasia, New Zealand was almost as popular as destination as Australia in the 1900s but fell back as the Australian economy improved.

From about 1880 to 1930, Scottish migrants followed the general shift away from the rural world to urban-based manufacturing and service employment, a shift that was a mirror of Scotland itself. Over this period the number of urban dwellers in Scotland rose from 52 to 67 percent and the number employed in primary occupations (agriculture and mining) fell steadily from 22 to 6 percent. As the typical Scottish migrant was much more likely to be an urban dweller than before, they could move with greater ease into the urban worlds of North America, South Africa, and Australia. It would seem from all this that the Scots were following economic opportunities rather than creating them.

WHERE DID THEY COME FROM?

Like many migration questions, the regional sources of Scottish emigrants should be easier to answer than it is. From about 1750 to about 1840, it is generally agreed that most emigrants came from the western side of Scotland. Rent increases, as much as the eviction of traditional land occupiers in the Highlands, forced waves of involuntary emigration to England and British North America. The 1911 census for England and Wales published the birthplaces of its Scots-born by county, and this, combined with Scottish county birthplace figures, enables an estimation of the outlines of Scottish migration by region for the previous forty years (Table 3).

These results confirm some longstanding views and amend others. As expected from later evidence, those born in Strathclyde were the largest source of emigrants both overseas and to England, but much more so for overseas. Those born in the Lothian and Tayside regions were, like those born in Strathclyde, more likely to go overseas than to go to England, but England was preferred choice for those born in the border regions (Borders and Dumfries and Galloway), the Central and Fife region, and the Highland region. Those who left the Grampian region were divided between going to England and overseas.

THE SCOTTISH PRESENCE, C. 1930

In the early 1930s, the number of Scots-born living outside Scotland was a quarter of Scotland's residential population. Bad as it was, it was the same for the Welsh and was less than for the Northern Irish (37 percent). Of those who left, 62 percent went to North America, 20 percent to England, and 17 percent to Australasia. With no jobs in Scotland, the great majority of these emigrants had no choice but to leave. The United States was the most popular destination, taking 38 percent of all Scottish emigrants, and nearly 60 percent claimed to be either professional or skilled. In 1930, there were 354,000 Scot-born in the United States, their highest ever level and double the number of 1880. Almost 40 percent had come in the 1920s, which was twice the proportion for English, Welsh, and Northern Irish emigrants, and their coming rejuvenated the American Scots.

The Scots headed for the cities and towns. In the United States, 83 percent of Scots were urbanized compared with 71 percent in Canada, 90 percent in South Africa, 72 percent in Australia, and 57 percent in New Zealand. Half of the 1.2 million Scots outside Scotland in the early 1930s lived in large cities. Predictably, London had the largest number (55,000), followed by Toronto (40,000), and, less expectedly, Sydney (33,000). New York was next with 29,000, but Detroit was not far behind (24,000). The early 1930s was the high water mark of the tide of overseas Scottish migration to North America and New Zealand, but not in South Africa or Australia. It had already peaked in South Africa in 1911 but South Africa was a special case because unlike North America or Australasia it demanded proof of means from intending European migrants, thereby excluding the less well-off.

WHAT FUTURE?

When the preliminary results of the 1931 census for Scotland were published in late 1931, they found that the population had fallen for the first time in its history; it was nearly 40,000 less than in 1921. It was a blow to national pride, expected for Ireland but not for Scotland, and it gave rise to a new kind of Scottish writing: the literature of anxiety. At stake was not what kind of future Scotland would have; it was whether it had a future at all. The noted Scottish poet Hugh MacDiarmid began the process with his *Albyn: or, Scotland and the Future* in 1927. He was followed by Alexander M. MacEwen, *The Thistle and the Rose: Scotland's Problems To-day* in 1928 and by Andrew D. Gibb's *Scotland in Eclipse* in 1930. There was heightened concern too about how Scotland always had higher rates of infant and maternal deaths, malnutrition, overcrowded housing, and unemployment than England.

Only one historian seems to have been directly influenced by the spirit of the times. In 1937 Donald F. Macdonald published *Scotland's Shifting Population, 1770–1850*, a pioneering study of population change, the impact of the Industrial Revolution, and internal, seasonal, and external migration. His book included the first general investigation of Irish immigration to Scotland, but he was exceptional. His study belonged as much to the literature of anxiety of the 1930s as it did to the history of Scottish migration because, as the dust jacket for his book explained, it was an "admirable, indeed an indispensable introduction to the study of present-day problems." Anxiety about Scotland's future continued. In 1944, Catherine Snodgrass, reviewing recent population changes in Scotland in the *Scottish Geographical Magazine,* concluded that its natural resources were sufficient to provide well for its five million inhabitants. She was the first researcher to draw attention to the consistently high level of emigration since 1901 and called the loss of

80,000 people in 1923 a "veritable national debacle." Combined with a trend toward smaller families, she feared that the Scots might have started "on the way to dying out" in their homeland.

She was concerned too that Scotland paid for raising and educating potential emigrants but that other countries reaped the benefits. Hers was hardly a new complaint. As early as the 1790s Sir John Sinclair complained that the "flower of our young men, of every class and description" were leaving because they were "incited by the prospect of making a fortune." Sir John also complained about the cost to Scottish society of "fitting them [emigrants] out," one of the earliest references to the cost in human capital emigration. Mass emigration did not just mean that there were fewer Scots at the time and later on. Concerned contemporaries were always well aware that its effects were corrosive and costly. These costs were especially evident for education. There were some groups, apart from the Irish, for whom Scotland was a land of opportunity—or at least its medical schools were. Because they provided a cheaper education than England, they were attractive for the less well-off medical students who could get a medical degree that was recognized and respected in the United States and throughout the British empire. In 1881, there were 2,364 medical students or assistants in Scotland of whom 43 percent were born outside Scotland, mainly English. In that year, there were 1,708 Scottish-born physicians and surgeons in practice in Scotland compared with 1,207 in England and Wales, 172 in Canada, and 398 in the United States; that is, there were as many Scots-born physicians practicing outside Scotland as in it.

The medical profession illustrated one of the main costs of emigration to Scotland: It paid to train these people but it was unable to reap the benefits of their skills. Nevertheless, emigration was not a complete economic loss to Scotland. The high levels of temporary return migration from the United States from 1870 to 1890 hint at a flow of remittances that would have supplemented the low wages of the Scottish economy. There is also evidence from North America that the Scottish migrants did not abandon elderly family members and either took them with them or arranged their passage later, which would have removed their cost from the Scottish economy.

The mass emigration of the 1920s also had the unintended effect of giving birth to the modern Scottish nationalist movement, signaled by the formation of the National Party of Scotland in 1928. Yet despite the scale and depth of the economic and social crises of the 1920s and 1930s, Scottish nationalism failed to attract a mass following. My mother assured me that at this time a Scot had three political choices: Labour, Conservative, or Communist. They may have disagreed just about everything, but they did agree on one thing: Scottish nationalism was madness. Mass emigration from Scotland continued, even in the 1930s when 57,000 returned from overseas but about the same number left Scotland, mainly to England. By 1960 over 500,000 Scots left, and in the 1960s 290,000 did so. In the wake of these losses, Scottish nationalism, previously a fringe option, began to attract widespread support. The nationalists' historical claims may have been attacked by the English historian Hugh Trevor-Roper in *The Invention of Scotland: Myth and History* in 2008, but the nationalists not only failed to go away, they went on to become part of the Scottish political landscape.

NO EASY ANSWERS

The history of Scottish migration from 1750 to 1930 defies any single explanation because its size, nature, and reasons changed according to what period is being considered. It is not a straightforward story but a succession of responses to various kinds of challenges—environmental, political, and economic—and people also entered Scotland as well as left it.

Four distinct phases of migration are evident before 1821. The first was the creation of something of a "second Scotland" in the settlement of Ulster before 1700. The second was the large-scale but short-term movement by ethnic Scots from Ulster to Scotland from about 1750 to 1775 to earn enough to go to North America, where they became known as the Scotch-Irish. The third was the creation of a pool of about 200,000 Scottish expatriates between 1755 and 1776, some of whom settled in North America but most of whom were British army recruits. Many of this original group failed to survive the wars between 1756 and 1815 but enough of their wives and children must have done to make up a fourth phase: the return of about 144,000 of them to Scotland between 1800 and 1820. The loss of males in military service was the principal reason why Scotland continued to have a female majority, exaggerating the effects of generally lower female mortality.

The century and ten from 1820 to 1930 were for the Scots, as for other Europeans, marked by mass emigration, mainly to North America and Australasia, and, as before, it was characterized by distinctive phases. Before 1900 Scottish migration was based on the desire not just for land but also for higher wages, a consequence of Scotland's success as an industrialized nation based on its payment of wages lower than England. Scottish wages were also kept down by sustained labor market competition from the Irish who came in large numbers from the late 1840s. This phase ceased after 1900 when the Scottish economy switched from just a low-wage economy to a low-wage no-new-jobs economy. Demand for labor dried up and Scots wanting jobs had to leave, propelling a surge in emigration that was only interrupted by World War I. It amounted to the economic eviction of nearly a million urban wage earners; and unlike the Victorian era few high flyers emerged from their ranks. The following chapters chart the course of this migration to England, North America, South Africa, and Australasia.

Chapter Four

England

After the Act of Union in 1707, England gradually became an important destination for Scottish migration. Dr. Samuel Johnson's well-known jibe of 1763 that "the noblest prospect which a Scotchman ever sees, is the high road that leads him to England" was meant figuratively, not literally, because there was no high road; indeed the southward roads were so dangerous that it was common for would-be coach travelers in the eighteenth century to make a will before going. The Scots preferred to go by sea. Few went to Wales, then or later; it was too much like Scotland.

Despite its economic attractiveness, the Scots seemed to have regarded England, especially London, as more a place of temporary migration than permanent settlement before 1800. This was most evident among those living in the border counties. One clergyman in Kirkcudbright County claimed in the 1790s that Scottish peddlers from these counties "commonly return, after 10 or 12 years" with £800 or even £1,000 after plying their wares in London. These were large sums for the time and they may be fanciful than fact; but the point of the journey being worthwhile was well made. Another clergyman in Roxburgh County claimed that about 10,000 tradesmen worked in London for part of the year leaving from Berwick and Newcastle-upon-Tyne. There was also seasonal migration to farms in northern England from about 1780. Seasonal migration continued, but the growth of the English economy encouraged more Scots as settlers.

Scottish migration to England, Wales, and Ireland is harder to study than for North America, South Africa, and Australasia. With its long history of emigration, Britain did not see itself as a nation where immigrants were a significant part of the population before the 1960s. People certainly entered Britain from other countries, but they were always an insignificant proportion of the population. Country of birth was asked at each census from 1841, but before 1971 the outside-born were not asked how long they had been there. England may have been a place of secondary migration for the Scots but the extent of this is unknown and the evidence points to the contrary, that their movements to England and overseas before 1930 were largely separate. Within these limitations, this chapter sets out the main trends of Scottish migration to England up to 1930, using not only printed sources but also unpublished information from the 1881 census.

THE MANCHESTER SCOTS, 1837

It is uncertain how many Scots settled in England before 1841. As discussed in chapter 3, about 200,000 left Scotland between about 1755 and 1775 and from about 1800 most of these expatriates and their children returned. As many of them would have been part of the British armed forces, it is reasonable to expect that some of them might have decided to stay in England after completing their tour of duty in North America, India, and Western Europe. As well, their numbers would have been raised by other Scots going to England directly to get work, but how many did so is unknown. Fortunately, the main outlines of Scottish migration from 1820 can be estimated with some confidence thanks to what must be one of the earliest surveys of an immigrant community anywhere. It was undertaken by the Scotch Church Young Men's Society and published as the *Statistical Report of the Scottish Population of Manchester, taken in 1837*. Based mainly on married couples, the survey's team had the foresight to ask about how long they had been living in England, and the investigators were surprised to discover that nearly one in four had been there since 1817.

The survey also charted the start of the assimilation of the Scots-born into English society: of the 1,455 married respondents 63 percent were both Scots-born, but 24 percent had an English or Welsh spouse and 12 percent an Irish spouse. Not all the results were positive: the survey also found that many were neglecting their children's education and sending them out to work, just like the locals. In another first, the survey asked respondents for their county of birth. As might be expected given the poor land transport of the time, 69 percent came from counties on the western side of Scotland. The authors of the survey recognized this bias and claimed that the main flow of Scots to London was from the southeastern countries. If their survey was representative of all Scots in England—and taking likely deaths into account—it suggests that Scottish migration into England in the 1820s was steady, not sudden, rising from about 35,000 in 1821 to about 54,000 by 1831. If these figures are right, they show that their numbers must have doubled in the 1830s to 102,000 when they were first counted at the 1841 census. Wales was not an important destination, and only 1,500 Scots were counted there in 1841.

HENRY MAYHEW'S LONDON SCOTS, 1856

In 1856 the renowned social investigator Henry Mayhew (1812–1887) interviewed some London Scots as part of his mass interview project later published in the third volume of his *London Labour and the London Poor*. By this time, the number of Scots living in London and southeast England had risen by 11,000 to 52,000. Two of those he interviewed, Mr. Grant and Mr. Campbell, were pipers, the sons of soldiers and ex-soldiers themselves, and part of the street culture that Mayhew recorded with such clarity and compassion. The first piper, Mr. Grant, was a twenty-six-year-old who had been born in Inverness. His father had been in the 42nd regiment, the Black Watch, for seventeen years and he had joined the 93rd Southern Highlanders. He saw service in Canada (1843) and India (1848–1849) but was forced to leave the army because of increasing blindness and was unable to claim a pension because he only had ten of the twenty-one years of service required. Interestingly, he complained about competition from the Irish dressing as Scottish pipers.

The second piper was a fifteen-year-old, Mr. Campbell, whose family came from Argyll. His father had joined the 92nd regiment at fourteen or fifteen and had lost a leg during the first Afghan War (1839–1842). Although he was paid a pension of a shilling a day, his family failed to receive any money while he was in India, and he and his brothers were sent out by his mother to earn money by playing the bagpipes. Mayhew's evidence is significant for showing how sons followed their fathers into the military. He also interviewed a blind musician who had been plying the streets of London for thirty years who supported Grant's claim that "a good many London Highlanders" were Irish. So even Scottish pipers in London could not escape competition from the Irish. Table 4 sets out the scale of Scottish migration up to 1930.

IMPORTANT AND DISTINCTIVE, 1820–1930

Between 1820 and 1930, England absorbed 700,000 Scots or 30 percent of all those who left permanently. Although some subsequent migration from England to overseas must have occurred, most likely in the 1850s to Australia, there is no evidence that it was significant aspect of this migration; on the contrary the evidence points to the decisions to go either overseas or to England as being separate.

The Scots who settled in England differed from those who went overseas in two ways. First, they were younger; in 1881, half the Scots in England and Wales were under age thirty-two compared with forty-eight for the Scots-born in Canada and thirty-nine in the United States in 1880. By 1911 the age difference had narrowed with only half under age thirty-seven compared with thirty-four for the Scots-born in Canada and forty-two for the United States. By 1931 the ages of the Scots-born in England and Wales were comparable with those in North America and still younger than those in Australasia. The Scots who settled in England were mostly under forty without the middle-aged who were more evident among those who went to North America.

Second, as England offered no opportunity for acquiring land as there was in North America and Australasia, the Scots conspicuously avoided rural England and settled almost exclusively in the cities and towns; even as early as 1851 nearly two-thirds of them lived in the largest cities and towns, and London and Liverpool between them accounted for a third.

NORTH ENGLAND AND LONDON, 1841–1931

By 1881 the number of Scots living in England had grown to 248,000. Then, as before and later, they were concentrated in three regions: the north, northwest, and southeast/London. Together, these three regions accounted for 82 percent of the Scots-born in England. The northern region included the former counties of Durham and Northumberland, famous for their coal mining, and the northwest region was essentially the manufacturing powerhouse of Lancashire (Table 5). The southeast (including London) consisted of greater London and the former counties of Essex, Kent, Sussex, Surrey, and the intermediate counties to Oxford and south to the Isle of Wight.

During the Victorian era, the regional distribution of the Scots-born in England was fairly stable, but from 1901 to 1931 there was a notable shift to the southeast and London region and away from the north and northwest as a result of the declining fortunes of heavy industries such as steel making and mining in these regions. This is indicated too by an increase in the number of Scots in both the East and West Midlands following the emergence of lighter forms of manufacturing such as car making in these regions. From the start, the great majority of Scots were urban dwellers, and there was no switch from rural to urban settlement as occurred in North America and Australasia after 1880.

PRESBYTERIANISM

Religion was not included in the regular census of England and Wales until 2011. A special census of church attendance was held in 1851; but as it showed that the strength of the non-established faiths was comparable to that of the Church of England, it was not repeated. Analysis of the 1851 results and later information on the distribution of religion by John D. Gay in 1971 revealed that Presbyterianism was strongest in the north in 1851, weak in the

Midlands and London, and largely absent elsewhere. By 1877 its geographical reach had broadened to most of the other English counties, essentially following Scottish migration.

WHERE DID THEY COME FROM?

The 1911 census of England and Wales was unusual for publishing the birth counties of its migrants from other parts of the United Kingdom. Predictably, one in three Scots-born came from the Strathclyde region and 17 percent from the Lothian region; that is, half came from Glasgow and Edinburgh and their surrounding areas. The Highland regions (Highland and Grampian) contributed 18 percent and 15 percent came from the border regions (Dumfries and Galloway and Borders). Glasgow and Edinburgh may have provided half the Scots-born, but compared with their 1901 populations, the level of migration from the border regions was double that of the other regions, presumably just because they were closer to England (Table 6).

WHAT DID THEY DO?

England was a particularly desirable for certain groups of Scots. Unpublished information from the 1881 census makes it clear that for the Scots qualified in education, finance, and health, it offered opportunities and careers as well as for artists and entertainers. It confirms the long-held view that compared with Scotland the Scots were over-represented in the skilled white-collar industries, namely information and communication, finance, property and business services, professional, scientific and technical, public administration, defense, and health. These figures testify to an early "brain drain" from Scotland to England even though the difference for artists and entertainers was less evident.

The industries that employed the Scots-born in 1881 were remarkable for three reasons. First, some industries employed about the same proportion as in Scotland; these included manufacturing, construction, wholesale and retail trade, education, and general laborers. The top three industries—manufacturing, construction, and transport and storage—employed half the Scots-born labor force. Second, the proportion of employed in agriculture was only 6 percent, well below that for Scotland (23 percent). Similarly, mining and quarrying employed only 3 percent of the Scots compared with 7 percent in Scotland. Third, fewer Scots-born women worked in manufacturing than in Scotland, and their employment was far more concentrated in the accommodation, food, and personal services. This industry accounted for 60 percent of Scottish women compared with 44 percent in Scotland, mainly as domestic servants. Education was the only other industry of note: it employed 7 percent of Scots-born women compared with only 2 percent in Scotland.

WERE THEY MARRIED?

Marriage rates among the Scots-born in England and Wales were much higher than for the Scots-born in Scotland, according to unpublished census figures for 1881. Not only that, the figures for those ages sixty and older show that this had been probably the case since about 1840. Of Scots-born men ages fifteen and older, 58 percent were married compared with 48 percent in Scotland; among Scots-born women, the difference was twice as large, 62 to 43 percent. Only a third of Scots-born men had Scots-born wives in 1881, and only 40 percent of Scots-born wives had Scots-born husbands. This was a significant difference from the 1837 Manchester survey, which found that about two-thirds of its Scots had a Scots-born spouse. If its results were representative of all the Scots-born at that time, it would signal a marked decline in in-marriage and their relatively fast assimilation into English society by 1881.

FEW SURPRISES

Even without the benefit of unpublished information, there were few surprises in the nature and trends of Scottish migration to England between about 1820 and 1930. England was always going to have appeal for the Scots; it was close, offered work, and required less adjustment and travel than North America, let alone Australasia. It was also much easier for family members in Scotland to pay visits. In 1911 there were 3,200 Scots-born in England and Wales who were visitors, not residents; they could have just been better-off Scots tourists but some may also have been there mainly to visit family members. As there were no opportunities to take up land on a significant scale, the Scots avoided agricultural employment and rural living. Theirs was always a big city movement that rewarded the better educated or those with marketable skills. England's appeal was that it offered jobs, but, if as happened, a Scot could get a job back in Scotland, he took it. For example, James Meikle (1870–1948) left his native Glasgow in the late 1890s for England and married an English wife, Janet Basford, in St Albans after a four-year courtship, in 1902. An appointment as manager of the Oxford University Press in Glasgow in the mid-1900s enabled him to defy the migration trends of his day and to move back to his native city where he stayed until 1938 when he and his family moved to Bilton near Rugby.

Chapter Five

North America

Immigration to North America is forever colored by century-old images of the Statue of Liberty, Ellis Island, and the huddled masses yearning to be free. Those granted entry work hard to build the nation, suffer crowded housing and disease, and if they do not prosper, the chances are that their children will. The homeland is a memory, something left behind and not revisited. The vision is compelling and enduring; it is also American without regard for the Canadian experience. It fits persecuted groups, most famously Eastern European Jews, but not the Scots. Their migration to North America was nothing like that of the Jews and to apply Jewish terms such as "exodus" and "diaspora" to their migration history is simply wrong. The Bible tells us that the Jews left Egypt; it does not tell us that many went back for a time. "Diaspora" means the forced eviction or "scattering" of the Jews after the Second Revolt CE 132–135; it does not mean planned, purposeful migration to selected countries, which was the hallmark of Scottish migration from 1820. The Scots were not yearning to be free but to be paid.

 The contours of Scottish migration to North America in the eighteenth century were traced in Chapter 3 where it was suggested that the traditional view needs to be modified in two respects. First, many of the Ulster-born of Scottish descent (the Scotch-Irish) who went to the American colonies before 1776 probably earned their passage in Scotland. Second, between about 1755 and 1776 about 200,000 left Scotland, most of them for North America. Some went as settlers, but most were part of the British army as at least 70,000 were counted as having been recruited in Scotland for both the Seven Years War and the American War of Independence. Two Scots were among the signatories of the Declaration of Independence, but they were exceptions. Most Scots sided with the British, and as Loyalists they were expelled to British North America (later Canada) after the war; Scots-born are hard to find in the United States again until the 1820s. In British North America, the European population trebled from 233,000 to 750,000 between 1790 and 1820, not just because of the end of the American war but also because of the closing of the former American colonies to British migrants. Scottish emigration to the United States seems to have not only ceased but reversed in this era, although there was some to British America. Nearly 5,400 were sent there between 1800 and 1803, and between 1811 and 1817 the Earl of Selkirk tried to establish a settlement for Scots and Irish at Red River in modern Manitoba that was violently suppressed. Nearly 1,300 Scots were counted in Nova Scotia in 1817 but the total number of Scots was small; modeling based on their survivors at the 1901 census puts their original number at only about 11,000.

The contrast with the next 110 years could scarcely have been greater, with North America emerging the leading destination for Scottish overseas migrants, accounting for half the Scots who emigrated, 1.1 million in all. Canada was their preferred choice in the 1820s, and although it continued to be popular up to 1860, it was overtaken by the United States thereafter; indeed, the number of Canadian Scots fell steadily from 1860 to 1900, although their numbers rebounded strongly between 1901 and 1930. After the American Civil War ended in 1865, the United States drew increasing numbers of Scots until the depression of the 1890s. As in Canada, this migration was mostly male before 1850 with only about 40 percent of migrants being female; but as shipping conditions and technology improved, females made up an increasing proportion of immigrants to both countries. After 1900, large-scale Scottish migration to both Canada and the United States resumed until 1930 and stayed strong until the Great Depression. In all, 574,000 Scots settled in North America in this period and in a reversal of the previous pattern, Canada's intake of Scots exceeded that of the United States, drawing 309,000 or just over half, although the United States attracted more Scots in the 1920s (Tables 7 and 8).

MAKING THE SOURCES SPEAK

The first general counts of the Scots in what is now Canada were made between 1842 and 1844, covering modern Ontario and Quebec. There were counts made earlier than this that included birthplace, but they only covered the small settlements of Red River and Nova Scotia (1817). Details of all these counts were published in Volume 4 of the 1870–1871 Canadian census. The Scots-born were first identified in the US census in 1850. The printed versions of these and later censuses usually showed only their location; the numbers of males and females were not published until 1900 in the United States and 1911 in Canada. This information can be supplemented by unpublished information from the North Atlantic Population Project for the United States (1880) and Canada (1881); as well, the printed US census for 1870 gives labor force figures for the Scots-born for persons age 10 or older, and the 1890 census published them by sex.

The bald figures for the Scots in these printed censuses disguise how the two countries offered different things to different groups. Canada offered opportunities in agriculture and the reassurance of staying a British subject, and it also seems to have been generally easier for poorer migrants to establish themselves there. The United States offered greater and wider economic opportunities but more for those migrants with money or skills in demand. Both nations viewed the Scots positively and they were ideally placed to use North America as they wished. They could go there as settlers or as seasonal workers. If they did not like Canada they could try the United States, and if they did not like either, they could go back to Scotland. So what did they do?

On their own, the printed censuses of both countries are incapable of answering questions such as these, not just for the Scots but for any immigrant group. What is required is information on when immigrants arrived by age and sex, information that was not published in Canada until 1931 and never for the United States. Limited, general information on when immigrants arrived was published for the United States from 1890 and for Canada in 1901, but this is of little value for particular immigrant groups. To fill these gaps, I searched publicly available genealogical sites for the Canadian census for 1901 and the US census for 1910; this yielded samples of 10,000 commonly occurring Scottish family names for Canada and 7,300 for the United States. The family names searched for both countries were Brown, Campbell, MacDonald, Smith, and Stewart. Because less information was published about the Scottish population of Canada, I added Anderson, Cameron, Fraser, Johnson, MacKay, MacKenzie, Miller, Morrison, Reed, Robertson, Ross, Scott, Sutherland, Thompson, and Wilson to the search.

Knowing the ages by sex of immigrants for particular decades enables their past numbers to be reconstructed by restoring to them the expected deaths that would have occurred after arrival. Not all the Scots told the census collectors when they came, and the quality of their responses may have degraded with failing memories too. Nevertheless, this approach is the only feasible way of finding out how many of those who arrived in a particular decade actually stayed and how many there were before they were first counted by the census. This technique, like other demographic methods, has its drawbacks, mainly because its estimates take no account of those who left before the last census was held, leading to undercounting of the true level of earlier arrivals. That said, it is the only way of establishing how many migrants came in the economically depressed 1890s when Scottish settler arrivals were outnumbered by deaths among the previous arrivals, causing their total numbers to fall in both Canada and the United States.

Departures from Scottish ports to British America/Canada and the United States were counted from 1825, Scottish arrivals in United States ports from 1820, in British America/Canada ports from 1829 to 1880 and again from 1901. Scots who returned to Scotland were recorded from 1895 as were Scottish departures from the United States from 1908. This abundance of port statistics should not be reason for complaint, but as they stand they are often difficult to reconcile with census information before 1890, leading to long-held suspicions that they are incomplete and unreliable. This is certainly case for the US arrival statistics before 1908; they are highly incomplete and erratic but remain the only source for Scottish arrivals from 1820 to 1824. The British port statistics are a different matter and need be understood before they can be used. First, they measured journeys and may include those who undertook multiple journeys. Second, they counted *intended* destinations as stated by emigrants, not necessarily *actual* destinations; migrants could, and did, change their minds about where they wanted to go after their original destination was recorded by emigration officials.

Taking these caveats into account and combined with early twentieth-century census information about length of residence information from later censuses, it is possible to reconcile the main apparent anomalies in the British port statistics and offer a revised account of Scottish migration to North America before 1860. During the 1820s Scottish migration was mainly to British America but the number of settlers was low, only about 22,000 in all. Emigration jumped in the 1830s and 1840s to both countries but there were important differences; more went to the United States than British America in the 1840s and about 20,000 who told emigration officials that they were going to British America changed their minds and disembarked in the United States. This change of heart happened again in the 1850s when about 12,000 said they were going to the United States but actually went to Australasia, a change that would explain why the United States had only 108,000 Scots in 1860 when it should have had about 120,000. So despite their reputation and against expectations, the British departure statistics for North America from Scotland do seem to be reliable when these adjustments are made. Checked against census counts, they also show that most of those who emigrated before 1870 did not make a return journey, but afterward this was less true.

DID THEY STAY?

In the 1870s and 1880s, 320,000 journeys were made from Scottish ports to North America; but nearly of half of those who made a journey did not stay—only 179,000 did. Most return journeys were from the United States. Even though a certain level of return migration is to be expected in free societies, especially in times of economic depression, this was abnormal and calls for examination. Little is known about Scottish returnees from North America. Some undoubtedly would have been disappointed job seekers. Others are known to have been seasonal workers who never intended to settle permanently. In 1953 Rowland Berthoff, the pioneering American historian of British migration to the United States, found that there was some evidence of this by Scottish stone cutters and building workers in the late 1880s and early 1890s, but this was too limited to be the whole explanation. Using the length of residence figures in the Canadian censuses of 1901 and 1911, and the 1910 US census, as well as the Scottish census, it is possible to offer a new reason why return migration was so high in this period. The first clue comes from the 1891 Scottish censuses, which revealed low numbers of North American–born under 20 years of age; there were only 4,808 for the United States compared with at least 120,000 return journeys in the 1870s and 1880s. In Canada, about 21,000 return journeys were made in this twenty-year period but there were only 946 under 20 years of age in Scotland born in Canada in 1891, indicating that most returnees had not stayed long enough in either country to come back with children.

This is supported by the length of residence figures in the Canadian censuses of 1901 and 1911 and from the 1910 US census, which modifies the common assumption that married immigrants emigrated together. Before 1900 this view applies well for Scottish migrants to Canada but far less so for the United States, which absorbed most Scottish migrants. In Canada about 95 percent of Scottish married couples arrived together but only about 62 of those who settled in the United States came together between about 1870 and 1910; in some cases they took up to four years to move permanently with their families, but most took two. These findings cast the migration history of North America between 1870 and 1900 in a different light and flag the need for a re-examination of the migration histories of other groups to see if the Scots were typical. For many Scottish emigrants the United States was enticing but expensive, necessitating multiple journeys to get enough money to finally enable permanent settlement. This new evidence reinforced the view that the decision to settle in the United States was well planned, that its implementation was taken with resolve, that the apparent large gap between outward journeys and permanent settlement may not have existed, and that those making the outward and return journeys and those who became settlers were really the same people moving at different times. For Scotland itself, the lack of growth members' spending in cooperative societies per head suggests that wages were flat between 1872 and 1888, making paying for cost of emigration especially hard. The puzzle of large-scale return Scottish migration in the 1870s and 1880s now looks less of a mystery and more like an elliptical process that would have supplemented the notoriously low wages at home through remittances and helped sustain the Scottish economy if only temporarily.

WHERE DID THEY GO?

Quoting an 1875 article in *Harper's Magazine*, the 1880 US census said of the American Scots over the 150 years that they "were then, as they are now, everywhere." This was true in the sense that some Scots could be found in most places but it was also true that at the time of writing about 80 percent of Scottish settlement in North America was in the Northeast region of the United States or around the Great Lakes and shores of the St Lawrence River. Few went to either the South of the United States or the western parts of either country. In this, the distribution of the Scots was much like that of other migrants of the time and, as so often happens, their distinctiveness can be noted but neither should it be overstated.

From 1860 to 1930 half the American Scots lived in the Northeast census region, which covered the states of the New England division plus those of the Middle Atlantic (New Jersey, New York, and Pennsylvania). For much of this period New York state had the largest number of Scots-born, accounting for a third of Scots-born in 1850, a quarter in 1860, and a fifth in 1870 and 1930. Before 1870 about 30 percent of Scots in New York state lived in New York City and about 60 percent between 1890 and 1930. Pennsylvania was home to the second largest number of Scots in 1850, from 1870 to 1910, and again in 1930. The North Central census region, which covered the triangle of states between Ohio, Kansas, and North Dakota, contained a third of Scots from 1860 to 1930, the South region only accounted for 6 percent, and the West 11 percent.

Before 1880 the majority of American Scots outside the Middle Atlantic region were rural dwellers even if they were not necessarily farmers. After 1880, there was a pronounced shift to urbanization among the Scots, although its scale and pace of urbanization differed. In the North Central and West regions, an urban majority among the American Scots was not reached until 1890 and in 1910 in the South. The traditional view that urbanization was fed from newer waves of immigrants rather than from existing rural dwellers is borne out by the Scots, particularly during the decisive decade of the 1880s when the majority of the 100,000 newly arrived Scots bypassed the rural areas and headed for the cities, lifting their national urbanization level from 45 to 66 percent and making them a predominately urban group for the first time. By 1910, 72 percent of Scots were urbanized compared with 62 percent in Scotland. This was comparable with the English-born in the United States, but higher than the Welsh (66 percent) and lower than the Irish (85 percent). By 1920, urbanization among the Scots had risen to 77 percent and to 83 percent by 1930, which was higher than the English or Welsh, comparable with the Northern Irish but well below those from the Irish Republic.

In Canada, Scottish settlement was far more concentrated than in the United States with Upper Canada (later Ontario) accounting for about 70 percent of Scots-born between 1842 and 1891. French-speaking Quebec held 23 percent in 1844 and 16 percent in 1851, but thereafter its appeal waned as better opportunities became available elsewhere. With the linking of Quebec with Vancouver by rail in 1886, the Scots joined in the settlement of Manitoba, Saskatchewan, Alberta, and, most popular of all, British Columbia. Between 1891 and 1911 these four provinces increased their share of Canada's Scots-born from 11 to 50 percent, and they still held 46 percent in 1931. Despite this westward shift, Ontario continued to be the main province of the Scots-born, accounting for 38 percent in 1911 and 42 percent in 1931.

Direct comparisons of urbanization among the Scots in Canada and the United States are misleading. To begin with, the official definitions of urbanization before 1950 were not the same. To qualify as "urban" in the United States required a minimum population of 2,500 compared with only 1,000 in Canada, and this tended to overstate Canadian urbanization. More important, the national US level was boosted by the greater size, diversity, and longer urban history of its Northeast census region. A fairer comparison is between Canada and the US North Central region where the level of urbanization among the Scots was comparable with Canada (24 percent in 1880 compared with 27 percent in Canada in 1881). After that, there was significant divergence because the industrialization of the North Central region in the 1880s led to its faster and higher urbanization; by 1890, 52 percent of its Scots were urbanized compared with 35 percent in Canada. In the 1900s this was abruptly changed by the entry of 109,000 Scots into Canada of whom about two-thirds settled in urban areas, making the Canadian Scots an urban people for the first time at 58 percent in 1911, approaching their urbanization in the North Central region (62 percent in 1910). Later Scottish arrivals in Canada raised their urbanization level to 71 percent by 1931. Compared with other British groups in 1931, urbanization among the Scots in Canada was, like in the United States, higher than the English or Welsh but only just above the Irish.

WHAT DID THEY DO?

The emphasis on later urbanization among European migrants to North America is fair, but it must be remembered that what most of the earlier migrants really wanted was land of their own. Like other migrants, the Scots who settled in North America before 1880 were more attracted to a life on the land than those who came later. Traditionally, farming appealed to those wanting personal independence and a satisfying lifestyle even if it did not bring wealth.

There was no opportunity for doing this in Scotland. Quite apart from its natural poverty, all the land was monopolized by about 630 owners who had no desire to part with any of it. North America was one place where those Scots who wanted a life on the land could find it. In 1870, one in four Scots in the United States worked in agriculture, which was comparable with the English-born and higher than the Irish. In nine states—North Carolina, Wisconsin, Iowa, Minnesota, Vermont, Kansas, Nebraska, Utah, and Washington state—40 percent of more of the Scots-born labor force worked in agriculture. These figures capture the closing of the American farming frontier, not its beginning and, ironically, the economic success of agriculture in North America, to which the Scots along with other migrants contributed, had the unintended result of destroying agricultural employment in Scotland after 1870 through cheaper food imports. By 1890, 54 percent of Scots-born farmers owned their farms outright, 31 percent were mortgaged, and the rest were tenant farmers, which was comparable with farmers from other parts of the British Isles. The level of outright ownership varied greatly between states. In the older areas of settlement along the east coast, farm ownership tended to be higher, but the highest levels were in the West (Oklahoma, Arizona, and Utah). In the central northern States, about two-thirds of farms were owned outright.

Nevertheless, the best prospects for Scots who wanted to be farmers were in Canada, not the United States where there were only 17,100 farmers by 1880 compared with 29,600 in Canada. One of these farmers was Robert Brown (c. 1796–1889) who disembarked in Upper Canada (Ontario), in 1836 and began farming at Lambton West district. He came his wife Janet (1801–1902), Ann, their two-year-old daughter, and John, their one-year-old son, along with 2,220 other Scots in that year. In many ways the Browns fit the stereotypical view of the Scots who came in this period; they also show what could happen to families at this time. John Brown joined his father in farming and married Margaret A. Clark (1835–1904), who was born in Ontario to Scottish parents, by whom he had a daughter, also called Margaret, in 1872. Normally, he would have been expected to take over the farm, but instead he predeceased his father in 1876, leaving him, now 80, to work the farm. Robert Brown's daughter, Ann, later Annie, never married and was still listed at the 1901 census with her mother, now 100 and Canada's oldest Scottish household head. Margaret, her niece, the last surviving family member, died in 1919.

In 1881, Canadian agriculture employed 54 percent of Scots, which was comparable with Scotland but well above the United States (21 percent). As a result, the proportion of Canadian Scots employed in other industries such as manufacturing was less than in the United States. Jobs for women were restricted in both nations; in Canada, a third of working Scots women were domestic servants compared with half in the United States. Between 1880 and 1910 there was a shift away from rural to urban occupations among the Scots in both Canada and the United States. In Canada the number of Scots-born farmers fell by nearly half to about 16,000 and in the United States by 40 percent to 10,200. In Canada, Scots still settled on the land after 1910, but far fewer did so than before 1880; and by 1931, 72 percent of Canada's 14,800 Scots-born farmers had been in Canada for twenty years or more. This is not to say that farming wholly lost its appeal, even for second-generation Scots. For instance, one of the farmers counted in Saskatchewan at the 1911 census was John J. Rathjen who had been born in Australia in 1884 to Scottish parents but who went to Canada in 1904. And in his reminiscences about growing up Ontario in the 1910s and 1920s, John Kenneth Galbraith claimed that the Scots considered agriculture to be "an inherently superior vocation" giving "peace and independence" compared with the "artificialities of urban existence."

As mentioned previously, the majority of Scots in both Canada and the United States by 1910 were urban dwellers doing urban jobs. In Canada, the number of Scottish men employed in construction seems to have been about the same as in agriculture, a result of the influx of Scottish construction workers escaping the collapse of their industry in Scotland in the 1900s. Scottish men's employment in manufacturing and transportation was comparable with construction, each accounting for about 14 percent. The employment prospects for women remained much the same with 42 percent working as domestic service and 24 percent in manufacturing. In all, about 83 percent of the Scots in Canada in 1911 worked in nonfarm occupations compared with about 94 percent in the United States in 1910.

WHAT WERE THEIR NAMES?

In his recollections of the Scottish-Canadian community of Elgin County, Ontario, in the 1910s and 1920s, the noted economist John Kenneth Galbraith (1908–2006) grumbled about how few first names were used and the resort to nicknames to separate the many individuals with the same first name. His complaint was justified. John was by far the most common first name of Scots-born males in Canada and the United States in 1900, followed by James, William, and Alexander. Girls fared no better. Mary, Margaret, and Elizabeth were the top three names for girls in both Canada and the United States. Annie was the fourth most popular name in Canada compared with Agnes in the United States but the margin was small. In all, the ten most common first names covered about 13 percent of Scots in Canada and about 22 percent in the United States.

Changes in the frequency of family names give some clues about migration changes in migration. As in Scotland, the most common family name among the Scots in 1900 was Smith, but this had not always been true in Canada. In Canada Campbell was the most common family name in 1881 and other family names associated with the northwest—Cameron, Fraser, Ross, and Sutherland—were also relatively more numerous, indicating a higher level of migration from that region. Some of these findings are consistent with previous research, but others are not. MacDonald, for example, Scotland's second-most common family name, was relatively underrepresented in North America whereas Stewart, Scotland's sixth-most common family name, was overrepresented. The emergence of Smith as the most common family name among the Canadian Scots-born by 1900 suggests that the 36,000 Scots who settled there between 1881 and 1901 were more geographically representative than previous migrants.

WHAT DID THEY BELIEVE IN?

The religions of Scottish migrants were not necessarily as might have been expected from its relative strength in Scotland itself. Presbyterianism may have been the dominant religion, but its strength varied among Scottish migrants. Religion was not included in the US census but it was in Canada, and the religions of its Scottish migrants are known from a sample of 1,000 from the 1911 census. Before 1901, 75 percent of Scottish migrants to Canada were Presbyterians of some kind, the same percentage as those who went to New Zealand and higher than those who went to Australia (70 percent). The next largest faiths were Methodists (7 percent), Anglicans (6 percent), and Baptists (4 percent), which was comparable to their shares among the Scots of Australia and New Zealand. In all three countries, Roman Catholics were conspicuously underrepresented. Based on marriages in Scotland, about 9 percent of Scottish migrants might have been expected to have been Catholics, but only 2 percent were in Canada, 1 percent in New Zealand, and 4 percent in Australia. Judaism was almost absent among Scottish migrants to Australia and New Zealand, but among Scottish migrants to Canada, Judaism had more adherents than Catholicism because some Eastern European Jews went to Scotland first before going to North America.

WERE THEY MARRIED?

Where the figures are available, marriage is one of the most interesting aspects of migration. In the case of Scottish migration, there was a gulf between the level of marriage among those who migrated and those who stayed at home. Unpublished census figures for North America uncover a much higher level of marriage among Scottish migrants by 1880. Most adult Scottish migrants were either married when they came or married soon after their arrival, and most migrant couples seem to have had their children after their settlement according to a sample of 277 Canadian Scots in 1881. The contrast with Scotland was stark; there, twice as many were unmarried (refer to table 9)

Inter-marriage among the Scots-born was far higher in Canada than in the United States in 1881 (Table 10). In Canada, nearly 70 percent of spouses had a Scottish-born spouse and of the rest nearly all of the Canadian-born spouses claimed Scottish ancestry, another indication that their migration was based on tight family ties. In the United States, there was far more inter-marriage with non-Scots-born, with more spouses being born in either England or Wales or outside either Scotland or the United States, presumably suggesting that more males who settled in the United States were less likely to be married on arrival than those who went to Canada. That said, it is not hard to find Scottish migrants to the United States who conformed to the standard view of migrants as families coming with children. For instance, William Macdonald came to the United States in 1883 as a thirty-one-year-old with his thirty-four-year-old, Janet, and their four daughters, Jeana, Margaret, Jess, and Daisy, ages one to eight. They settled in Paterson, New Jersey, which then had a Scottish community of about 1,800.

A WORLD OF KITH AND KIN

The traditional obsession with the economic side of Scottish migration to North America, particularly the United States, can easily give the impression that it was just about inputs of labor—faceless, nameless units of production, responding to the economic stimuli of trade cycles, effectively denying their humanity. It must be modified by seeing Scottish migration as a process based on families and kin. Sampling of the censuses 1901 for Canada and for pre-1900 arrivals from the 1910 census of the United States reveals an array of household relationships, making it clear that Scottish migration was very much a family affair (Table 11).

Some of these results might have been expected; nearly three-quarters of males were heads of households and about half the females were wives, but the remaining results provide new benchmarks for the family and household structures of immigrants of this period. Among males, about 7 percent were sons, and about one in ten was a boarder. Among females, 16 percent were heads of households through widowhood, and about 9 percent were daughters. At a glance, the results suggest that the makeup of Scottish migrants to Canada and the United States were much the same, but they contain notable differences too. In Canada, nearly a quarter of Scots who arrived before 1901 were under 15 years of age when they came compared with only about 5 percent for the United States. In Canada too, 12 percent of females were mothers of household heads, whether men or women, compared with only 3 percent in the United States, a result of more extended family members among the Scottish migrants to Canada.

This is borne out too by the higher proportion of elderly migrants among the Scots who came to Canada before 1900 compared with the United States, particularly women; in the United States, 6 percent of Scottish migrants were 65 years of age or older when they arrived whereas in Canada it was 9 percent. For men, the difference was less: 5 percent for the United States and 7 percent for Canada. These findings prove that, at least for the Scots, elderly family members were not abandoned but were brought across to join other family members once the heads of households had found work and established themselves in their new societies. As well as testifying to the strength of family ties, it had economic consequences too, for it transferred the cost of their upkeep from Scotland to North America. For the Canadian Scots the additions of the elderly speeded up the aging of their group, but over the next ten years this trend was abruptly reversed.

THE 1900S

During the 1900s Canada absorbed a million migrants, raising its population by a fifth; Scots accounted for nearly one in eight of these migrants, 109,000 in all. It was the largest number of Scots ever to settle in Canada in any decade, easily surpassing the number who went to the United States (78,000); and it was not until the 1920s that more Scots went to the United States than Canada. Most Scottish overseas migration at this time happened between April and October to avoid the cold and storms between November and March. The 1900s was a special decade for Scottish migration to Canada not just for its size but also because its makeup is known from sampling the 1911 census.

The 1900s marked the start of the Scots' flight from the slow death of their economy, the start of an economic eviction of its urban wage earners that lasted for sixty years. As mentioned many of the new arrivals were construction workers (about 17 percent of men), fleeing the collapse in demand for their services in Scotland. No less than 60 percent of immigrants came as married couples or as dependent children, but they did not necessarily arrive at the same time. Among married couples, about 28 percent arrived separately: the husband came first and having earned sufficient to afford permanent settlement—a process that could take up to four years—returned to Scotland to arrange for his wife and family members to emigrate. Others made more than one journey. For instance, Matthew Kerr, a stonecutter, his wife Martha, his brother George, and Kerr's three children arrived in Canada in 1910; but their eldest son, Cecil, had been born in Ontario in 1906, proving that this was their second journey.

Married Scottish migrants typically had a Scots-born spouse, and of the few that did not, nearly all had Protestant spouses born in either England or Ireland. Nearly a quarter of married couples came with no children, and of those with children, half came with one to three. The remaining 40 percent of arrivals were unmarried and over age 15. About half of this group were either lodgers or were domestics or assistants who lived in the households in which they worked; the rest lived with family members of some kind. Lodgers (also called "roomers") simply paid for a room whereas boarders had their meals with the family. It was common for Scottish families to take in a Scottish lodger to help pay the bills, probably someone they had known back in Scotland.

Compared with those who went to the United States, the Scots who chose Canada were more likely to be male, to be wives, and to have daughters under age fifteen (Table 12). Like those who emigrated before 1900, fewer married couples came together to the US—57 percent compared with 72 percent in Canada—and they were more likely to come with no children (37 percent) than those who arrived in Canada (23 percent). About a third of males in both countries were boarders, lodgers, or roomers, which signified their recent arrival, a necessary stage for many trying to establish themselves in their new societies and a reminder that the Scots were not the privileged migrants so often assumed. For most, being a boarder or lodger was a temporary stage, but for others it was a long-term relationship; among the Scots who arrived before 1901 in both countries about 10 percent of men and 4 percent of women were boarders or lodgers.

The 1900s migration rejuvenated the aging Scottish population. At the end of the decade, two in three of the Scots-born in Canada and the United States had only been there for ten years or less, giving them the age profile of the so-called "new" immigrants, such as Italians and Jews from Eastern Europe. But the Scots were not fleeing persecution; they were fleeing the implosion of their economy. The 109,000 Scottish migrants to Canada were far more likely to be Presbyterians than those who settled before 1901, and this diluted the representation of the other Protestant faiths; 85 percent of those who came in the 1900s were Presbyterians and only 1 percent were Catholics, even though Catholics accounted for 11 percent of marriages in Scotland in the 1900s. Again, more Jews (about 1,650) entered Canada in the 1900s than Catholics (about 900) because Scotland was a refuge for Jews fleeing Russian Poland in the 1890s but its ailing economy made it too difficult for them to stay. For example, Jacob and Sarah Samuels were Polish-born Jews who arrived in Canada in 1906 and settled in Toronto. Both their children were born in Scotland, their daughter in 1898 and their son in 1900.

MOVING ON

One of the choices that migrants have to make in a new land is to whether to move on to somewhere else. Of those Scots-born in Canada in 1901, very few left Canada, but over the next twenty years about 4,600 moved out of Ontario and the other eastern provinces to the Prairie provinces and to British Columbia. Of those who came in the 1900s, most went directly to the province of their choice rather than settling in one province and moving later. About 15,000 of those who came in the 1910s left Canada and about 2,700 of this group went to British Columbia, but most of the rest remained in the province where they had first settled. John Kenneth Galbraith judged those who moved westward unkindly, saying that they were the "more unsettled and frivolous." In the United States, there was only limited subsequent movement by those Scots present in 1900 up to 1930, notably to California, which gained about 3,600 from this group. As they did in Canada, Scots who settled in the United States in the 1900s usually stayed in the states where they had first settled, apart from Michigan which gained about 2,300 from this group by 1930. There was no obvious later movement among those who arrived in the 1910s.

JOHN KENNETH GALBRAITH'S *THE SCOTCH*

The world of the rural Canadian Scots was given literary form in 1964 by one of its most celebrated sons, the noted economist John Kenneth Galbraith (1908–2006). *The Scotch* was his wry and perceptive recollections of growing up in Elgin County, southern Ontario, from the late 1910s to about 1930, a work he called an "exercise in social anthropology." His book is important for many reasons. Reviewers of the day praised its style, humor, and insights. Galbraith himself was the product of two generations of Ontario-born of Scottish descent; his paternal grandfather, John Galbraith, was born in Ontario in about 1836. The family were Baptists, not Presbyterians, and nowhere did he speak of those about him as well-off; they are presented as frugal and hardworking: "some were poor, none was rich."

His complaint that "personal nomenclature" was an "enduring problem among the Scotch" was soundly based; as mentioned earlier, he preferred being called Ken, not John, because so many males of his day were also called John. At the time of his birth, John was the first name of about 12 percent of Scots-born males in Canada. Had he been born into a Scottish community in the United States, he would have even more cause for complaint; there, 16 percent were called John. More than any other work before or since, *The Scotch* drew attention to the strength of Scottishness in Canada, even after two generations. As an account of Scottishness, it is possibly unique, for it describes generations of Scottish settlement in Ontario with no need for new arrivals to maintain its social cohesion and traditions. By 1931 when his recollections stopped, rural Ontario had long ceased being attractive to Scottish immigrants and the number of rural Scots-born in Ontario had dropped to 26,000, compared with 90,000 living in cities or towns.

RELUCTANT AMERICANS?

Emigration to the United States did not just mean a change of country; it also presented Scots with a decision about their allegiance: they could opt to become American citizens and thereby renounce their British nationality. The US census first asked about citizenship in 1890 but only for men ages 21 and older, and it did not ask about the whole population until 1920. The results for 1890 showed that the Scots' rate of take-up of American citizenship was the same as the English (about 70 percent) but lower than the Welsh and the Irish. In 1900, most Scottish men and Englishmen over twenty-one were American citizens (87 percent). Both the Scottish and English citizenship take-up rates had fallen by 1910; the Scots went down to 56 percent compared with 59 percent for the English. These differences may have been simply the result of not being resident in the United States for long enough rather than lack of interest in becoming citizens because at this time an alien had be resident for at least five years.

The longer British migrants stayed in the United States, the more likely they were to take out American citizenship, regulations permitting. By 1920, it was still the case that fewer Scots were American citizens (54 percent) than migrants from the rest of British Isles (61 percent). It was even truer in 1930 when their citizenship rate was 51 percent compared with 66 percent for the English. Again, this could be explained by the higher proportion of recent arrivals among the Scottish migrants—they had not been resident long enough to qualify for citizenship—but it is much harder to explain for 1940 when their citizenship of 67 percent still lagged behind that of those from other parts of the Britain (72 percent).

HOW WELL DID THEY DO?

The Scots have long had a reputation for being more successful than most other migrants. Studies of the Scots in North America and Australia support this view, but such studies have been largely confined to pre-1900 migrants. The high achievers who were so easy to find earlier were far less evident from the 1900 to 1930 period when nearly a million left Scotland. Most of these migrants were urbanized wage and salary earners who bypassed the agricultural life that attracted the pre-1900s migrants. They were essentially economic refugees whose migration history was not much different from that of other British migrants of the time.

The US census enables the relative success of Scottish migrants to be tracked using one of the best indicators available: home ownership, which was an achievable aspiration for Scottish migrants to North America, unlike Scotland. In 1890, 65 percent of Scottish migrants to the United States lived in tenanted homes, which was slightly higher than for other British migrants, including the Irish. Only a quarter owned their homes outright, and in the fifty-eight largest cities, 76 percent were tenants. In 1930, the Scots' tenancy rate was still high (54 percent) compared with other British migrants, because many had not been working long enough in the United States to become homeowners. The US evidence demonstrates that the general level of economic success of the Scots-born was comparable to that of other British migrants, and there is little reason to doubt that this was probably true of Canada too.

Household structure provides another means of comparing the Scots with other British migrants. The 1930 US census found that 11 percent of Scottish families had at least one lodger living with them, which was slightly more than other British migrants (10 percent). It also found that half the families from Scotland had 3.3 members—the same as for Northern Ireland but lower than England and Wales. The proportion of families with no children under ten was 68 percent, which was lower than all the other British groups (about 74 percent). Yet despite these differences—which could largely be explained by there being twice as many Scots arriving in the 1920s than other British immigrants—the general impression of these findings was the Scots were really not that much different from other British migrants of the time.

SOUTHWARD BOUND?

Rightly or wrongly, Canada has the reputation as a transit lounge for migration to the United States—good at attracting migrants but less successful in retaining them. Does the evidence for the Scots support this view? As discussed previously, there is no evidence of any significant movement between the Scots who settled in Canada and the United States before 1860; but was this true over the next forty years when the number of Scots in Canada fell continually from 139,000 to 84,000? Over this same period, about 65,000 Scots settled in Canada but this was not enough to halt their aging; by 1881 half the Canadian Scots were ages 48 or older compared with ages 39 and older for the Scots in the United States.

Again, the paradox of the gap between journeys and settlement has to be faced; 104,000 journeys were made from Scotland to Canada in this era but only 63 percent of them stayed. This was only about a quarter of those made to the United States, of whom even fewer stayed, only half in fact. The severe depression that blighted the 1890s readily explains this decade, but this reason cannot apply to the three previous decades. Earlier, it was suggested that high level of return journeys from the United States mainly came from married men preceding their families before settlement, but this explanation does not fit Canada where virtually all the Scottish families came together. As with the United States, return journeys were regular and the absence of large numbers of children in Scotland under age 20 who were born in Canada shows that they did not stay long; there were only about 1,000 of them throughout the 1880s. Although the evidence is indirect, it likely that these return journeys were made by seasonal migrants. Many of Canada's Scots were rural dwellers and farmers before 1900, and Scots going there on a short-term basis would have provided welcome additional labor, particularly with the collapse in rural employment in Scotland after 1870. If this is correct, it rules out any significant movement from Canada to the United States, at least for the Scots, before 1900.

Length of residence data from the Canadian census makes it possible to estimate that possibly as many as 15,000 Scots of the 109,000 who came in the 1900s had left Canada by 1921, doubtless returning to Britain to take part in World War I. Otherwise, there is no clear evidence that there was large-scale movement from Canada to the United States, although some would have occurred. There is no doubt too that United States attracted more Scots than Canada in the 1920s, but it should not be assumed that this movement was all one way; official figures show that 5 percent of the 86,000 Scots who entered Canada between 1926 and 1931 came from the United States. Perhaps the last word on this topic should be left to John Kenneth Galbraith who said that the Scots of his time were only attracted to the United States after World War II.

Chapter Six

South Africa and Australasia

Most Scots who settled south of the equator between 1820 and 1930 did so either in South Africa or Australasia, that is, along what were then the southern sea lanes of the British empire. These lands may have shared the same general latitude, but their settlement histories differed despite having some common themes such as frontier settlement and gold rushes. Scots were also prominent among the achievers in all three societies. But whereas Australia and New Zealand actively encouraged immigration—even to the extent of their governments providing financial assistance to immigrants—the policy of the various administrations of South Africa was passive and by the early twentieth century only those with sufficient means to prevent them being a charge on the public purse were admitted. With this less welcoming policy, it was hardly surprising that South Africa never became a place for large-scale European migration, Scottish or otherwise.

A VARIABLE PRESENCE

Establishing the scale of Scottish migration to South Africa before 1900 is much harder than for Australia or New Zealand. Birthplace was not asked in any census before 1875 and then only for the colony of the Cape of Good Hope; there was no census covering all of modern South Africa until 1904. The Boer Wars (1881, 1899–1902) also added to the problem of incomplete census coverage. Similarly, the British emigration statistics collected from 1825 have totals for Australasia but did not count South Africa until 1877. Settler arrivals and departures by European migrants, including the Scots, were published by the South African government from 1913 to 1940; this series was resumed in 1945 and discontinued in 1956.

Using the 1921 Australian census as its model, the South African census of 1926 included critical information on length of residence on its European migrants back to 1851, and this can be used to reconstruct the likely size of the Scottish-born, even though this method takes no account of departures before 1926. The size of the Scottish presence in South Africa, Australia, and New Zealand to about 1931 is set out in Table 13, which makes it clear that Scottish migration to all three countries was variable. Only Australia had a notable number of Scots before 1850 with few Scots living in either South Africa or New Zealand. There was no steady upward progression; rather all three had fluctuating flows shaped by the fortunes of their economies and that of Scotland itself.

SOUTH AFRICA: FAILURE TO THRIVE

Scots were absent from South Africa before 1820 and few came before the 1880s. Their history up to 1914 has been explored by John M. MacKenzie and Nigel R. Dalziel in *The Scots in South Africa: Ethnicity, Identity, Gender, and Race, 1772–1914* (2007) and readers wanting a detailed account of the pioneering period covering the traditional topics of land settlement, missionary activity, military affairs, education, trade, and politics should consult this work. In contrast, Scottish settlement, like European settlement generally after 1914 in South Africa, has attracted little interest. And in the absence of an obvious account of the post-1914 period, only the main trends are sketched here.

Between 1851 and 1881 the number of Scots who settled in South Africa rose from about 500 to about 6,300 and then jumped to 9,400 by 1891. As this growth was consistent with departures from Scottish ports between 1877 and 1890, it suggests that most who went there, stayed there. The Scots of this era seemed to have been mainly the educated or better-off but this changed with the discovery of gold in the southern Transvaal in 1886, which attracted 23,000 Scottish migrants in the 1890s. This was a larger influx than for Australia, a result of the depression and drought that crippled the Australian economy. The Boer War (1899–1902) slowed Scottish migration but only temporarily. Some Scots fought with the British army, although there is an oral tradition in my family that no member serving in the British army fought against the Boers; it was considered an unjust war waged against farmers. Once the war was over, South Africa attracted its largest number of Scottish immigrants—45,300, higher again than for Australasia (31,100); but, tellingly, 60 percent of these arrivals had left by 1926.

The restrictions on entry and the racially segregated society made South Africa an unappealing prospect for large-scale Scottish settlement. The number of Scots peaked at 37,100 in 1911, declined a little later, and remained stable until the 1950s. As in Australia, the frontier society before 1900 gave way to a largely urban people afterwards; in 1921, 84 percent of South Africa's Scots were urban dwellers: 46 percent lived in the Transvaal, 27 percent at the Cape, 22 percent in Natal, and 5 percent in Orange Free State. Scots still went to South Africa, but many left too. Between 1921 and 1950, 24,300 arrived but a third left. Consequently the new arrivals failed to make up for losses from deaths, and the total number of Scots fell to about 30,100 by 1951.

The decision to migrate to South Africa was a difficult one, even in the workless mid-1930s. In 1937, Thomas Docherty, then a 23-year-old resident of St Andrews, decided against migrating to South Africa because of its racial strife. Instead, he went to Australia in December 1938 as an assisted migrant and got a job as a poultry abattoir worker in Double Bay, Sydney. As a prisoner of war at Stalag VIIIB in southern Poland, he became friends with a locomotive driver from South Africa in 1944 and considered going there, but changed his mind and went back to Australia. The 1950s marked the effective end of Scottish settlement in South Africa: 4,300 arrived between 1951 and 1956 when the official figures ceased to be published, but 1,900 left. By 1961, there were only 23,100 Scots-born remaining and they stopped being identified in the census after that time, effectively closing the Scottish chapter in the European settlement of South Africa.

SUCCESS IN THE ANTIPODES:
AUSTRALIA AND NEW ZEALAND

In contrast to South Africa, Australia and New Zealand were success stories of Scottish migration and settlement. Scottish and British settlement generally in Australia has been well covered by the entries in James Jupp's *Encyclopedia of the Australian People* (1992). But all credit for attempting something new in this field must go to Jock Phillips and Terry Hearn in their *Settlers: New Zealand Immigrants from England, Ireland and Scotland, 1800–1945* (2008); an expanded version of their work can be found online. They used samples of death records to reconstruct the characteristics of British migrants to New Zealand. Their results are important, although readers should note that the sample sizes used for the Scots are often too small to be reliable for particular decades; but if they are combined for 1840 to 1915 and for the post-1915 period, they can be used with more confidence. Also it needs to be remembered that their results only capture those who died in New Zealand and miss those who died outside it. No similar work exists for Australia.

The Scots were recorded by gender in the Australian census from 1846 and in the New Zealand census from 1858, something that was not done in the printed censuses of the United States until 1900 and Canada until 1911. Like them, the census recorded only their location, but from 1891 some important additional characteristics were collected, mainly for New South Wales and Tasmania. As in South Africa, and unlike North America, the censuses of Australasia did not retain the original schedules and so they cannot be used to trace individuals. The first national Australian census was conducted in 1911. Although under the authorship of George Knibbs, the head of the newly formed Commonwealth Bureau of Census and Statistics, it drew its intellectual power from his second-in-charge, Charles Wickens, an actuary and statistical visionary from Western Australia. Between them, they designed the 1911 census that created a benchmark for the Australian population, both present and past, and was the model for the census for the next fifty years. Much of this chapter is based on the information they so expertly assembled. It also draws on the vital statistics collection that Wickens created from 1909 that recorded births, deaths, and marriages for all the outside-born, including the Scots, until 1940 and provided the model for the national Canadian collection from 1921 to 1940. Deaths among the Scots-born were also published in lesser detail for New Zealand from 1909 to 1940.

GOLD AND DISTANCE

Scottish migration and settlement in Australia and New Zealand had a distinctly different history to that of either North America or South Africa. There is no evidence for any substantial numbers of Scots-born in Australia before the late 1820s and before 1848 for New Zealand. Very few Scots came as convicts; it has been estimated that there were only 8,600 Scots-born convicts out of 160,000 who were dispatched to Australia between 1788 and 1868. These differences arose from a combination of geography and economic conditions as well as government policy. Whereas most Scottish settlement in Canada before 1900 was in Ontario, the Scots in Australasia were divided among seven widely separated colonies—the six colonies of Australia plus New Zealand—up to 1901. Moreover, the long sea voyage and the generally robust state of the Australasian economy between 1860 and 1890 inhibited large-scale return migration.

Large-scale Scottish migration to Australia first occurred in the 1850s caused by a series of gold rushes in the southeast. The United States had gold rushes too—notably in California from 1848—but access to them was by a long and difficult overland or sea journeys; the route to the Australian gold fields was easier through the ports of either Melbourne or Sydney, and the diggings were government regulated with little of the violence of California, apart from the shared hostility toward the Chinese. The Australian gold rushes of the 1850s attracted nearly 600,000 immigrants and their coming doubled the population to 1.1 million. About 79,000 of these arrivals were Scots, and they created a bulge in the Australian Scottish population that was still evident in 1911 and well above the number who went to the United States.

As is so often the case with migration research, the census figures can give a false sense of stability when in fact there is much secondary movement taking place. New Zealand had gold rushes too—the first in the South Island starting in 1861 and the second in the North Island from 1867—and this drew thousands from Australia as the original gold rushes there petered out in the 1860s. Scots must have played a significant part in this migration; in just three years, from 1861 to 1864, their numbers in New Zealand doubled to 32,000 but eased off to finish at 37,000 by 1871. Gold rushes do not last, and it is likely that many of those Scots who went to New Zealand from Australia drifted back in the ensuing years to be present at the 1911 Australian census when they would have reported their arrival as the 1850s, disguising their time in New Zealand. In the 1870s Scottish settlement in both countries was about the same, about 21,000 each. There was a second, smaller bulge in Scottish immigration to Australia in the 1880s that was almost entirely directed at the cities and towns. The acute depression of the 1890s and prolonged drought from 1895 to 1903 brought an abrupt halt to large-scale migration to Australia. The depression was less severe in New Zealand, and for the first and only time it attracted about the same number of Scottish settlers. As a result, the 1850s gold rush influx easily retained its importance within the pre-1901 Scottish population of Australia (Table 14).

DID THEY STAY?

Scottish migrants were never separately identified in migration statistics for Australia although they were for New Zealand from 1922. The British departure figures from 1825 to 1938 give total departures and return migration (from 1895) but only for Australasia. The results suggest that return migration from Australasia was limited before 1890. Some return migration did occur as the Scottish census for 1891 records 486 people under age 20 who were born in Australia, 268 in New Zealand, and 427 in South Africa. There was also some interchange between Australia and New Zealand, but the extent of this movement over the longer-term seems to have been small. The high level of temporary return Scottish migration evident for the United States in the 1870s and 1880s was not a feature of Australasia; on the contrary, the British departure statistics and reconstructions from the Australian and New Zealand census are in close accord.

Return migration rose during the depression of the 1890s when about 5,900 journeys were made back to Scotland from Australasia between 1895 and 1900—about the same number as for Canada but well below the 42,000 from the United States. Some of those who left Australia went to Canada. For instance, Maggie Cockrone, who was born in Australia in about 1876 to Scots-born parents, returned to Scotland (presumably with them) in about 1892. She married there and had two sons, one in 1895 and the other in 1897. After her husband's death, she went to Canada in 1910 and worked as a waitress in Winnipeg, Manitoba. William Sage, a carpenter, migrated to New South Wales probably in the 1880s with his wife where their first son, William, was born in about 1892. They returned to Scotland where they had three more children between 1897 and 1902. He left for Canada in 1905 and the rest of the family followed the next year; by 1911, they were living in Saskatoon City, Saskatchewan (table 15).

As in North America there was some return migration from Australia and New Zealand in the 1910s response to the call for soldiers and skilled metal workers to assist the British war effort. In the 1920s, again as in North America, return migration fell off as the Scottish economy descended into even deeper depression than before. Between 1922 and 1932 the New Zealand government published the most detailed immigrant figures for any part of Australasia. Used with British port statistics, they enable Scottish migration to Australia to be separated out, showing that about 21 percent of journeys from Scotland to New Zealand ended with a return trip compared with 16 percent for Australia. But the New Zealand figures also show something that is often overlooked: that by no means all Scottish journeys were intended for settlement, even in this extreme period. Of those Scots who came to New Zealand, 9 percent had no intention of staying; they were there mainly as tourists with the others coming for business or just in transit. In all, 1,674 Scottish tourists came to New Zealand in the 1920s; they were from "have" Scotland, enjoying the international cruises of the day, while many from "have not" Scotland had to leave.

GOVERNMENTS LEND A HAND

Unlike in North America, governments in Australasia actively assisted migration to fill shortages in certain occupations and to promote economic growth by boosting the labor supply. Sales of government land were used to fund these programs from 1831 based on the ideas of Edward Gibbon Wakefield (1796–1862). Assisted migration to Australia began in 1837, ceased during the gold rushes of the 1850s, and resumed in 1862 when immigration slowed down. Under the first scheme, 10,000 Highland Scots were brought to Australia by 1851 to escape famine. The second scheme was less successful, attracting only 13,000 over thirty years. The first program had the most impact, causing the number of pre-1850 Scots to double, but the second program accounted for only 17 percent of Scots who had arrived by 1891. In 1871, the New Zealand government began a program of assisted and nominated immigration that attracted more Scots than Australia did—19,600, or nearly two-thirds of those who came in the 1870s and 1880s. Both countries stopped these programs in the early 1890s because of the depression. As in Canada, farm workers and domestic servants were the most desired occupations in Australasia, but it is unclear that these were the ones who actually arrived; more likely, they were just the poor. Assisted migration programs were resumed in both Australia and New Zealand from the early 1900s to about 1930 and again from 1938 (Australia) and 1947 (New Zealand) and continued to the 1970s, but their published figures no longer distinguished how many Scots were assisted.

WHERE DID THEY GO?

In Australia, the distribution of population was the product of history and its physical geography. Although Australia is about the area of the United States without Alaska, about 70 percent of it is desert or arid; it receives only about a quarter of the US's rainfall, and that rainfall is also less regular. Only the eastern highlands and Tasmania are relatively well-watered, and droughts are common. The northern periphery is monsoonal. These limitations meant that European settlement in Australia has been largely in the southeast of the mainland, mostly the main ports and their hinterlands. For many of the first generation of Scottish immigrants, the chance of a life on the land made Australia attractive, but there was far less good agricultural land available than in North America, especially Canada. Also, the use of land sales by governments to assist immigration made setting up as farmers more expensive. Consequently, most Australian Scots were less likely to be rural dwellers than in Canada, and their urbanization levels were comparable to those of the Scots living on the US West Coast between 1890 and 1930. By 1861 when the main gold rushes had passed, 59 percent of Scots-born migrants were living on the land compared with 67 percent for the general population, and over the next twenty years the towns and cities gained at the expense of the rural areas. There was a more pronounced shift to the towns and cities after 1881, not just to the strongly growing mainland capitals but also to the other cities such as Newcastle. By 1891 there were 124,000 Scots in Australia, a number that was not exceeded until 1933, of whom 60 percent were urban dwellers.

The depression of the 1890s and the sluggish recovery of the Australian economy before the mid-1900s reduced the Scottish population to 93,000 by 1911. It also ended the dominance of Victoria as the main center of Scottish migration; and although some Scots left Victoria for New South Wales, most stayed in the colony where they had first settled. Between 1891 and 1911 Victoria's share of Australia's Scots fell from 41 to 29 percent, mainly through aging and the growing preference of Scottish migrants for New South Wales after 1901. By 1911 New South Wales had more Scots-born than Victoria, and Sydney had more Scots than Melbourne for the first time. Over the next twenty years, the Australian capitals increased their share of the Scots-born at the expense of the rural areas and smaller cities and towns. By 1933, Australia's capital cities were home to 57 percent its Scots-born of 132,500, and Sydney easily dominated the others accounting for nearly a quarter of Australia's Scots-born (32,800). Comparisons with Canada in 1931, the closest country in area and size of its Scots-born, are instructive. Although their level of urbanization was almost the same, 72 percent in Australia and 71 percent in Canada, in Canada there was far less concentration in the two cities with the largest numbers of Scots; Toronto and Vancouver held only 22 percent of Canada's Scots compared with 39 percent in Australia's two largest cities, Sydney and Melbourne.

In New Zealand, the main division of the population was between the North and South Islands. Much of the original European settlement was in the South Island and this was true of the Scots as well. It was not until 1901 that the North Island overtook the South Island as the home of most New Zealanders, but the difference was small; the North Island held 51 percent of the population in 1901 but by 1936 had increased its share to 63 percent. In contrast, the Scots-born much preferred to stay in the South Island, which was still home to two-thirds of them in 1901. Between 1916 and 1921 the number of Scots in the North Island slowly overtook the aging Scots in the South Island for the first time and a majority of the Scots also became a mainly urban group also for the first time. The four largest cities—Auckland, Wellington, Christchurch, and Dunedin—held 38 percent of New Zealand Scots in 1921 and 45 percent in 1936. Unlike North America, where the Scots were the second highest group of urbanized British migrants, in Australia urbanization among the Scots in the early 1930s was less than among the Welsh, English, and Irish. In New Zealand in 1936, the Welsh and Irish were also more urbanized than the Scots, who were only just above the Irish.

WHAT DID THEY DO?

Census information on the occupations of the Scots-born for Australasia before 1945 is confined to New South Wales (1901) and New Zealand (1936). Neither of these collections is truly representative of their historical experience, if for different reasons: the New South Wales figures capture a society still gripped by depression, and the New Zealand figures record a mainly urban population at the end of the period of mass migration. Both collections were made too late to capture the early dominance of agriculture. Nevertheless, the occupations of Scots in New South Wales were not much different to the labor force generally. The Scots were under-represented in agriculture, about average in pastoralism, and almost absent from dairy farming, an occupation that blossomed in the 1890s. Scottish men had about the same representation in farming as the English and Welsh, but both were below the level for the Irish. Otherwise, the Scots' share of men's occupations was similar to the other British groups, even in religion, health, and education where they might have been expected to be over-represented according to the usual stereotypes. That this was not the case may well have been the result of the erosion of the superior literacy that Scottish migrants were supposed to have had over others. During the 1880s the percentage of grooms and brides in Australia and New Zealand who were unable to sign their names decreased to as their public education schemes took effect, and by 1900 Scottish migrants had lost the relative advantage in literacy that they seem to have had before.

Well-watered and fertile, the South Island of New Zealand was attractive for immigrants wanting a life on the land without the severe winters of North America. According to Phillips and Hearn, 31 percent of Scottish migrants to New Zealand were farmers or farm laborers before 1890, rising to 36 percent between 1891 and 1915 and falling to 17 percent between 1916 and 1945. Farm laborers, a minority before 1890 and after 1916, made up nearly half this intake between 1891 and 1915, a comment on the steady decline of agricultural employment in Scotland from the 1870s and 1880s. Their figures indicate that those who went to New Zealand before 1915 were more likely to come from the rural parts of Scotland.

The Scots' occupations at the 1936 New Zealand census showed similar trends to those of New South Wales thirty-five years before. Compared with the total New Zealand labor force, Scottish men were under-represented in agriculture (18 percent for Scottish men compared with 27 percent for all men) and only slightly higher in health and education. The New Zealand results were shaped by the shift in the migration composition of the Scots from about 1901 if not earlier; they were predominately urban dwellers used to doing urban occupations. Many were also relatively recent arrivals too—37 percent had only been resident since 1922—which accounted for their higher levels of unemployment. These qualifications aside, the Scots-born in Australasia in the early 1930s were a well-integrated economic group, and this was demonstrated too by the annual incomes they reported at the 1933 Australian census, which were comparable to those of most Australians.

Chapter 6
WERE THEY MARRIED?

From the early 1890s to the mid-1900s Australia suffered one of its worst depressions. It began with the global financial crisis (1893) and was exacerbated by one of the worst recorded droughts, from 1895 to 1903. The Victorian economy was hit hardest and many left for Western Australia. The depression also brought a reduction in the birth rate, causing alarm in conservative ranks that the trend was not just a response to the depression but also the result of immorality in the form of use of artificial contraception. Their concerns resulted in the appointment of a royal commission into the subject in New South Wales (1903–1904), which was predictably critical of the moral state of society. As often happens with population debates, "sin" was never far away, but in this instance it did have useful consequences. The commission collected much evidence for contraceptive use in its second volume, which, because of its highly sensitive nature, had a severely restricted print run. Assumed lost, it was rediscovered by Neville Hicks in the National Library of Medicine, Bethesda, Maryland, who used it for his book *'This Sin and Scandal'* (1978). The debate had another, less well-known result: the 1901 census of New South Wales included new questions on marriage and fertility by birthplace, which enabled the Scots to be studied in a way not available for anywhere else. It showed, for example, that the median age at marriage of Scots-born wives in New South Wales between about 1851 and 1901 was 23.5, which was about nine months less than in Scotland over the same period.

Although the marital status of the Australian Scots is only known for New South Wales and Tasmania before 1911, this provides enough information to estimate that about 55 percent of Australian Scottish men over age 15 in 1891 were married, which was roughly comparable with the Scots in England but well below that among the Scots in North America ten years earlier, most likely the result of the arrival of more single men among its Scottish migrants. For Scottish women, about 59 percent were married, which was comparable with England and Canada but less than the United States. Even so, the marriage level in Australia was still much higher than Scotland, especially for women.

Over the next twenty years, the number of married Scots in Australia fell with aging; the Scots still got married but they were outnumbered by the rising number of deaths among the older married Scots. Immigration after 1911 slowly reversed this decline. The recording of deaths among married Scots and Scots marrying in Australia can be used to work out how many Scottish migrants were married on arrival; it was 37 percent in the 1910s and 31 percent in the 1920s, but there was a notable disparity between the sexes. In the 1910s, 30 percent of arriving Scottish men were married compared with 46 percent of Scottish women. In the 1920s, only a quarter of men were married compared with 38 percent of women, showing that Australia continued to be attractive for single Scottish men. The impression that many of the adult Scottish migrants to Australasia were single on arrival is also supported by the evidence for New Zealand, which shows that of those who arrived before 1916, 31 percent of men and 42 percent of women arrived married.

Whom did they marry? New South Wales was the only part of Australia that asked this question in its census before 1911. In 1891 it found that 41 percent of Scottish husbands had Scottish wives but that 59 percent of Scottish wives had Scottish husbands. Not only that, 29 percent of Scots husbands had an Australian-born wives but only 10 percent of Scots-born wives had an Australian-born husband. Apart from Scotland or Australia, the most popular birthplace of spouses was England and Wales; they accounted for 12 percent of the wives of Scots-born husbands and 17 percent of the husbands of Scots-born wives.

The first Australian national census in 1911 reported that 31 percent of Scots-born husbands had a Scots-born wife and 45 percent of Scots-born wives had a Scots-born husband. The annual marriage figures from 1907 to 1940 demonstrated a greater willingness by the Scots to marry those not born in Scotland, supporting the previous finding that many Scottish men arrived unmarried. These results differed from the marriage pattern of Scottish migrants in Canada. In the 1920s, 29 percent of Scottish grooms in Australia married a Scottish bride compared with 37 percent in Canada. The difference was even greater for brides; in Australia, 22 percent married a Scottish husband compared with 38 percent in Canada. The relatively high degree of in-marriage among the Scots in Canada probably meant that they were joining Scottish communities on a scale that was not possible in Australia where the Scots were more dispersed and had no choice but to join mainstream society somewhat faster.

CHILDREN

From about 1870 there was a slow decline in the number of children produced by married couples in Western European societies. The decline began in France in the 1830s, slowing its population growth and enabling Germany's population to overtake it by 1870. This decline became an international issue during the 1900s—largely in response to war preparations—as more people were needed to fight wars. Infant mortality attracted new attention and governments began supporting baby health clinics less out of humanitarian caring and more to improve the efficiency of the supply of men for armies. These developments were faithfully followed in Australia whose censuses were exceptional in examining many of these issues by birthplace, included those of their Scots-born.

The 1901 census in New South Wales found that those Scottish wives married before 1870 had an average of 6.6 children but thereafter their fertility declined, as it did in other Western nations. The census also found that about one in eight Scots-born wives had no children and of those who did, they had an average of 3.8 children. Australia-wide figures on the completed fertility of Scots-born wives in 1911 confirmed the main findings of the 1901 New South Wales census; their average number of children had risen to 4.9 compared with 4.0 previously. About half of this rise in the number of children came from the high level of migration from Scotland in the 1900s when about 13 percent of the women of child-bearing age—15–44 years of age—left. The average number of children born to Scottish wives in Australia was higher than that of English wives (4.7), about the same as Welsh wives (5.0), and not far behind Irish wives (5.3). By the early 1930s, the number of children born to Scottish wives was broadly comparable to those from other parts of the British Isles.

WHAT DID THEY BELIEVE IN?

The religions of the Scots-born are known from the 1911 Australian census and from deaths among those in New Zealand before 1915. Again, comparisons with the Scots-born in Canada are illuminating. In Australia, 70 percent of the Scots in 1911 were Presbyterians, as were about 75 percent who arrived in New Zealand by 1915. In Australia, there was only a slight difference between the sexes. In Canada, Presbyterianism was far stronger—83 percent in 1911—stronger even than in Scotland itself where 72 percent of marriages in the 1900s were conducted by the Presbyterian Church.

Presbyterianism in Australia was weakened not so much by the dispersal of the main areas of settlement but more by out-marriage among the Scots to non-Presbyterians, mainly Anglicans. As in Canada in 1911, Roman Catholics were greatly underrepresented among the Scots of Australasia; only 4 percent were Catholics in Australia and only about 1 percent were in New Zealand, the same as in Canada. Based on Scottish marriages, about 9 percent of Scottish migrants might have been expected to have been Catholics if they had been a true cross-section of their society. Australian Catholicism before the 1950s was the history of Irish Catholicism, so it was truly remarkable that Australia's first saint, Mother Mary MacKillop (1842–1907), was the daughter of Scottish rather than Irish immigrants. Jews were largely absent among Australasian Scots; only forty-eight individuals claimed Judaism as their faith in Australia in 1911, a result that was consistent with their tiny representation in Scotland.

HOW HEALTHY WERE THEY?

Writing in the *Scottish Geographical Magazine* in 1913, Ralph Richardson observed that "our Scottish emigrants are usually men and women in the prime of life, full of health and energy." Was this common view of migrants, not just Scots, correct? Recorded Scots deaths in Australia for 1911 can be compared with those for Scotland. For males, the rates were comparable for those under age 30, higher for 30- to 44-year-olds, and comparable again for those under 60. For those over 60, the death rate among the Australia's Scottish men was much lower, especially for those born in the 1830s. The death rates for Australian Scottish females were comparable with males. These differences were a comment on the degree of physicality needed by migrants to Australia before the 1880s.

They confirm Richardson's claim but only up to a point; for example, the death rates among those in their twenties was almost identical in both sexes in Australia and Scotland. The Australian figures also record the cause of death for 1911. About 90 percent of deaths among the Australian Scots occurred among those ages 45 and older and the causes were similar to those in Scotland but with some notable differences. Cancer and bronchitis killed fewer Australian Scots, but more died from liver disease, accidents, and homicide. The incidence of suicide was also higher, an indication of the greater social isolation suffered by migrants. By the early 1930s, the death rate among the Australian Scots-born was still lower than for Scotland for those ages 5–69 but much lower for those ages 70 and older—that is, for those born before 1861. In making these comparisons, it is important to remember that the Scottish migrants were self-selected and included more of those "full of health" than those who stayed in Scotland; emigration, by leaving the less healthy behind, made Scottish death statistics for the 1930s look even worse than they might otherwise have been.

ONLY IF NECESSARY

Compared with North America, Scottish migration and settlement in South Africa and Australasia was a rather dull affair in the 1900s; it increased certainly, but it could hardly be called a flight, unlike the Scots' movement to Canada. About the same number went to South Africa as New Zealand (13,000), and even Australia only attracted 18,000 Scots despite the improvement in its economy after 1903. Indeed, the number of Scots who arrived in Australia was not sufficient to outweigh the deaths among their aging members, reducing their total number in 1911 to 93,000, compared with 102,000 in 1901. In New Zealand, their arrivals managed to restore their 1901 total, but in South Africa, they doubled it to 37,000, although there was little growth thereafter.

Australasia was very much the less desired choice for Scottish migrants. Being on the other side of the planet demanded a long sea voyage, meaning the decision to go there was much harder to reverse than for North America or even South Africa. The stereotype that the Scots were prepared to venture far from home is true, but their settlement record in Australasia suggests that it was only as far as was necessary. Bypassed by the surge in Scottish migration of the 1900s, they were an older population that those in Canada or the United States in 1911, and subsequent Scottish migration to Australia was a steady process with nearly the same number settling in the 1920s as the 1910s (41,000), in contrast to North America. There was no repeat of the great immigration surge of the 1850s when 79,000 Scots came to Australia, even in the 1950s.

By 1931 there were 132,000 Scots in Australia, certainly their highest number, but not that much higher than their previous peak of 124,000 in 1891. Similarly, the number living in New Zealand was also at its highest of about 61,000, but, as in Australia, this was not much more than their 1886 peak of 55,000. Considered this way, the scale of Scottish migration to Australasia was less impressive that it first seems, even though it was undeniably a success story in that it attracted nearly 400,000 Scots settlers by 1930. As elsewhere, the Scottish high achievers who seemed so numerous before 1901 were far fewer among those who came from 1900 to 1930, and they became part of their new societies with little comment. Of those who arrived in the 1920s nearly four in ten had come in the past ten years; one those who came was Jane Gray (née Cant) (1901–2014) who was born in Newtyle, near Dundee. She met her husband Jock in 1922 and they were engaged for five years before they emigrated, settling in the southern Sydney suburb of Matraville in 1927 where they married. Jock died in 1987, and in 2011 she was Australia's oldest woman living independently.

Chapter Seven

A Changed World

After 1930 mass Scottish migration overseas largely petered out and shifted to England. This happened less because conditions in Scotland improved and more because the world about them had changed. Increasingly, the traditional overseas destinations wanted only skilled migrants. Before 1930 Scottish rural workers and domestic servants had been sought-after migrants, but demand for these workers ended after 1930. Neither was there was a need to import manufacturing workers, as most countries, with the exception of Australia, could provide their own. Even so, Scotland remained extraordinary for the size of its expatriate population; in 1991 about a quarter of Scots-born still lived outside Scotland, a figure that had hardly changed since 1931. Those who left after 1930 were much the same sort of people who had left thirty years earlier, mainly urban wage earners, unable to stay because of the inability of the Scottish economy to provide enough new jobs. Before 1900 the Scots had often been notable as high achievers in North America, South Africa, and Australasia; but as these societies invested more in education, the advantages the Scots once had were gone and there were far less opportunities for them to shine. After 1900, too, the Scottish became increasingly less distinctive, and to the outside world they seemed much like other Britons.

The slowdown in British emigration meant that there less interest in their migration generally in the censuses of North America after the early 1930s, although their immigration statistics continued to separate Scottish immigrants. The United States published separate figures on Scottish arrivals and departures from 1908 until 1975. In Canada, the immigration authorities restored the Scots to their statistics in 1901 after a twenty-one-year absence and published a much expanded collection from 1966 to 1996. Perversely, though, the Scots, along with the English, Welsh, and Northern Irish, were no longer separately identified in the Canadian census after 1961 and were lumped together in the "United Kingdom" category. It was an illogical decision, followed by no other nation with a significant number of Scots-born. It was especially hard to understand for a nation that continually proclaimed its pride in being multicultural as it discriminated against the British heritage of most Canadians.

Within Scotland, the office of the registrar general for Scotland assumed greater importance for the study of migration, especially under Edmund A. Hogan, who served as registrar general from 1948 to 1959, a man whose achievements have been forgotten. In 1953 he published the first historical review of Scotland's population since 1861 that included estimates of migration by county and how many Scots had died during World War I. He also prepared annual estimates of out-migration since 1931 and in 1951 he initiated a new series of estimates of Scots leaving for other parts of the United Kingdom and overseas, which his successors continued to 1999. His work was supplemented by the Office for National Statistics, which published estimates of overseas movements to and from Scotland from 1975 to 1990 based on passenger surveys.

STILL DISTRESSED: SCOTLAND C. 1930–1970

Scottish migration after 1930 was, as before, caused by its parlous economy. More Scottish economic measures become available, but they gave scant cause for cheering. There was some growth, but Scotland still lagged significantly behind England as it had done previously. This was made plain in the contributions to Alec K. Cairncross's *The Scottish Economy* (1950); C. E. V. Leser found that the value of net output per head in Scotland between 1907 and 1948 was about 5 percent below that of England and Wales. And A. D. Campbell estimated that Scotland's national income was not only about 10 percent lower than England and Wales between 1924 and 1948 but that it was also far less stable. He also pointed out that Scottish salaries still lagged behind those in the United Kingdom as a whole even though, surprisingly, the share of national income from wages was comparable.

Such high-level analysis hardly conveyed the misery of mass unemployment, poverty, and malnutrition of the 1920s and 1930s that was only alleviated in the early years of World War II. Despite their ever-presence, the unemployed were not counted by labor exchanges until 1923 and by the census until 1931, by which time they could no longer be ignored. The census found that 21 percent of male and 12 percent of female wage and salary earners were jobless, 371,000 in all, and the figures would have been far worse had not about the same number emigrated in the 1920s. The flatness of sales by the Scottish Co-operative Wholesale Society testified to an economy that largely failed to recover from the depression of 1921–1922 until 1940. The Scottish people paid for their depressed economy in continued high rates of tuberculosis, overcrowded housing, and a lack of improvement in life expectancy among mature and older people, even though the death rate fell among babies and the very young. World War II may have killed 34,000 Scottish military personnel and at least 1,500 civilians from air raids, but it also brought better nutrition for young people through equitable food rationing.

As elsewhere, the 1930s abruptly halted mass overseas emigration. More Scots returned to Scotland than left it—42,000 according to the registrar general for Scotland—adding to the burden on relief efforts. Yet although the balance switched to return migration, emigration leading to settlement still occurred: about 14,000 went to North America, about 9,000 to South Africa or Australasia, and it took World War II to shut it down. When the war was over, emigration resumed in 1946 and gathered pace as pre-war shipping services were restored. There were improvements in the health of the Scottish but not enough to discourage rising numbers leaving. The fundamental problem then, as before, was a lack of new jobs. Mass unemployment disappeared, mostly because so many left, but the economy remained stagnant. Employment in the construction industry, a good bellwether of general economic health, only just exceeded its level of fifty years earlier in 1951; and although it grew by a fifth in the 1950s, it hardly changed in the 1960s.

Scotland's total labor force growth can only be described as woeful, being almost flat between 1921 and 1961. In 1971 the Scottish labor force was only 9 percent higher than in 1901, making the 29 percent growth in Wales over the same period look impressive. Scotland continued to be "distressed" and in their despair increasing numbers came to embrace the idea of Scottish independence, which gained a mass following in the 1960s for the first time. Others turned to the traditional solution—emigration—with 537,000 leaving between 1946 and 1960; but there were distinct changes compared with the pre-1930 era, which are outlined in the rest of the chapter.

FIRST CHOICE: ENGLAND

During the 1930s about 32,000 Scots left for England compared with 23,000 for North America, South Africa, and Australasia. It was a watershed decade, making England the clearly preferred country for Scottish migrants (Table 16). The change was obscured by the largest English influx in Scottish history when about 95,000 people were evacuated to Scotland to avoid German bombing during World War II. Most returned to England during 1946 and about 177,000 Scots went to England during and just after the war. By 1951, there were 575,000 Scots in England and Wales, 44 percent of them born in the Strathclyde region, up from to 34 percent in 1911. The only other notable change in the regional origins of the Scots was the increase from Central and Fife from 7 to 10 percent and the fall in those born in the border regions (Dumfries and Galloway and Borders) from 15 to 6 percent.

In the 1950s, about 152,000 Scots migrated to England and Wales; of those, about 104,000 stayed there and most of those who left went to Australia or New Zealand. Another 115,000 Scots settled in England in the first half of the 1960s but only 23,000 in the last half because of the deterioration in the English economy, although this did nothing to change the Scots' general preference for England after 1930. Between 1931 and 1951 the percentage of expatriate Scots living in England and Wales rose from 29 to 47 percent in 1951 and to nearly 60 percent by 1971, by which time 735,000 lived there, rising slowly to 767,000 by 1991.

LESS POPULAR: CANADA

Part of the shift in the distribution of Scottish expatriates can be explained by the general improvement in living conditions in United Kingdom which made it more attractive to stay there. But their traditional overseas destinations changed too. The special case of South Africa has already been discussed, and in any case it was never a place of mass Scottish migration. Less easy to explain is Canada, where there was distinct decline in official interest in the Scots and other British groups after World War II as evident from their treatment in the population census. For instance, the 1951 census did not differentiate the British-born by the length of residence as it had done in 1941, and, as mentioned, after 1961 they were dropped altogether and amalgamated with the other United Kingdom–born.

Scottish arrivals were still recorded in the immigration figures and in great detail from 1966 to 1996; but without census counts, this information lost much of its value. In particular, it no longer becomes possible to know with certainty how many Scots stayed to become permanent settlers after 1961. I have tried to fill this gap with estimates of the Scots-born based on expected deaths but they are just that—estimates that take no account of later departures. Scottish migration continued after 1945 but it seems that their retention rate was low; in the 1950s, 93,000 Scots arrived in Canada but only about two-thirds seem to have stayed. So from their high water mark of 280,000 in 1931, the Scots-born became an aging population falling to 244,000 by 1961, and maybe to about 157,000 by 1991. In the 1960s their migration was the mirror opposite of England and Wales with more coming in the last half of the decade than in the first, yet more evidence of just how closely migration follows economic opportunity. After 1970, Scottish immigration fell sharply; only 31,000 came in the 1970s and 11,000 in the 1980s, a mere tenth of those who had settled in Canada in the 1900s (Table 17).

NOT REALLY WANTED: UNITED STATES

The United States began to restrict immigration in 1921, and further restrictions followed in 1924, 1952, and 1965. But it seems these restrictions made little difference to Scottish migration. The 1924 restrictions definitely caused concern—the number of Scots fell from 33,500 in 1924 to 12,400 in 1925—but the fall was temporary and emigration quickly resumed after the initial shock. Rising unemployment was another matter; 16,700 arrived in the twelve months to June 1930 as the Depression took hold, and they probably made up most of the 21,800 who had left by 1940. By this time, the number of American Scots had fallen by a fifth to 279,000, and their economic condition was much like other British migrants. With nowhere else to go, the Scots seem to have made the best of their circumstances and decided to hang on. As observed in Chapter 5, their citizenship rate lagged behind those of the English and Welsh and the Irish (all on 72 percent) in 1940. By 1980, 71 percent of the 142,000 Scots in the United States had become US citizens; this was higher than the Welsh (67 percent) but still below those from Ireland (81 percent). The citizenship rates for the English (58 percent) and the Northern Irish (66 percent) were also lower than for the Scots, but this could simply have been because more of them were relatively recent arrivals who would not have met the residential requirements. That said, there was no obvious reason why the citizenship rate of the Scots still lagged behind the Irish, the most comparable group in size and length of residence, just as it did in 1940.

In all likelihood, most Scots found the United States a difficult and expensive destination, more suited to those with means or skills in demand much more than Australasia. They kept going to the United States, but their mass movement was a thing of the past, and not enough came to stop the American Scots from becoming a declining, aging group; by 1950 their numbers had fallen to 244,200 or by nearly a third compared with 1930. Between 1950 and 1980, Scottish migration to the United States was less than to Canada but they were more likely to settle because many had married US citizens; about 5,000 Scottish women seem to have entered the United States as war brides in the last half of the 1940s. By 1990, of the 131,000 Scots who came before 1980, 61 percent were female and nearly all over age 15 (93 percent) had been married at some time.

Despite their pre-1900 reputation for being widely distributed, most Scots in the 1930s lived in only ten states—New York, Michigan, New Jersey, Pennsylvania, Massachusetts, California, Ohio, Illinois, Connecticut, and

Washington—which together accounted for about 83 percent from 1920 to 1970, in other words, the Northeast, West Coast, and a few central states. In the 1970s California finally overtook New York as the state with the most Scots, but only by a small margin. A better indicator of Scottish preference was the growing popularity of Florida, as more aging Scots sought refuge from the northern winter. In 1950 Florida ranked twelfth for its number of Scots-born but fourth by 1980, easily beating traditional favorites such as Michigan and Massachusetts. There was nothing out the ordinary about these trends, which were the result of general shifts in employment as well as aging; that was the point: the Scots had become unremarkable. Table 18 sets out the size of Scottish migration to the United States from 1930 to 1990.

STILL WELCOME: AUSTRALIA AND NEW ZEALAND

Unlike North America, Australasia positively encouraged mass British emigration and was prepared to pay for it. In Australia, immigration was seen as essential not only for economic growth but also for defense, and it was a significant destination of Western European migration after 1945, not just of Scots. The Depression killed off assisted migration for the first half of the 1930s but as the economy began to slowly improve from 1936, the Australian government reintroduced assisted British migration on a limited scale in May 1938. No figures were published for the origins of these immigrants and only 852 had actually arrived by end of the year, but one Scot who did was Thomas Docherty (1914–2003), who was recruited from St Andrews. He reached Sydney in late December 1938 and lived with an aunt, Jessie, and her husband, Henry George, who had emigrated in 1912, at Hurstville. After a week he got a job with Glazbrooks, a poultry abattoir in Double Bay that serviced the central business district. He got to work by bicycle, journey of about 18 kilometers, a comment not just on his fitness but also on the lack of cars in Sydney of that time; today the life expectancy of an unescorted cyclist making the same journey would be measured in minutes if not seconds. His journey to work was one thing; making himself understood another. He had to drop his Scottish east coast, working-class accent by reading in front of a mirror, a reminder that integration into new societies, even English-speaking ones, was not quite the straightforward business that is so often assumed. About 3,800 Scots settled in Australia between 1931 and 1940 and about 1,800 in New Zealand. Two of those who settled in Australia were my uncles, Tommy and Bill; they came under the Big Brother Movement in 1934 and were exploited as farm workers in Victoria.

After World War II, the Scots continued to migrate to Australia and New Zealand along with large numbers of British immigrants. But the total British figures were less than desired, and this led Australia to broaden its intake to other countries in Western and Southern Europe (Table 19). The Scottish component of the British intake was higher than previously; surprisingly, more Scots settled in Australia in the 1950s than in the 1920s. Unlike the Scots who went to Canada, many of those who went to Australasia seem to have made their way there from England rather than directly from Scotland. Of the 33,000 Scots who settled in New Zealand between 1956 and 1975, 36 percent had previously been living in England, compared with only 4 percent who settled in Canada. There are no similar published figures for Australia, but the pattern was probably comparable, as many more Scots moved to England than stayed there permanently and much of Australia's official efforts to attract British migrants in the 1950s and 1960s were based in England.

In the 1970s, the scale of Scottish migration changed as Canada and Australasia abandoned policies that promoted British migration on principle with policies based on job skills in demand, family reunions, or refugees. Scottish immigration to Australia continued to be relatively strong, actually increasing in the 1980s, whereas it fell in North America and New Zealand (Table 20). Like their predecessors, the Scots preferred to live in the cities and towns where the jobs were. By 1966, 92 percent of Scots in Australia were urban dwellers compared with 77 percent in 1947, and 69 percent lived in the capital cities. Post-1950 studies of the Australian Scots have also confirmed that they were little different from other British migrants. In New Zealand (Table 20), Scottish migration was relatively high in the 1950s and 1960s but fell thereafter and was not enough to cause a continual decline in their numbers after 1971.

PUTTING IT TOGETHER

In the last half of the eighteenth century, the Scots had a reputation of brilliance and exoticism. Edinburgh was the brilliant aspect, the beacon of the Enlightenment in Britain, whose achievements reached far beyond Scotland. The western archipelago was the exotic aspect, the long-desired goal of Samuel Johnson, which he finally visited in 1773. He was famously disappointed; instead of the exotic he found the conquered often living in desperate poverty. The rest of Scotland seems to have been of little real interest. On his way back, he inspected a school in Edinburgh where the deaf and dumb were being successfully taught, a seemingly impossible task. Johnson was not only impressed by what he saw, he recognized its underlying message that Scotland surely needed then and always: hope. The wars and politics of his day obscured the underlying problem that long predated him and continued until recent times: the oversupply of Scots either for their environment, their society, or their economy.

The Scotland that Johnson saw was a profoundly conservative world that was much closer to its feudal past than England and, unlike England or Ireland, lacked the large tracts of arable land that could have supported a larger and better-off people. Scotland's population is thought to have been relatively small until about 1,000 years ago when it was probably only about 200,000, and to have doubled during the more benign Medieval Warm Period (CE 1000–1300) to about 400,000. Despite repeated attacks by the bubonic plague from 1349 to 1648, six famines between 1540 and 1592, the arrival of smallpox in 1567, and incessant warfare, the population still managed to rise to about 776,000 by 1650. From then on, its growth was driven by a series of small but lasting improvements in mortality rates. This was why births exceeded deaths; the Scottish birth rate was mostly stable between 1650 and 1880, but life expectancy increased.

Why this happened before 1750 is unclear. There is some evidence of an improvement in growing conditions from about 1650—despite the threat of famine in the 1690s—but it was not enough to explain the growth in the Scottish population. The most likely reason may simply have been the general peace of the era, in contrast to the internal violence and wars that characterized 1550 to 1650. Because these improved mortality rates were greater among females more than males, they gave Scotland an excess of females, mainly for those over age 30, from at least about 1680 but more likely from about 1650. This female majority is one of the defining characteristics of Scottish population history, and it was strengthened by the withdrawal of thousands of men to fight in the Seven Years War (1756–1763), the American War of Independence (1775–1783), and later the wars against Revolutionary France and Napoleon (1793–1815).

Neither was Scottish economy always depressed; it seems to have been prosperous in 1300 and was definitely so from about 1725 to 1775, attracting ethnic Scots back from Northern Ireland even if only temporarily to earn their passage to the American colonies. About 200,000 left Scotland between about 1755 and 1776 of whom about a third were soldiers. And although about 144,000 of these expatriates and their children reentered Scotland between 1800 and 1815, there were still not enough males among them to overturn the female majority. Their return helped to raise the population to 2.1 million by 1821, or double what it had been in 1700. It was not caused by the Irish who only began to enter Scotland in large numbers from the 1840s to escape famine. They may have been unwelcome but the Irish made a substantial contribution to building the infrastructure of Victorian Scotland, and in the process they also helped to maintain it as a low-wage economy and as a land of large-scale emigration. With 80 percent of Scotland owned by about 630 individuals, it was not just a land without opportunity—those who wanted a better life after 1820 were faced with living in overcrowded cities and towns or leaving altogether.

Scottish emigration from 1820 to 1930 falls into two parts: before 1900 and the thirty years after it. Before 1900 there was considerable internal movement within Scotland, movement that often preceded going overseas. Nearly 1.3 million people left Scotland, 62 percent of them for overseas and the rest to other parts of Britain. Their reasons for leaving differed. Some were poor and were assisted to go; others were determined for a life on the land; and others wanted achievement and adventure. It was the heyday of the high-achieving Scots. A large volume of return migration from the United States was an important feature of this migration. Not all families could afford to emigrate together, particularly in the 1870s and 1880s when wages seem to have been flat in Scotland, and nearly half the journeys made to the United States in this era seem to have been made by married men going first. Only when they had made enough money were they able to send for their families, or go back to collect them to make the last journey together to an expensive if desirable nation.

The Scottish people remained mainly female, a fact long blamed on emigration. It certainly lowered the number of males compared with females, but the evidence, surprisingly, does not support it being the primary cause. If the 716,000 Scots-born living outside Scotland in 1881 were restored to the Scottish population they would have reduced the female majority from 52.2 to 51 percent; and if this exercise were repeated for 1931 its effect would have been even less, only lowering it from 52.2 to 51.4 percent. The reason for Scotland's female majority in 1930 was the same as it had been in 1690: female mortality was lower than males even though the gap narrowed after 1880.

Queen Victoria's death in 1901 coincided with the beginning of the slow implosion of the Scottish economy and the opening of a new phase of Scottish migration that, apart from the interruption of World War I, lasted until 1930. Ships were still launched on the Clyde, but they could not disguise the nation's descent into a distressed region by 1911, Britain's first. The nearly million urban wage earners who left between 1901 and 1930 did not want to go; they were forced out by the failure of the economy to produce new jobs, expressed well by one of their dockyard placards that declared "We Want Jobs, Not the Dole." Emigration peaked in the 1920s but it was the culmination of a process that had begun twenty years earlier, making Scotland's loss North America's gain, causing the Scottish population to actually fall by 1931 for the first time in its recorded history. They were wise to go because the Scottish economy failed to really recover before the 1970s, ensuring that Scots often had no choice but to leave. Another million left between 1931 and 1990, half of them to England up from about one in five between 1901 and 1930.

Was emigration a bad thing? The traditional answer is yes, because Scotland lost out on the investment it made in the education of its people and the cost of raising them, adding to its impoverishment. But this assumes that all those who went away stayed away. The evidence in this work revises this interpretation in some ways. Sir John Sinclair's *Statistical Account* of the 1790s showed that seasonal and return migration was commonplace. With their long tradition of seasonal and short-term migration combined with low wages, it was to be expected that many Scots would continue to be short-term movers in the nineteenth century. The difference between when many husbands first came and when their families came to the United States in the 1870s and 1880s points to a remittance flow with thousands of these married men returning temporarily with their earnings, a process that must have helped the Scottish economy by supplementing its meager wages. The assisted immigration programs of the Australian and New Zealand governments in the 1870s and 1880s would also have removed many poor who would otherwise have required support. Lastly, there is also evidence for both Canada and the United States that elderly relatives were included in the families of Scottish migrants; they were not abandoned, and the cost of their upkeep would have gone with them.

Scottish migration made an undeniable contribution to the peopling of North America and Australasia where about 17 million people claimed some degree of Scottish ancestry at the end of the twentieth century. Canada had the highest proportion who claimed some Scottish descent: 5.2 million in 2001 or 15 percent. This figure is usually claimed to be an understatement, yet it is in line with the 1961 census when one in ten Canadians claimed some Scottish ancestry. In Australia and the United States, about one in twenty-two claimed some degree of Scottish ancestry. The numbers are important but they cannot disguise the fact that all too quickly the Scots became just like those around them.

THE MAN ON THE BRIDGE

Contrary to most television documentaries about the end of World War II in Europe, the last battle was not fought in Berlin but to the south, on the eastern side of a much older city, Prague. There, the remains of the German Army Group Centre, under its commander Field Marshal Friedrich Schörner, fought on for three days after Germany's official surrender. They fought because their commander had not told them the war was over and any German soldiers who tried to escape his brutal savagery were hanged as deserters. When they finally surrendered on May 11, 1945, 780,000 became Soviet prisoners of war. On that day, too, the Soviets released a starving Scots-Australian soldier, who had escaped from German captivity in November 1944 and had been fighting with a small band of communist Czech partisans in the hills of Moravia. Of course they were not true communists; they would come in 1948.

Weak from hunger, he worked his way across the King Charles Bridge, clinging to lampposts for support. Ahead of him lay a city that had been liberated by an uprising that had left over 3,000 Czechs dead or seriously wounded. After showing Prague's new rulers his safe pass, he was given some bread, his first food in over a week. He traded his coat for a lift in a truck to Pilsen where he reached the US Third Army where he was given K-rations, rations that many US soldiers disdained. He barely made it out alive. Ahead of him lay liberation, behind him a new tyranny was being planned. This work was inspired by the memory of this man, Thomas Hill Docherty (1914–2003), my father, and by that of his wife of fifty-five years, Annie Cairns Meikle (1912–2011), my mother.

Appendix A: Population Timeline

c. 8500 BCE: Evidence of human settlement in Scotland is found at Cramond, near Edinburgh, in 2001.

c. 4000 BCE: Agriculture begins in the Orkney Islands.

c. 32000–2400 BCE: Neolithic settlers build a large settlement and stone monuments on the Orkney Islands at Skara Brae and Ness Brodgar.

c. 50 BCE: Classical authors note the low value on human rights in Celtic society. Caesar claims that the common people in Gaul were virtually slaves. The Greek author Diodorus of Sicily observes that the Gallic Celtic chiefs would willingly sell their people for wine.

43 CE: The Romans invade modern southeast England supposedly to assist the chieftain Verica.

71: The romans begin their conquest of modern northern England.

79–84: The Roman general Agricola wages a successful war along the coastal areas of eastern Scotland culminating in a victory over the "Caledonians" at Mons Graupius, northwest of Aberdeen.

c. 122: Unable to hold their conquests in Scotland, the Romans withdraw and begin building Hadrian's Wall to keep the northern tribes out.

c. 165: The Romans complete the Antonine Wall between the Firth of Forth in the east and the northern side of the Clyde estuary in the west.

209–211: The Roman emperor Septimius Severus invades eastern Scotland.

297: The orator Eumenius makes the first recorded mention of the Picti (Picts) who seem to have been a confederation of Celtic peoples. Over the next century, they raid northern Roman Britain repeatedly, along with the Scoti from Ireland.

c. 500: The Scoti (or Scotii), an Irish Gaelic people, begin to colonize parts of southwestern Scotland. At this time, the Picts are the dominant people in Scotland. The two groups fight each other for centuries.

760–800: Vikings from Norway settle in the Shetlands, Orkney Islands, and Hebrides.

889: Donald II becomes the first king of the Scots and Picts.

1171: The presence of Jews in Scotland is recorded for the first time.

1124–1153: King David I founds fourteen burghs or townships surrounding castles; they include Aberdeen, Dundee, Edinburgh, and Perth and represent the beginning of urbanization. He also mints the first silver Scottish coins.

1237: The Treaty of York sets the border between Scotland and England.

1249: Feudal lords define Scotland's border with England although the north of England remains subject to ongoing military contests and raids by mounted robbers ("reivers") until 1504.

1266: Norway cedes the Hebrides to Scotland.

1291: Church revenues raised in Scotland are 19 percent of those of England.

1349: The Black Death reaches the Scottish Lowlands and the Highlands in 1350. Three Scottish chroniclers claim that it kills a third of the population. There are three further outbreaks of the plague by 1401 and other outbreaks up to 1649.

1380: John of Fordun, an Aberdeen chronicler, writes the first description of the cultural and linguistic divisions between Scottish Lowlanders and Highlanders.

1389: The first law is passed to regulate sea travel between England and Scotland.

1396: The population of Aberdeen is about 3,000.

1410: Scotland's first university is founded at St Andrews; it is followed by the establishment of universities at Glasgow (1451), Aberdeen (1494), and Edinburgh (1583).

1420: There is evidence of trade between Glasgow and France in cured salmon and herrings.

1449: The Scottish parliament bans food exports because of famine; a second such act follows in 1455.

1472: Scotland formally annexes the Orkney and Shetland islands; the Shetlands has previously been part of what is now Norway.

1474: The Dublin parliament claims that 10,000 Scots are living in what is now Ulster.

1476: Froissart's Chronicles is published in France; it includes a detailed account of the Scots invasion of northern England in 1327.

1497: The Scottish parliament enacts an education law.

1507: The first Scottish printing press is established.

1526: Food exports are banned by parliament because of famine; further bans follow in 1540, 1551, 1567, 1581, 1587, and 1592.

1524: The Scottish parliament prohibits Protestantism, thirty years after its first appearance in the form of the Lollards.

1533: In Ulster, English officials note an increase in Scottish immigration.

1553: A parish register is begun for Errol, Perth County. The register is one of the very few from this period that survives.

1556: Concerned about Scottish immigration to northern Ireland, the Irish parliament forbids all contact with Scots including intermarriage.

1559: John Knox introduces Presbyterianism into Scotland, and Roman Catholicism is abolished in 1560; the new religion of Presbyterianism is fully established by 1592, but the Highlands remain largely Catholic.

1560: The population of Glasgow is about 4,500.

1562: The registers for Perth show that there were 225 baptisms and 182 burials, suggesting a population of about 5,600.

1567: The first case of smallpox in Scotland is recorded in Glasgow.

1572: Scottish mercenaries are mentioned as fighting against the Spanish in the Low Countries.

1591: The word Scots as a general term for the inhabitants of Scotland enters the English language.

1603: King James VI of Scotland becomes James I of England and Scotland.

1608: Sir Cahir O'Doherty leads a rebellion in Donegal, Ireland. After its suppression, many of his clan or "sept" flee to Scotland.

1608–1618: Lowland Scots start to migrate to the English plantations in Ulster.

1610: Smallpox breaks out in Aberdeen, its second recorded occurrence since 1567; the disease remains a leading cause of death for the next 200 years. There are other outbreaks in 1635, 1641, and 1672.

1618–48: Possibly as many as 30,000 Scottish mercenaries take part at some time in the Thirty Years War in central Europe.

1622: James I of England approves the founding of Nova Scotia ("New Scotland"). The venture fails, but later it attracts refugees from the failed Jacobite uprisings of 1715 and 1745.

1623: Widespread famine in Scotland is caused by crop failures.

1640: Birth registers are in common use in most parishes, but very few survive to 1801.

1644–1648: Repeated outbreaks of the plague cause many deaths in Scotland.

1650: Despite famine in the Highlands in 1650, the general death rate begins to slowly fall from about 1651; as the decline is somewhat greater among females than males, they tend to outnumber males from about 1680.

1656: Scotland is united with England following its defeat in the English Civil War; the union is dissolved in 1660.

1690: Presbyterianism is re-established in Scotland after the religious turbulence of the previous half-century.

1691: A hearth tax is introduced and continues until 1695; although the results are incomplete, it gives the first indication of the size of the Scottish population.

1695–1699: Widespread famine in Scotland prompts large-scale emigration to Northern Ireland. Archbishop Edward Synge estimates that 50,000 Scots migrate to Ireland between 1688 and 1715.

1696: Presbyterian schools are to be set up in every parish by law, eventually resulting in Scotland becoming one of the most literate countries of Western Europe.

1703: Martin Martin publishes Description of the Western Islands of Scotland, a work that inspires Dr Samuel Johnson to visit the islands seventy years later.

1707: The Act of Union with England is established. The Union opens up direct trade between Scotland and the American colonies. From about this time, mortality in Scotland begins to fall gradually. The population of Scotland is estimated at about 1 million.

1716: 639 Jacobite rebels are transported to the American colonies.

1717: Significant emigration by Irish of Scots descent from Ulster to Scotland and North America begins; about 160,000 migrate to the American colonies by 1775.

1726: Daniel Defoe publishes the last part of his Tour through the Whole Island of Great Britain, which includes a detailed description of Scotland.

1736: General James Oglethorpe founds New Inverness, now Darien, in Georgia with 177 Scottish Highlanders and their families.

1739: Potatoes and turnips start to become staple crops, boosting the food supply and helping to sustain the growth of Scotland's population. About 500 Highlanders settle in New York.

1746: The Duke of Cumberland's victory over the Scottish Highland army at Culloden eliminates Scotland as a military threat to England. Over the next 180 years, a combination of military policy, environmental and economic pressures, and forced evictions lead to the depopulation of much the Highlands.

1750: Literacy has become commonplace in rural Lowland Scotland and is believed to have been higher than in the urban areas; literacy seems to have fallen with increasing urbanization after 1780.

1752: David Hume, the Scottish philosopher and historian, publishes an essay "Of the Populousness of Ancient Nations" in which he questions the standard view that the current population is lower than in ancient times.

1753: Robert Wallace, a Presbyterian minister, publishes A Dissertation on the Numbers of Mankind in Ancient and Modern Times in which he argues that the current population is lower than in the past. Wallace also produces a table showing how population could grow geometrically based on the Bible. Together, Wallace and Hume began a debate about population that continues until the end of the century.

1755: Alexander Webster, an Edinburgh minister, completes a census of Scotland's population on behalf of the Presbyterian church; it reveals a total population of 1.3 million. It is the first British census and one of the earliest national censuses in Europe.

1759: The first arrivals of Scottish Highlanders in North America are forced out after the failure of the 1745 rebellion. An iron-smelting works is established near Falkirk in Sterling Country; it signals the start of the industrialization of much of southwestern Scotland.

1762: Sheep farming is introduced into the Highlands, eventually replacing subsistence agriculture. The change results in the displacement of thousands over the next thirty years.

1763: Sustained emigration to the American colonies commences; about 25,000 Scots emigrate by 1775.

1771: Thomas Pennant's Tour of Scotland 1769 is published. The first emigrants from the Isle of Skye leave for America; a total of 2,400 emigrate by 1790.

1772: The first Scots arrive at Prince Edward Island, British North America.

1770–1815: About 15,000 Highland Scots move to British North America (what is now Canada) during this period.

1773–1776: The British government's emigration register shows that of the 10,000 emigrants to North America, about 2,600 were from Scotland.

1775: Samuel Johnson's Journey to the Western Islands of Scotland describes a poor, defeated land outside of the towns.

1776: The US Declaration of Independence is signed; two Scottish-born men, James Wilson and John Witherspoon, are among the signatories. Adam Smith links the lower demand for labor in Scotland with higher emigration compared with England in The Wealth of Nations.

1777: Employers of male servants are required to pay a tax until 1798.

1782–1783: Eight months of eruptions from a volcano in Iceland disrupts weather patterns in northern Europe and causes harvest failures in Scotland.

1783: A tax on the registration of birth, marriages and deaths reduces compliance; the tax is repealed in 1794. After the British defeat in the American War of Independence, about 30,000 Scottish Loyalists leave.

1785: Employers of female servants are required to pay a tax until 1792.

1788: Transportation of British convicts to Australia begins; by 1868 about 8,640 Scots were transported.

1790: The first population census is held for the United States; it shows that about 260,000 are of Scottish stock; by this time most were probably "Scotch-Irish" (originally from Ulster rather than Scotland).

1791: Sir John Sinclair publishes the first volume of his Statistical Account of Scotland; twenty volumes are published by 1799. Credited with using "statistics" in its modern sense, his count of Scotland's population shows a total of 1.5 million.

1792: The Rev. Mr David Wilkie constructs a life table based on the parish of Torthorwald, Dumfries, for 1763–1790; it is one of the earliest life tables in Britain.

1798: The Rev. Thomas Malthus publishes the first edition of his Essay on the Principle of Population, in which he argues that unchecked population growth tends to exceed the food supply. He notes the poverty of Scotland's peasants and its Highlands. The failure of the rebellion in Ireland causes some to immigrate to southern Scotland.

1799: Scottish coal miners are finally emancipated from serfdom.

1800: Some Scots migrate to Upper Canada (what is now Ontario); a total of 5,391 arrived by 1803.

1801: The first government census of population is held; it shows a total Scottish population of 1.6 million, of whom about a quarter live in cities or towns. It excludes 70,0000 men serving in the British armed forces and merchant navy; they are not included in the census count until 1841.

1803: British parliament passes the first Passenger Act to regulate emigration. Lord Selkirk brings 800 Scottish Highlanders to Prince Edward Island; he also founds the Red River settlement in what is now Manitoba.

1811: The second British census finds that Scotland's population has grown to 1.8 million and that 78,000 Scots were serving in the armed forces against Napoleon. The French ban of British exports to Europe causes depression in Glasgow in 1811–1812.

1815: The economic hardship that follows the end of the Napoleonic wars encourages more Scots to emigrate. Hardship is also aggravated by harvest failures in 1816–1817.

1817: The census in Nova Scotia lists 1,280 Scots-born.

1820: About 1,200 handloom weavers from the Glasgow area are assisted to emigrate. Arrivals by country are first recorded in the United States; the figures are very incomplete. Some Scots go to South Africa.

1821: The government assists 1,883 industrial workers in and around Glasgow to emigrate to New Lanark, Upper Canada. The census shows that half the Scots are under twenty-one.

1822: James Dixon's Narrative of a Voyage to New South Wales and Van Diemen's Land, a handbook for emigrants, is published in Edinburgh. The spread of the power loom and the influx of lesser-paid Irish weavers displace Scots-born in the textile industry.

1825: Those leaving Scottish ports are counted for the first time in official statistics.

1829: Scottish arrivals are first recorded in the port statistics for British North America.

1830s: The widespread poverty and limited food choices of the Highlands are noted by commentators.

1831: Sir John Sinclair publishes Analysis of the Statistical Account of Scotland, a summary of his life's work. It contains much valuable information on the population history of Scotland.

1831–32: The European cholera epidemic kills about 10,000 Scots; other outbreaks occur in 1848–1849, 1853–1854, and 1866–1867.

1832: James Cleland, the supervisor of public works in Glasgow, publishes an account of the population of Glasgow and the County of Lanark based on the returns from the 1831 census.

1836–39: Harvest failures cause famine in the Highlands and encourage greater efforts to promote emigration.

1837: An assisted migration program of Scots to Australia is initiated; 3,000 Highlanders are assisted to emigrate by 1840. The Scotch Church Young Men's Society conducts a survey of the Scots in Manchester, England; it is one of the first surveys to be conducted of an immigrant community.

1840: The introduction of the first steamships by the Cunard company improves conditions for British emigrants.

1841: The Scottish census collects birthplace information for the first time. It shows that the population had reached 2.6 million or double what it had been in 1751. The census also collects the first detailed information on occupations by sex.

1842: The Scottish Patriotic Society is formed; one of its aims is to promote emigration. The census in Upper Canada asks about birthplace for the first time: 59,000 are identified as Scots-born.

1843: The annual reports of the Colonial Land and Emigration Commissioners present statistics on steerage passengers from Scotland by sex for the first time. A schism occurs in Scottish Presbyterianism when the Free Church of Scotland splits from the Established Church, an event known as the "Disruption."

1845: Scottish Poor Law Act denies benefits to the unemployed; parish welfare was only available to those who had resided in the parish for at least five years. The legislation encourages emigration during depressions.

1846: In Australia, the New South Wales census identifies the Scots-born for the first time; it shows a total of 16,464 Scots.

1847: The failure of the potato crop causes famine in the Highlands and the offshore islands that continues until 1850. Some landowners assist a total of about 10,000 to emigrate by 1856, mainly to eastern Australia. Two Presbyterian denominations, the Relief Church (established in 1761) and the United Succession Church (formed in 1820), merge to form the United Presbyterian Church.

1848: The economy of the industrial Lowlands is in a depression that continues during 1849. The discovery of gold at Coloma, California, begins the first US gold rush. The first Scottish settlers arrive in the south island of New Zealand; they name the settlement Dunedin after the Celtic name for Edinburgh. The future industrialist and philanthropist Andrew Carnegie (1835–1919) migrates to the United States.

1850: The Scottish male death rate starts to fall somewhat faster than for females, gradually eliminating the trend from about 1680 to produce a surplus of females; thereafter emigration maintains the Scottish population as predominantly female. The US census collects birthplaces for the first time; it counts 70,550 Scots-born.

1851: The Scottish census collects ages by five-yearly groups for the first time. It shows 7 percent of Scotland's population are Irish-born, many of whom have been forced out of Ireland by famine. Lured by the gold rushes in the United States and the Australian colonies of New South Wales and Victoria, 254,000 Scots emigrate in the 1850s, the largest number for any decade until the 1900s. The first statistics on attendances at Scottish churches for all denominations are collected for Sunday, March 30. An emigration society is set up on the island of Skye. The labor market in Upper Canada is buoyant because of railway construction.

1853: Violent evictions of Highlanders are carried out at Glengarry, Inverness. A society to assist emigration from the Highlands is formed.

1855: The official registration of births, deaths, and marriages in Scotland begins.

1857: Scotland's population passes the 3 million mark.

1859: Nearly all Scottish bridegrooms (90 percent) are able to sign their names in the marriage register, a level not achieved in England and Wales until 1886; among Scottish brides, 78 percent could sign the marriage register, a figure not matched by English and Welsh brides until 1876.

1860: The registrar-general for Scotland publishes the results of an enquiry into the most frequent family and first names for 1855–1858.

1861: The Scottish census is conducted by the registrar general for Scotland for the first time; previously, the census had been under English control. William P. Dundas, the registrar general, publishes a survey of the ages of mothers by the number of children they have ever had for Edinburgh City during 1855; it is the first investigation of its kind. He also investigates deaths by marital status and finds that the married and widowed had lower death rates than singles. In New Zealand, the discovery of gold in Otago and Westland in the South Island attracts a flood of immigrants, and the number of Scots-born doubles from 15,500 to 31,700 by 1864, some of whom are Scots from Australia.

1862: The American Civil War stops cotton supplies and disrupts trade; the war is blamed for causing large-scale destitution in Scotland, increasing the death rate, and boosting emigration. Ironically, the cotton shortage helps the jute mills of Dundee. About 120,000 Scots who had emigrated in the 1850s return to Scotland. The Australian colonies initiate assisted migration programs; 13,089 Scots arrive by 1892.

1863: Although Scottish trade improves, the American Civil War still depresses cotton manufacturing.

1864: Smallpox kills 1,741 Scots; another epidemic occurs in 1871–1872.

1867

1870: In New Zealand, there is a second gold rush, this time in the North Island, which attracts a wave of immigration from Australia.

The inventor of the telephone, Alexander Graham Bell (1847–1922), migrates to Canada with his father; he moves on the United States in 1871.

1871: The Canadian census shows that there are 125,000 Scottish-born and 550,000 who claim Scottish descent. The New Zealand government introduces a program of assisted and nominated immigration; 19,623 Scots are assisted to emigrate by 1891.

1872: Scotland introduces universal education for children ages five to thirteen.

1874–1875: Scarlet fever epidemic kills 4,921 Scots.

1875–1877: Economic conditions in Scotland are depressed, particularly in agriculture.

1877: Dr William Robertson constructs the first full life table for Scotland based on the 1871 census.

1881: For the first time, the number of urban dwellers in Scotland equals those living in rural areas. The number of Irish-born in Scotland reaches their highest level, 219,000; thereafter their numbers start to slowly decline as Scotland's largest immigrant group.

1885–1887: The Scottish economy is generally depressed.

1886: Montreal and Vancouver are connected by the Canada Pacific Railway, which makes migration to the West Coast easier. The discovery of gold in the southern Transvaal, South Africa, leads to a rush of migrants.

1880s: 217,000 emigrate from Scotland, the highest number since the 1850s.

1891: Scotland's population reaches 4 million. Over the next decade, 186,000 Scots make an overseas journey, but lack of employment elsewhere in Britain and overseas forces all but 77,000 to return.

1892: The registrar-general for Scotland publishes the first analysis of occupational mortality among males for 1890–1892 and conducts a second investigation for 1900–1902.

1895: British government statistics first record return emigration from North America and Australasia; South Africa is not included until 1913.

1900: The Free Church and the United Presbyterian Church join to form the United Free Church.

1901: The school-leaving age is raised to fourteen and it is compulsory to attend school until twelve. There is a sustained rise in Scottish emigration.

1904: Dr James C. Dunlop provides abridged life tables for 1861 to 1900 in the detailed Annual Report of the Registrar-General for Scotland. New Zealand resumes assisted immigration; the previous program had been suspended in 1892.

1900s: The improvement in the economies of English-speaking countries from about 1904 brings about a resumption of large-scale Scottish emigration.

1907: Australia begins to publish figures on the deaths of Scots-born by sex and age.

1908: US official statistics first distinguish immigrants from Canada, the British isles, and elsewhere; they also identify Scottish emigrants until 1957. In Australia, the Scots-born are included in the marriage statistics.

1909: New Zealand begins to publish statistics on the deaths of Scots-born by sex and age.

1910: The registrar-general for Scotland begins to check the correctness of deaths among those claimed to be age one hundred or older; the information is published up to 1967. Age and sex data are collected in the US census for the main immigrant groups, including the Scots; the information is not published until 1933.

1911: Scotland's rural population is at its highest level—1.9 million—accounting for 40 percent of all Scots; thereafter it falls. At least 83,000 Scots emigrate, the highest number in one year until 1923. The registrar-general for Scotland begins to publish deaths by marital status, figures that had been first published on a trial basis in the early 1860s. The Australian census publishes detailed age and sex figures on the Scots-born for the first time.

1912: Scotland's estimated population falls for the first time since official statistics began in 1855.

1914–1918: During World War I, over 600,000 Scots serve in the armed forces. The war claims 81,000 Scottish lives directly, mainly in northern France and Belgium, not counting deaths among Scots who emigrated after 1911 and enlisted in other Allied armies.

1915: Total civilian deaths in Scotland are 81,631; it is the highest figure since 1900 when 82,296 died. By August, 27 percent of Scottish coal miners, nearly 36,000, had enlisted in the army.

1916: Scotland introduces conscription for men ages eighteen to forty-one unless they are married or widowed with children or in a reserved occupation.

1918–1919: The Spanish Influenza pandemic kills 17,575 Scots.

1920: A severe depression in Scotland starts in late 1920 and continues for three years, causing a wave of emigration.

1921: The English-born replace the Irish-born as the largest immigrant group in Scotland. Divorce is included as one of the marital states in the Scottish census for the first time. The New Zealand census publishes detailed age and sex statistics on its Scottish-born. Canada begins to record deaths of Scots-born in its towns and cities with 10,000 or more and continues to do so until 1950; it includes the Scots-born in its marriage statistics.

1923: 86,600 Scots emigrate, the highest recorded number for any year before or since.

1925: In Canada, about two-thirds of Presbyterians agree to join with the Methodists and Congregationalists of Ontario and Quebec to form the United Church.

1926: The South African census publishes detailed age and sex statistics for its Scottish-born for the first time.

1927: The noted Scottish poet Hugh MacDiarmid publishes Albyn: or, Scotland and the Future, in the wake of especially high levels of emigration.

1928: Alexander M. MacEwen publishes The Thistle and the Rose: Scotland's Problems To-day.

1929: The United Free Church and the Church of Scotland merge to form the Church of Scotland, uniting the Church for the first time since 1733.

1930: Andrew D. Gibb publishes Scotland in Eclipse. Adoptions are registered for the first time. The Australian government restricts assisted immigration to the wives and dependants of men who arrived before January 1, 1930.

1932: The registrar-general for Scotland publishes a third report on occupational mortality among males for 1930–1932.

1931: As a result of a net loss by emigration of 390,000, the highest for any decade, the Scottish population is lower than in 1921. The number of Scots in North America is at its highest. The onset of the Depression together with World War II halt mass Scottish emigration. The census for England and Wales publishes the first detailed age and sex data on the Scottish-born.

1933: The registrar-general for Scotland records divorced persons separately in marriage statistics for the first time.

1934: The Scottish National Party is established in its present form; the core of the party had existed since 1927.

1935: The registrar-general for Scotland conducts the second survey of the most frequent family and first names.

1936: Scotland's oldest woman dies; her age was verified as 109. The Irish Republic census publishes ages for the Scots-born, and the New Zealand census gives information on its Scots-born for their marital status, industry, and occupation.

1937: Donald F. Macdonald publishes Scotland's Shifting Population, 1770–1850, the first academic study of population movements in and out of Scotland and their relationship to economic changes.

1938: The Divorce Act comes into force. In Australia, the federal government re-introduces assisted immigration for selected occupations.

1939: A wartime population register is established in Scotland, and stillbirths are officially registered for the first time. The population reaches 5 million. The first German attack on British territory happens when the battleship Royal Oak is torpedoed at Scapa Flow in the Orkney Islands (October 14). Men ages eighteen to forty-one are required to undertake military training, preparatory to conscription. The Marriage (Scotland) Act introduces civil marriages and abolishes "irregular" marriages; it comes into force on July 1, 1940.

1940: About 60,000 people move to Scotland from England to avoid German bombing; as the bombing lessens, all but 14,000 return by mid-1944.

1944: The German V-bombing of southern England results in 35,000 being evacuated to Scotland in September and October.

1939–1945: During World War II, 34,000 Scots die in military service and at least 1,523 are killed in German bombing raids in Scotland. The US Congress enacts the War Brides Act (December 1945) which allows the entry of the European wives and children of American servicemen for the next two years.

1946: Large-scale migration from Scotland resumes. Most English evacuees return to England.

1947: James E. Handley publishes The Irish in Modern Scotland. The registrar-general for Scotland publishes the first annual Scottish life tables.

1951: Edmund A. Hogan, the registrar-general for Scotland, begins publishing annual statistics on total net migration, to other parts of the United Kingdom and overseas.

1952: James G. Kyd, the former registrar-general for Scotland, publishes Alexander Webster's census completed in 1755.

1953: Edmund A. Hogan, the registrar-general for Scotland, publishes the first detailed account of Scottish population history from 1861 to 1951 in the annual report to mark the centenary of the collection of the first national statistics of births, deaths, and marriages.

1955: The registrar-general for Scotland releases the results of an investigation into occupational mortality among both sexes for 1949–53; a fifth report follows for 1959–1963.

1956: The South African government ceases to publish immigration data. By 1960, the number of Scots-born in South Africa is 23,000 compared with 30,000 in 1951.

1958: Richard H. Osborne, a geographer at Edinburgh University, publishes the first detailed study of internal migration in Scotland from 1851 to 1951. The registrar-general for Scotland conducts a third survey of the most frequent family and first names.

1961: The Scottish census asks about internal migration for the first time. In Canada, the census records 244,000 persons of Scottish birth; it is the last time the census identifies the Scots, Welsh, English, or Northern Irish.

1962: Canada abolishes preferences for British and French immigrants.

1966: Canada begins publishing detailed information on immigrants, including the Scots-born, until 1996. John Kenneth Galbraith publishes The Scotch, his memoir of the community on Lake Erie where he grew up.

1968: The registrar-general for Scotland publishes migration figures from British International Passenger Survey; the figures are not published after 1978.

1970: Scottish death statistics give some information on birthplaces for the first time.

1971: The number of Scottish-born in Australia is at its maximum: 159,300. The registrar-general for Scotland begins publishing estimates of internal and external migration; it ceases to do so after 1980.

1974: Scotland's population reaches its highest ever level (5.2 million); but because emigration exceeds natural increase, the population still tends to gradually fall.

1975: Scots cease to be separately identified in migration statistics in New Zealand.

1977: Michael Flinn, Duncan Adamson, and Robin Lobban publish their landmark work, Scottish Population History. The Marriage (Scotland) Act modernizes marriage law.

1986: Nearly 5 percent of Australians claim some Scottish ancestry at the census.

1989: Scotland records a net gain from migration of 7,500, the first recorded since 1946.

2000: The US census estimates that 4.9 million Americans claim some form of Scottish ancestry.

2001: Scotland's population—of just over 5 million—is about the same as in 1951. The census asks about religion for the first time since 1851.

2003: Murray Watson publishes Being English in Scotland.

2005: Duncan Macniven, the registrar-general for Scotland, publishes a survey of 150 years of Scottish population history in his annual report.

2006: 4.7 million Canadians—15 percent of the population—claim some Scottish ancestry at the population census, the highest level for any country. The number of Scots-born in the Irish Republic is almost 17,000, its highest recorded level.

2011: The England and Wales census includes a question on national identity for the first time.

2014: A majority of the Scottish electorate votes against independence in a referendum, but a significant minority (45 percent) vote in favor (September 18).

2015: At the national election, the Scottish Nationalist Party wins fifty-six of the fifty-nine parliamentary seats in Scotland.

Appendix B:
Scotland: The People's Names

This appendix sets out the names of the Scottish people in three parts. The first part is a listing of the principal family names by region and county in about 1650 drawn from R. F. Treharne and Harold Fullard, eds., *Muir's Historical Atlas: Ancient, Medieval, and Modern*, 6th ed. (London: George Phillip, 1963), 37. Conspicuously absent from this list are two of the most common later Scottish family names, Smith and Brown.

The second and third parts rank the most common family and first names in 1858, 1935, and 1958 as determined by the registrar-general for Scotland and reported in the *Annual Report* for 1962, pp. 67–72. The 1858 survey covered fifty names and the later surveys covered the top one hundred.

PART 1: SCOTLAND: PRINCIPAL FAMILY NAMES
BY REGION AND COUNTY, C. 1650

Strathclyde:

Argyll: Campbell; MacDonald; MacFie; MacGregor; MacLean; Stewart
Ayr: Kennedy
Bute: Brodick
Dumbarton: MacGregor
Lanark: Hamilton
Renfrew: Hamilton

Dumfries and Galloway:

Dumfries: Armstrong; Johnstone

Kirkcudbright: Gordon; Maxwell
Wigton: Stewart

Borders:

Berwick: Home
Peebles: Scott
Roxburgh: Armstrong; Elliot
Selkirk: Scott; Selkirk

Lothian:

Haddington: Lindsay

Central and Fife:

Fife: Bethune; Lindsay
Stirling: Stirling

Tayside:

Forfar:Lindsay
Kinross: Kinross
Perth: Campbell; Macnab; Menzies; Murray; Robertson

Grampian:

Aberdeen: Farquharson; Forbes; Gordon
Banff: Gordon
Elgin: Grant

Highlands:

Caithness: Sinclair
Inverness: Cameron; Chisholm; Frazer; Grant; MacIntosh; MacNeil; MacPherson; Moray
Nairn: MacIntosh
Ross and Comarty: Comarty; MacDonald; MacKenzie; Ross
Sutherland: MacKay; MacLeod; Murray

See tables 21, 22, and 23

Appendix C:
Some Vital Data

This appendix makes available selected information about Scotland that I would like to have had when I was writing this book. They came mostly from my calculations and were not simply taken from official publications. There are a number of reasons for doing this. The first is that, although Scotland can lay claim to having population statistics that rival those for Scandinavia before 1850 in the form of age data for 1751, 1791, 1811, 1821, and 1841, this information has to be unzipped using the population models of Ansley J. Coale and Paul Demeny as published in *Regional Model Life Tables and Stable Populations,* 2nd ed. (New York: Academic Press, 1983). By matching the Scottish data before 1901 with particular models, it is possible to know accurately vital information such as birth, death, and growth rates as well as life expectancy.

The second reason is less obvious: underreporting in the official Scottish statistics before 1901, according to the models that match the age distribution for census years. About 10 percent of births were missed in the first year of registration, 1855, but coverage quickly improved, missing only about 2 percent up to 1862, and after that they seem to be complete. Deaths reporting was much poorer, and an annual average of 4–5 percent were missed. Much of this underreporting was for infant deaths; at least one in five infant deaths went unreported from 1861 to 1891 and about one in eight in the 1890s. This means that splicing the infant mortality rate from models before 1860 with the official series from 1861 to 1901 would create the false impression that there had been a sharp improvement when in fact it was only gradual.

Some explanations and comments are also required for the tables. Table 1 excludes men on military service from 1801 to 1841 to ensure that it covers the residential population only. The figures excluded were 1801: 70,000;

1811: 78,200; 1821: 45,800; 1831: 41,200; and 1841: 32,200. Tables 2 to 4 on birth and death rates and life expectancy combine data from models up to 1901 and my calculations from official statistics afterward. Table 5 on marital status uses a minimum age of twenty rather than the more common fifteen years because it was the unofficial minimum age for marriage in Scotland in the past. Table 6 on land ownership is entirely new and has been built from individual land holdings. Table 7 summarizes the main features of the labor force. Tables 8 and 9 chart Scottish urbanization using the pre-1950 US minimum size of an urban center of 2,500, not the traditional English minimum of 1,000. This was done not just for closer comparisons with the United States but also with England and Wales from 1801 to 1911, as calculated by C. M. Law in 1967 and available in Richard Lawton (ed.), *The Census and Social Structure* (London: Frank Cass, 1978), p. 97.

Tables 10 and 11 give a global summary of migration by the Scots-born based on unpublished as well as published information. More details are given in the chapters for particular countries. Tables 12 and 13 consider the effect of emigration on Scotland by restoring its emigrants to its population in 1881 and 1931 and in so doing demonstrate that it was not the main reason for its female majority.

LIST OF TABLES

A. Scotland

Table 24: Scotland, Population, Selected Features, c. 1000–2011
Table 25: Scotland, Births and Deaths, per thousand males, c. 1651–2012
Table 26: Scotland, Births and Deaths, per thousand females, c. 1651–2002
Table 27: Scotland, Life Expectancy at Birth and 20 Years by Sex, c. 1651–2012
Table 28: Scotland, Marital Status, Ages 20 and Older by Sex, c. 1791–1971
Table 29: Scotland, Land Ownership by Large Owners and County, 1882
Table 30: Scotland, Labor Force, by Sex and Type, 1841–1971
Table 31: Scotland, Urban-Rural Population, c. 1701–1971
Table 32: Scotland, Urban Population by Size of Center, percentage, c. 1751–1971

B. Scots-Born Migration

Table 33: Scots-Born Migration, thousands, 1820–1990
Table 34: Scots-Born Migration, by Sex, thousands, 1841–1930

Appendix C: Some Vital Data

Table 35: Scots-Born by Age and Sex, Scotland and outside Scotland, thousands, 1881

Table 36: Scots-Born by Age and Sex, Scotland and outside Scotland, thousands, 1931

Year	Population (thousands)
1000	200
1300	400
1450	300
1500	450
1600	600
1650	776
1700	994
1751	1319
1791	1526
1801	1608
1811	1806
1821	2092

Table 1. Scotland, Estimated Population, c. 1000–1821. Source: Author's estimates and population censuses from 1751.

Year	Number (thousands)	Percentage of Total Population	Net Migration at End of Decade (thousands)
1841	126.3	4.8	
1851	207.4	7.2	96.2
1861	204.1	6.7	20.0
1871	207.8	6.2	35.6
1881	218.7	5.9	41.2
1891	194.8	4.9	20.5
1901	205.1	4.6	30.2
1911	174.7	3.7	24.0
1921	158.7	3.3	27.8
1931	124.3	2.6	16.4

Table 2. Scotland, Irish-Born, 1841–1931. Source: Population census; the migration estimates are for net gains from 1841 to 1881 and for settlers from 1881 based on length of residence data in the 1931 census.

Birth Region	England and Wales (thousands)	Overseas (thousands)	Total (thousands)
Strathclyde	85.1	323.1	408.2
Dumfries and Galloway	22.3	6.9	29.2
Borders	14.2	6.6	20.9
Lothian	40.8	69.8	110.5
Central and Fife	16.5	9.4	25.9
Tayside	23.1	58.5	81.6
Grampian	29.9	28.6	58.5
Highland	15.9	10.9	26.7
Total	247.7	513.8	761.5

Table 3. Scots-Born, Net Migration by Birth Region, 1871–1911. Source: Author's estimates based on population censuses.

Period	Settlers* (thousands)	Population at End of Period		
		Thousands	% Males	% Females
1820s	22.8	53.6		
1830s	56.0	103.2	58.8	41.2
1840s	45.1	130.1	56.5	43.5
1850s	60.7	169.2	55.0	45.0
1860s	73.9	213.3	53.4	46.6
1870s	80.7	253.5	52.3	47.7
1880s	80.1	282.3	51.3	48.7
1890s	90.5	316.8	51.6	48.4
1900s	38.2	321.8	50.1	49.9
1910s	65.0	333.5	48.6	51.4
1920s	90.5	366.5	49.3	50.7

Table 4. Scots-Born Migration, England and Wales, 1820–1930. *Estimated net migration. Source: Author's estimates based on Scotch Church Young Men's Society, Statistical Report of the Scottish Population of Manchester, taken in 1837 (Manchester, J. Galt, 1838), p. 28, and the population census.

Region	1841 (%)	1851 (%)	1861 (%)	1871 (%)	1881 (%)	1891 (%)	1901 (%)	1911 (%)	1921 (%)	1931 (%)
North	25.2	25.4	24.8	26.3	24.2	23.4	22.1	19.0	18.0	14.2
Yorkshire and Humberside	5.8	6.1	6.1	7.2	7.6	7.6	7.6	8.0	8.7	8.2
Northwest	22.8	23.9	25.2	24.7	25.1	23.0	20.9	18.9	17.7	15.3
East Midlands	2.4	2.5	2.1	2.1	2.4	2.6	2.9	3.1	3.7	4.4
West Midlands	3.2	3.8	4.1	3.7	3.4	3.3	3.8	4.1	4.5	4.9
East Anglia	1.2	1.1	1.0	0.8	1.0	0.9	1.0	1.2	1.6	1.7
Southeast and London	34.3	31.5	30.7	29.9	30.8	33.3	35.7	38.9	38.0	44.0
Southwest	3.7	4.0	4.0	3.4	3.3	3.4	3.6	3.7	4.6	4.9
Wales	1.5	1.7	2.0	1.9	2.1	2.5	2.5	3.1	3.2	2.5
Total	100.0	100.0	100.0	100.0	100.0	100.0	100.0	100.0	100.0	100.0
Population (thousands)	103.2	130.1	169.2	213.3	253.5	282.3	316.8	321.8	333.5	366.5

Table 5. Scots-Born, England and Wales by Region, 1841–1931. Source: Population census.

Birth Region	Thousands	Percentage
Strathclyde	107.9	34.3
Dumfries and Galloway	28.3	9.0
Borders	18.1	5.8
Lothian	51.7	16.5
Central and Fife	20.9	6.6
Tayside	29.3	9.3
Grampian	38.0	12.1
Highland	20.2	6.4
Population	314.3	100.0

Table 6. Scots-Born, England and Wales by Birth Region, 1911. Note: Excludes those who did not state where they were born. Source: 1911 population census.

Period	Settler Arrivals (thousands)	Population at End of Period			
		Thousands	% Males	% Females	% Urban
1820s	16.4	27.0			
1830s	33.4	55.0			
1840s	31.9	90.4	60	40	
1850s	32.3	139.2	57	43	17
1860s	15.2	125.5	54	46	20
1870s	28.9	117.6	54	46	27
1880s	23.2	104.2	52	48	35
1890s	12.8	83.6	54	46	39
1900s	109.5	169.4	59	41	57
1910s	103.5	226.5	53	47	66
1920s	96.4	279.8	52	48	71

Table 7. Scots-Born Migration to Canada, 1820–1930. Source: Author's estimates based mainly on the 1901 and 1931 censuses.

Period	Settler Arrivals (thousands)	Population at End of Period			
		Thousands	% Male	% Female	% Urban
1820s	7.3	6.4			
1830s	11.0	29.0			
1840s	30.8	70.1	60	40	
1850s	45.4	108.5	60	40	39
1860s	39.6	140.8	56	44	39
1870s	46.6	170.1	56	44	45
1880s	100.0	242.2	55	45	66
1890s	39.9	234.7	55	45	69
1900s	77.5	261.1	56	44	72
1910s	47.4	254.5	53	47	77
1920s	139.9	354.3	51	49	83

Table 8. Scots-Born Migration to the United States, 1820–1930. Source: Author's estimates based the 1910 and 1930 U.S. censuses.

Marital Status	Scotland (Scots-born)		Canada		US	
	% Men	% Women	% Men	% Women	% Men	% Women
Married	48	43	68	60	66	65
Widowed	5	12	8	20	6	16
Single	47	45	24	20	28	19
Total	100	100	100	100	100	100

Table 9. Scots-Born Marital Status, Scotland, Canada, and the United States, c. 1880. Source: Unpublished population census figures for Scotland, Canada, and the United States. Figures apply to those ages 15 or older, and the US figures exclude divorcees.

	Percentage of Spouses Who Were Scots-Born	
	Canada	US
Birthplace of Wives		
Scotland	68	37
England or Wales	0	7
Canada	32	6
US	0	33
Other country	0	17
Total	100	100
Birthplace of Husbands		
Scotland	69	49
England or Wales	3	9
Canada	24	3
US	3	21
Other country	1	17
Total	100.0	100.0

Table 10. Scots-Born Birthplace of Spouses, Canada and United States, c. 1880. Sources: A sample of 159 couples from the 1881 census enumerators' sheets for Canada; unpublished data for all the Scots-born in the US in 1880 (157,885 persons). Totals may not add to 100 because of rounding.

	Canada	US
Males		
	Thousands	
Number	45.6	127.4
	Percentages	
Urban	39	65
Rural	61	35
Boarder/lodger	10	11
Brother	2	2
Brother-in-law	0	1
Employee of household	3	1
Father	3	1
Father-in-law	1	1
Head	72	74
Son	8	7
Females		
	Thousands	
Number	38.0	106.1
	Percentages	
Urban	39	65
Rural	61	35
Aunt	1	1
Boarder/lodger	3	4
Daughter	10	9
Employee of household	5	4
Head/widow	16	18
Mother	12	3
Mother-in-law	2	4
Sister	5	3
Sister-in-law	1	1
Wife	46	53

Table 11. Scots-Born Profile, Canada and United States, c. 1900. Sources: Author's samples of pre-1901 arrivals from the population censuses of Canada (1901) and the United States (1910). Sample sizes: Males 4,407 for Canada and 2,716 for the United States; Females: 3,059 for Canada and 1,900 for the United States. The totals exclude some minor categories. The urban/rural figures were estimated from the 1901 and 1931 Canadian censuses and the 1910 US census.

	Canada	US
Number (thousands)	109.5	77.5
Percentage		
Sex		
Males	62	57
Females	38	43
Males		
Urban	66	81
Rural	34	19
Husbands	29	29
Sons under 15	20	15
Sons over 15	10	7
Boarders/lodgers	30	34
Females		
Urban	74	81
Rural	26	19
Wives	44	37
Daughters under 15	27	19
Daughters over 15	8	9
Boarders/lodgers	4	7

Table 12. Scots-Born Profile, Canada and United States, 1900s arrivals. Source: Author's samples using unpublished census data for Canada (1911) and the US (1910). The urban/rural figures were estimated from the length of residence data in the 1931 Canadian census and the 1930 US census.

Year	South Africa (thousands)	Australia (thousands)	New Zealand (thousands)
1831		1.5	
1841		12.5	
1846		16.5	
1851	0.5	22.6	2.0
1861	1.0	97.2	15.5
1871	2.3	104.8	36.9
1881	6.3	98.3	52.8
1891	9.4	123.8	51.9
1901	18.2	101.8	47.9
1911	37.1	93.1	51.1
1921	35.9	108.8	51.7
1931	35.1	137.9	61.0

Table 13. Scots-Born, South Africa, Australia and New Zealand, 1831–1931. Sources: The population censuses, including author's estimates for some of the pre-1861 figures and 1931.

Period	Settler Arrivals (thousands)	Population at End of Period			
		Thousands	% Males	% Females	% Urban
1830s	8.4	10.0			
1840s	12.8	22.6	61	39	
1850s	78.7	98.9	59	41	41
1860s	22.7	99.4	57	43	44
1870s	21.2	98.3	58	42	51
1880s	33.6	123.8	59	41	60
1890s	8.7	101.8	58	42	64
1900s	18.3	93.1	59	41	66
1910s	40.5	108.8	56	44	69
1920s	46.2	132.5	55	45	72

Table 14. Scots-Born, Migration to Australia, 1830–1930. Source: Author's estimates based on the population census.

Period	Setter Arrivals (thousands)	Population at End of Period		
		Thousands	% Males	% Females
1840s	2.1	2.0		
1850s	12.9	15.5	62	38
1860s	20.8	36.9	62	38
1870s	21.3	52.8	59	41
1880s	8.4	51.9	57	43
1890s	5.9	47.8	57	43
1900s	12.9	51.7	59	41
1910s	13.0	51.7	55	45
1920s	20.2	58.2	53	47

Table 15. Scots-Born, Migration to New Zealand, 1850–1930. Source: Author's estimates of cohort survivors from New Zealand population censuses.

Year	Migration (thousands)	Population at End of Period (thousands)
1930s	32.0	330.0
1940s	177.0	575.3
1950s	104.0	641.2
1960s	138.0	734.9
1970s	50.0	752.2
1980s	37.0	767.0

Table 16. Scots-born, Migration to England and Wales, 1931–1991. Source: Author's estimates; they are approximate only.

Period	Migration (thousands)	Population at End of Period (thousands)
1930s	7.9	234.8
1940s	37.9	226.3
1950s	62.4	244.1
1960s	75.4	216.0
1970s	31.1	181.0
1980s	11.0	157.0

Table 17. Scots-Born, Migration to Canada, 1931–1991. Source: Population census and author's estimates after the1950s; they are approximate only.

Period	Migration (thousands)	Population at end of period (thousands)
1930s	7.5	279.3
1940s	16.7	244.2
1950s	32.9	213.0
1960s	29.8	170.0
1970s	14.4	142.0
1980s	21.9	152.7

Table 18. Scots-Born, Migration to United States, 1930–1990. Source: Population census and author's estimates.

Period	Migration (thousands)	Population at End of Period (thousands)
1930s	3.7	111.3
1940s	24.6	103.0
1950s	51.0	132.8
1960s	27.2	159.3
1970s	17.8	151.6
1980s	25.5	155.0

Table 19. Scots-Born, Migration to Australia, 1931–1991. Source: Population census and author's estimates.

Period	Migration (thousands)	Population at End of Period (thousands)
1930s	1.8	49.3
1940s	6.1	44.1
1950s	13.7	47.1
1960s	12.8	47.5
1970s	5.7	39.1
1980s	2.5	34.1

Table 20. Scots-born, Migration to New Zealand, 1931–1991 Source: Population census and author's estimates.

Name	1858	1935	1958	Name	1858	1935	1958	Name	1858	1935	1958
Smith	1	1	1	Kerr	41	37	35	MacIntosh		46	69
Brown	3	3	2	Hunter	37	43	36	MacIntyre		72	70
MacDonald	2	2	3	Davidson	32	36	37	Milne		53	71
Thomson	5	5	4	Ferguson	29	31	38	Murphy		80	72
Wilson	8	4	5	Simpson	44	40	39	Cunningham		71	73
Stewart	6	8	6	Martin	45	44	40	Williamson		81	74
Campbell	7	7	7	White	38	39	41	Ritchie		69	75
Robertson	4	6	8	Kelly		47	42	Fleming		94	76
Anderson	9	9	9	Allan	40	38	43	Crawford		77	77
Johnston	13	10	10	Grant	36	42	44	McLaughlin			78
Miller	14	12	11	Bell	43	41	45	Bruce		76	79
Murray	19	14	12	Black	46	45	46	Nicol		70	80
Scott	12	11	13	Wallace		52	47	Boyle			81
Reid	15	13	14	Russell		49	48	Hay		90	82
Clark	22	16	15	Marshall		56	49	Alexander		87	83
MacKenzie	11	15	16	MacMillan		48	50	Douglas		82	84
Paterson	17	17	17	MacGregor	42	51	51	Hughes		91	85
Taylor	26	22	18	Gordon		55	52	MacPherson		59	86
acKay	10	19	19	Kennedy		57	53	Shaw			87
MacLean	20	21	20	MacFarlane		58	54	Forbes		89	88
Young	23	25	21	Docherty		61	55	Lindsay		85	89
Ross	16	18	22	Wood		74	56	Boyd		97	90
Walker	30	28	23	Muir		62	57	Christie		86	91
Mitchell	27	20	24	Sutherland	49	54	58	King			92
Watson	28	23	25	Gallacher		84	59	Aitken		95	93
Morrison	31	27	26	Watt		64	60	Currie		88	94
MacLeod	25	26	27	Burns		67	61	Jamieson		99	95
Fraser	18	24	28	Stevenson		63	62	Findlay		75	96
Henderson	24	32	29	Wright		73	63	Donaldson		93	97
Gray	33	29	30	Sinclair	48	66	64	MacCallum			98
Cameron	21	30	31	Gibson	50	50	65	MacKie		83	99
Graham	39	35	32	Dickson		68	66	Weir			100
Duncan	34	33	33	Craig		60	67				
Hamilton	35	34	34	Munro	47	65	68				

Table 21. Scotland: The Most Common Family Names, 1858, 1935, and 1958. A. Family Names. Source: © Crown Copyright. Data supplied by National Records of Scotland.

Name	1858	1935	1958	Name	1858	1935	1958	Name	1858	1935	1958
John	1	1	1	Patrick		23	35	Roy		59	69
James	2	2	2	Steven			36	Scott			70
William	3	3	3	Alistair		24	37	Bernard		51	71
David	7	8	4	Martin		54	38	Ross			72
Robert	5	4	5	Raymond		64	39	Russell		99	73
Thomas	8	7	6	Christopher		62	40	Garry			74
Alexander	4	5	7	Daniel	22	22	41	Terrance		71	75
Ian		10	8	Anthony		52	42	Frederick		39	76
Brian		47	9	Keith			43	Albert		40	77
George	6	6	10	Malcolm	24	42	44	Craig			78
Alan			11	Graeme			45	Robin		93	79
Michael		28	12	Gerard		84	46	Grant			80
Andrew	9	9	13	Stewart		41	47	Harry			81
Peter	11	12	14	Alastair			48	Alasdair			82
Kenneth	32	27	15	Henry	21	17	49	Bryan			83
Gordon		25	16	Norman	31	29	50	Nicholas			84
Colin	19	44	17	Duncan	15	34	51	Adam	33	46	85
Stephen		67	18	Gary			52	Fraser			86
Charles	10	11	19	Kevin			53	Lindsay			88
Derek		58	20	Mark			54	Stanley		43	89
Douglas		26	21	Gerald		55	55	Leonard		70	90
Ronald	37	14	22	Leslie		50	56	Lawrence		49	91
Joseph	18	13	23	Samuel	20	31	57	Nigel			92
Graham		56	24	Archibald	13	20	58	Dennis		45	93
Donald	16	19	25	Philip		53	59	Vincent		87	94
Allan	29	21	26	Eric		36	60	Jack		65	95
Paul			27	Angus	14	35	61	Simon			96
Hugh	12	15	28	Matthew	26	38	62	Alfred		48	97
Iain			29	Roderick	27	60	63	Ralph			98
Edward	30	18	30	Bruce		81	64	Barry			99
Richard	28	30	31	Arthur		33	65	Cameron		83	100
Neil	23	37	32	Gavin		73	66	Ewan		76	87
Stuart			33	Frank			67				
Francis	25	16	34	Walter	17	32	68				

Table 22. Scotland: The Most Common Male First Names, 1858, 1935, and 1958.

Name	1858	1935	1958	Name	1858	1935	1958	Name	1858	1935	1958
Margaret	1	1	1	Heather			35	Alexandra			69
Elizabeth	3	3	2	Yvonne			36	Grace	17	22	70
Mary	2	2	3	Joyce		37	37	Carole			71
Linda			4	Christina	11	11	38	Wilma			72
Anne			5	Angela			39	Ruth		62	73
Catherine	9	4	6	Lorna			40	Sheena		74	74
Susan	26	36	7	Isabella	7	6	41	Theresa		45	75
Helen	10	9	8	Barbara	16	23	42	Gail			76
Ann			9	Marie	33	72	43	Louise			77
Fiona			10	Dorothy		19	44	Maria		85	78
Carol			11	Frances	43	30	45	Ellen	32	29	79
Jacqueline			12	Valerie			46	Josephine		57	80
Patricia		17	13	Rosemary		73	47	Rose	50	27	81
Christine			14	Diane			48	Norma		47	82
Elaine			15	Eileen		41	49	Carolyn			83
Maureen		25	16	Jennifer			50	Julie			84
Sandra			17	Lynn			51	Shona			85
Jane	5	13	18	Shirley		43	52	Doreen		38	86
Janet	6	10	19	Audrey		44	53	Alice	28	24	87
Caroline	37	92	20	Sarah	15	12	54	Annette			88
Jean	14	8	21	Pauline			55	Denise			89
Agnes	8	7	22	Morag		58	56	Wendy			90
Irene		18	23	Aileen		88	57	Sylvia		77	91
Janice			24	Janette		40	58	Avril			92
Alison	42	67	25	Gillian			59	Georgina	24	31	93
Kathleen		21	26	Bernadette			60	Deborah			94
Lorraine			27	Pamela			61	Isabel			95
Marion	13	16	28	Isobel			62	Laura			96
Lesley			29	Brenda			63	Jessie	12	14	97
Karen			30	Annie	4	5	64	Rhona			98
June		35	31	Eleanor		52	65	Lynda			99
Sheila		15	32	Evelyn		28	66	Teresa			100
Moira		33	33	Hazel		96	67				
Joan	29	20	34	Lynne			68				

Table 23. Scotland: The Most Common Female First Names, 1858, 1935, and 1958.

Year	Males (thousands)	Females (thousands)	Persons (thousands)	% Males	% Females	Marriages per thousand
1000			200.0			
1300			400.0			
1450			300.0			
1550			450.0			
1600			600.0			
1650			776.0			
1701	482.0	511.9	993.9	48.5	51.5	
1751	642.3	676.5	1,318.8	48.7	51.3	8.0
1791	702.7	823.8	1,526.5	46.0	54.0	8.4
1801	739.2	869.3	1,608.5	46.0	54.0	8.9
1811	826.3	979.6	1,805.9	45.8	54.2	7.9
1821	982.6	1,108.9	2,091.5	47.0	53.0	8.4
1831	1,114.5	1,249.9	2,364.4	47.1	52.9	7.4
1841	1,241.9	1,378.3	2,620.2	47.4	52.6	7.2
1851	1,375.5	1,513.3	2,888.7	47.6	52.4	7.0
1861	1,449.8	1,612.4	3,062.3	47.3	52.7	6.8
1871	1,603.1	1,756.9	3,360.0	47.7	52.3	7.3
1881	1,799.5	1,936.1	3,735.6	48.2	51.8	6.9
1891	1,942.7	2,082.9	4,025.6	48.3	51.7	6.9
1901	2,173.8	2,298.3	4,472.1	48.6	51.4	7.1
1911	2,308.8	2,452.1	4,760.9	48.5	51.5	6.7
1921	2,347.6	2,534.9	4,882.5	48.1	51.9	8.2
1931	2,325.5	2,517.5	4,843.0	48.0	52.0	6.8
1941	2,161.2	2,658.2	4,819.4	44.8	55.2	10.3
1951	2,434.4	2,662.1	5,096.4	47.8	52.2	8.0
1961	2,482.7	2,696.6	5,179.3	47.9	52.1	7.8
1971	2,514.6	2,714.3	5,229.0	48.1	51.9	7.8
1981	2,426.4	2,606.4	5,032.9	48.2	51.8	7.1
1991	2,469.0	2,637.3	5,106.3	48.4	51.6	6.8
2001	2,432.5	2,629.5	5,062.0	48.1	51.9	5.9
2011	2,571.1	2,730.5	5,301.6	48.5	51.5	5.6

Table 24. Scotland, Population, Selected Features, c. 1000–2011. Sources: For 1000 and 1450: Author's estimates based on Ian Morris, Why the West Rules— For Now (London: Profile Books, 2011), pp. 363, 437. For 1300: Thomas M. Cooper, "The Number and Distribution of the Population of Medieval Scotland," Scottish Historical Review XXVI (1947): 2–9. For 1550–1700: Author's modeling. For 1751: James G. Kyd, ed., Scottish Population Statistics, including Webster's Analysis of Population, 1755 (Edinburgh: T. and A. Constable, 1952). 1791: Sir John Sinclair, The Statistical Account of Scotland, vol. 21 (Edinburgh: William Creech). 1941: Estimates by the registrar-general for Scotland and the author. All other population counts were from the Census of Population and Housing. The pre-1790 marriage rates were estimated from Sir John Sinclair, The Statistical Account of Scotland (Edinburgh: William Creech, 1791–1799) and author's modeling.

Period	Births	Deaths	Infant Mortality
1651–1705	38.8	33.8	239.0
1706–1740	36.0	31.0	218.9
1741–1770	33.6	28.6	200.0
1771–1810	38.5	28.5	200.0
1811–1820	43.6	28.6	199.7
1821–1851	36.1	26.1	182.8
1861	38.9	23.9	167.2
1871	36.5	24.0	162.2
1881	36.5	21.5	174.6
1891	32.5	20.0	154.1
1901	30.4	20.4	152.0
1910–1912	27.2	15.6	119.6
1920–1922	27.2	14.8	105.8
1930–1932	20.3	14.0	93.8
1940–1942	21.1	16.8	87.2
1950–1952	19.3	13.2	41.5
1960–1962	21.2	13.1	30.0
1970–1972	17.2	12.9	21.8
1980–1982	14.4	13.1	12.9
1990–1992	13.8	11.9	8.4
2000–2002	11.0	11.3	6.2
2101–2012	11.6	10.1	4.4

Table 25. Scotland, Births and Deaths, per thousand males, c. 1651–2012. Sources: The pre-1920–1922 estimates were drawn from matching age structures with the population models from Ansley J. Coale and Paul Demeny, Regional Model Life Tables and Stable Populations, 2nd ed. (New York: Academic Press, 1983). Model North provided the figures for the period from 1651 to 1871 (Levels 6 to 10) and Model West from 1881 to 1901 (Levels 11 and 12). The infant mortality rates between 1861 and 1901 have been adjusted for underreporting using Models North and West. The figures after 1901 are three-yearly averages calculated from the Annual Reports of the Registrar-General for Scotland.

Period	Births	Deaths	Infant Mortality
1651–1705	35.6	30.6	205.1
1706–1740	33.1	28.1	187.6
1741–1770	31.0	26.0	171.2
1771–1810	35.7	25.7	171.2
1811–1820	40.7	25.7	171.0
1821–1851	31.4	23.9	156.5
1861	31.9	21.9	142.0
1871	31.9	21.9	140.8
1881	31.7	19.2	156.0
1891	28.8	18.8	130.6
1901	28.8	18.8	135.0
1910–1912	24.5	14.7	97.4
1920–1922	24.1	13.6	82.3
1930–1932	18.0	12.9	73.1
1940–1942	16.3	12.7	65.8
1950–1952	16.6	11.8	32.3
1960–1962	18.4	11.3	22.3
1970–1972	15.1	11.4	16.9
1980–1982	12.7	12.4	10.2
1990–1992	12.2	12.0	5.9
2000–2002	9.7	11.5	4.8

Table 26. Scotland, Births and Deaths, per thousand females, c. 1651–2002. Sources: The pre-1920–1922 estimates were drawn from matching age structures with the population models from Ansley J. Coale and Paul Demeny, Regional Model Life Tables and Stable Populations, 2nd ed. (New York: Academic Press, 1983). Model North provided the figures for the period from 1651 to 1871 (Levels 6 to 10) and Model West from 1881 to 1901 (Levels 11 and 12). The infant mortality rates between 1861 and 1901 have been adjusted for underreporting using Models North and West. The figures after 1901 are three-yearly averages calculated from the Annual Reports of the Registrar-General for Scotland.

Period	At Birth		At 20 Years	
	Males	Females	Males	Females
1651–1705	29.6	32.5	34.3	36.7
1706–1740	32.0	35.0	35.5	37.9
1741–1820	34.4	37.5	36.7	39.2
1821–1851	36.9	40.0	37.9	40.3
1861	40.4	43.1	39.1	41.1
1871	40.4	43.2	38.2	41.1
1881	43.2	44.8	38.8	40.9
1891	44.9	47.8	39.0	41.8
1901	44.8	47.5	38.8	42.0
1910–1912	50.5	53.5	43.3	45.4
1920–1922	53.4	56.5	44.8	46.8
1930–1932	55.8	59.4	46.0	48.3
1940–1942	56.8	62.0	45.3	49.3
1950–1952	64.4	68.6	48.3	51.9
1960–1962	66.2	71.9	49.0	54.2
1970–1972	67.3	73.6	49.5	55.4
1980–1982	68.8	74.9	50.3	56.0
1990–1992	71.4	77.1	52.5	57.9
2000–2002	73.3	78.8	54.1	59.4
2010–2012	76.7	80.9	62.1	66.2

Table 27. Scotland, Life Expectancy at Birth and 20 Years by Sex, c. 1651–2012. Sources: The data from 1651 to 1851 were drawn from the life tables for Model North (Levels 6 to 9) and Model West from 1881 to 1901 (Levels 11 and 12) in Ansley J. Coale and Paul Demeny, Regional Model Life Tables and Stable Populations, 2nd ed. (New York: Academic Press, 1983). The results from 1861were calculated from life tables available as an online template from the Office for National Statistics based on the method devised by Chin L. Chiang and the Annual Reports of the Registrar-General for Scotland. These data were also adjusted for underreporting using Model North (Levels 10) for 1861 and 1871 and Model West (Levels 11 and 12) for 1871 to 1901.

	Percentage				Total (thousands)
	Single	Married	Widowed	Divorced	
Males					
1791	27.5	65.6	6.8		387.8
1821	32.2	62.5	5.2		533.7
1851	35.2	57.9	6.9		707.9
1861	33.0	60.6	6.4		737.9
1871	33.0	60.5	6.5		810.3
1881	33.9	59.6	6.4		917.9
1891	35.6	58.1	6.3		1,015.1
1901	36.9	57.0	6.1		1,187.3
1911	36.6	57.1	6.3		1,301.5
1921	33.3	60.2	6.4	0.1	1,383.0
1931	33.1	60.3	6.5	0.1	1,448.3
1951	25.0	68.7	6.0	0.3	1,617.4
1961	33.3	62.1	4.3	0.3	1,909.3
1971	25.2	67.3	6.4	1.1	1,218.8
Females					
1791	31.5	54.7	13.8		452.6
1821	34.6	54.0	11.4		617.7
1851	36.1	49.1	14.8		854.3
1861	35.1	50.1	14.8		913.9
1871	33.9	51.0	15.1		981.3
1881	33.4	51.9	14.8		1,074.3
1891	34.5	51.4	14.1		1,169.3
1901	35.4	51.5	13.2		1,333.6
1911	35.5	52.1	12.4		1,458.2
1921	34.0	53.1	12.8	0.1	1,581.0
1931	34.0	53.6	12.3	0.1	1,649.6
1951	25.0	61.0	13.5	0.5	1,852.5
1961	20.3	64.6	14.4	0.7	1,856.1
1971	17.0	65.9	15.9	1.3	1,861.9

Table 28. Scotland, Marital Status, Age 20 and Older by Sex, c. 1791–1971. Sources: 1791 and 1821: Author's estimates based on two works by Sir John Sinclair, The Statistical Account of Scotland (Edinburgh: W. Creech, 1791–1799), and Analysis of the Statistical Account of Scotland (Edinburgh: William Tait, 1831). The 1851 to 1971 figures were summarized in the 1971 Census.

Region / County	Total Acreage (thousands)	% Owned	Annual Income (thousands)	Income per acre	Population (thousands)
1. Strathclyde					
Argyll	2,056.4	69	238.5	£0.17	78.1
Ayr	722.2	65	369.7	£0.79	199.4
Bute	139.4	96	40.4	£0.30	16.6
Dumbarton	154.5	72	62.9	£0.56	67.4
Lanark	564.3	56	197.6	£0.62	791.4
Renfrew	156.8	67	127.1	£1.21	188.5
Total	3,793.7	67	1,036.3	£0.61	1,341.3
2. Dumfries & Galloway					
Dumfries	680.2	74	267.9	£0.53	70.9
Kirkcudbright	574.6	64	163.6	£0.45	39.4
Wigton	310.7	88	174.7	£0.64	35.0
Total	1,565.6	73	606.3	£0.54	145.4
3. Borders					
Berwick	294.8	69	211.5	£1.04	32.5
Peebles	226.9	78	74.9	£0.42	13.1
Roxburgh	425.7	77	229.0	£0.70	48.5
Selkirk	164.5	68	43.8	£0.39	24.9
Total	1,111.9	74	559.2	£0.64	119.1
4. Lothian					
Edinburgh	231.7	45	151.6	£1.45	348.8
Haddington	173.4	77	196.9	£1.48	35.8
Linlithgow	76.8	42	53.6	£1.67	39.4
Total	482.0	56	402.1	£1.53	424.0
5. Central & Fife					
Clackmannan	30.5	81	25.5	£1.03	23.1
Fife	315.0	58	244.5	£1.34	166.7
Stirling	286.3	58	118.8	£0.71	100.3
Total	631.8	59	388.9	£1.03	290.1
6. Tayside					
Forfar	560.2	78	289.4	£0.66	249.9
Kinross	46.5	18	12.2	£1.45	7.2
Perth	1,617.8	80	504.9	£0.39	125.1
Total	2,224.5	78	806.5	£0.83	382.2
7. Grampian					
Aberdeen	1,251.5	80	467.5	£0.46	263.1
Banff	410.1	93	161.6	£0.42	59.0
Elgin	304.6	89	101.5	£0.38	44.2
Kincardine	245.3	75	125.7	£0.68	34.8
Total	2,211.5	83	856.3	£0.49	401.1
8. Highland					
Caithness	438.9	90	80.0	£0.20	39.4
Inverness	2,616.5	90	233.3	£0.10	84.5
Nairn	125.0	85	30.3	£0.29	8.7
Orkney	240.5	48	21.0	£0.18	31.7
Ross & Cromarty	1,970.0	100	201.7	£0.10	78.6
Shetland	352.9	20	5.8	£0.08	29.5
Sutherland	1,297.8	99	67.3	£0.05	22.1
Total	7,041.6	89	639.4	£0.14	294.5
TOTAL SCOTLAND	19,062.5	80	5,295.1	£0.35	3,397.8

Table 29. Scotland, Land Ownership by Large Owners and County, 1882. Source: John Bateman, The Great Landowners of Great Britain and Ireland, 4th ed. (London: Harrison, 1883), passim. The regions used were taken from Clive H. Lee, British Regional Employment Statistics, 1841–1971 (Cambridge: Cambridge University Press, 1979).

Year	Total Persons (thousands)	% Male	% Female	% Agriculture	% Manufacturing
1841	1,005.6	70.4	29.6	24.3	36.0
1851	1,271.2	67.4	32.6	24.9	41.3
1861	1,337.6	67.4	32.6	22.2	38.7
1871	1,464.3	69.6	30.4	22.2	38.5
1881	1,574.6	69.2	30.8	16.7	38.6
1891	1,747.7	68.9	31.1	14.0	39.6
1901	1,983.0	70.2	29.8	12.0	33.3
1911	2,067.0	71.3	28.7	11.0	34.2
1921	2,208.1	71.1	28.9	9.9	37.6
1931	2,221.4	70.0	30.0	8.9	33.2
1951	2,194.7	69.6	30.4	7.4	35.1
1961	2,199.8	67.7	32.3	5.8	32.4
1971	2,164.1	62.4	37.6	4.1	32.1

Table 30. Scotland, Labor Force, by Sex and Type 1841–1971. Source: Clive H. Lee, British Regional Employment Statistics, 1841–1971 (Cambridge: Cambridge University Press, 1979), passim.

Year	% Urban	% Rural	Total (thousands)
1701	10.0	90.0	993.9
1751	19.2	80.8	1,318.8
1791	23.9	76.1	1,526.5
1801	26.1	73.9	1,608.5
1811	28.9	71.1	1,805.9
1821	31.7	68.3	2,091.5
1831	34.9	65.1	2,364.4
1841	34.6	65.4	2,620.2
1851	39.6	60.4	2,888.7
1861	43.2	56.8	3,062.3
1871	47.8	52.2	3,360.0
1881	52.3	47.7	3,734.4
1891	56.9	43.1	4,025.6
1901	61.8	38.2	4,472.1
1911	61.7	38.3	4,760.9
1921	65.0	35.0	4,882.5
1931	66.8	33.2	4,843.0
1951	67.0	33.0	5,096.4
1961	68.1	31.9	5,179.3
1971	65.5	34.5	5,229.0

Table 31. Scotland, Urban-Rural Population, c. 1701–1971. Source: Author's estimates.

Year	Urban Center Size					
	2,500–9,999	10,000–24,999	25,000–49,900	50,000–99,000	100,000–499,000	500,000 or more
1751	37.3	28.4	11.8	22.5		
1791	32.9	30.4	0.0	36.7		
1801	35.3	18.3	6.4	40.0		
1811	31.8	21.1	5.7	0.0	41.5	
1821	28.1	15.3	12.6	0.0	44.0	
1831	27.0	11.3	16.7	0.0	45.0	
1841	26.8	8.5	8.9	6.5	49.3	
1851	28.5	8.0	6.0	11.6	46.0	
1861	28.4	8.4	6.8	10.9	45.5	
1871	22.1	15.2	3.0	7.3	52.4	
1881	19.8	15.6	6.6	10.7	47.3	
1891	18.3	16.4	6.1	8.3	26.2	24.6
1901	15.3	11.2	10.3	10.1	25.6	27.5
1911	13.3	13.9	11.9	9.7	24.4	26.7
1921	12.0	12.6	11.7	7.4	23.6	32.6
1931	12.2	10.2	12.7	7.1	24.2	33.7
1951	11.2	11.0	14.7	7.0	24.2	31.9
1961	12.1	9.1	13.6	11.5	23.7	29.9
1971	11.3	13.3	15.5	10.0	23.9	26.2

Table 32. Scotland, Urban Population by Size of Center, percentage, c. 1751–1971. Source: Author's estimates.

Period	England and Wales	Canada	US	South Africa	Australia	New Zealand	Total Overseas	Grand Total
1820s	22.8	16.4	7.3		1.5		25.2	48.0
1830s	56.0	33.4	11.0		8.4		52.9	109.8
1840s	45.1	31.9	30.8	0.2	12.8	2.1	77.8	122.9
1850s	60.7	32.3	45.4	0.5	78.7	12.9	169.7	230.5
1860s	73.9	15.2	39.6	0.8	22.7	20.8	99.1	173.0
1870s	80.7	15.4	46.6	3.3	21.2	21.3	107.7	188.4
1880s	80.1	23.2	100.0	4.2	33.6	8.4	169.3	249.4
1890s	90.5	12.8	39.0	10.3	8.7	5.9	76.7	167.2
1900s	38.2	109.5	77.5	14.1	18.3	12.9	232.2	270.5
1910s	65.0	103.5	47.4	7.9	40.5	13.0	212.2	277.2
1920s	91.5	96.4	139.9	5.1	40.5	20.2	302.1	393.6
1930s	32.0	7.9	7.5	3.2	3.7	1.8	24.1	56.1
1940s	177.0	37.9	16.7	7.6	24.6	6.1	92.9	269.9
1950s	104.5	62.4	32.9	2.4	51.0	13.7	162.4	267.0
1960s	145.6	75.4	29.8		27.2	12.8	145.2	290.9
1970s	54.1	31.1	14.4		17.8	5.7	69.0	123.1
1980s	52.4	11.0	21.9		25.5	2.5	60.9	113.4

Table 33. Scots-Born Migration, thousands, 1820–1990. Note: The estimates for England and Wales include Ireland up to 1911. Source: Author's estimates based mainly on length of residence data from the population censuses for the countries shown.

Period	England & Wales	Canada	US	South Africa	Australia	New Zealand	Total overseas	Grand total
Males								
1840s	24.6	17.5	19.3	0.1	7.7	1.2	51.1	75.7
1850s	32.9	17.6	30.0	0.3	46.2	7.7	101.8	134.8
1860s	38.8	8.8	21.1	0.5	12.4	12.7	55.5	94.3
1870s	42.3	9.1	26.1	2.2	13.5	11.9	62.9	105.2
1880s	40.6	13.4	54.7	2.6	20.3	4.8	95.9	136.5
1890s	48.1	7.0	21.1	7.6	5.6	3.8	45.1	93.2
1900s	18.4	67.7	44.3	7.6	12.2	7.8	139.6	158.0
1910s	31.3	48.5	22.0	3.7	20.7	6.5	101.4	132.7
1920s	45.8	48.5	70.9	2.7	20.7	10.5	153.2	199.0
Females								
1840s	20.5	14.4	11.4	0.1	5.1	0.9	31.9	52.5
1850s	27.8	14.7	15.4	0.2	32.5	5.1	67.9	95.7
1860s	35.1	6.4	18.4	0.3	10.4	8.1	43.6	78.7
1870s	38.4	6.3	20.5	1.0	7.7	9.3	44.8	83.2
1880s	39.5	9.7	45.3	1.6	13.2	3.6	73.5	113.0
1890s	42.5	5.7	17.8	2.8	3.1	2.1	31.6	74.1
1900s	19.8	41.7	33.2	6.5	6.1	5.1	92.6	112.5
1910s	33.6	55.0	25.4	4.2	19.8	6.5	110.8	144.5
1920s	45.7	47.9	69.0	2.5	19.8	9.7	148.9	194.5

Table 34. Scots-Born Migration, by Sex, thousands, 1841–1930. Source: Author's estimates based mainly on length of residence data from the population censuses for the countries shown.

Ages	Males			Females		
	Scotland	Outside Scotland	Total	Scotland	Outside Scotland	Total
0–4	249.8	6.4	256.2	243.2	6.4	249.6
5–9	216.2	10.6	226.8	210.7	10.6	221.3
10–14	192.2	14.9	207.0	186.0	14.3	200.3
15–19	173.4	19.9	193.2	173.5	19.1	192.7
20–24	141.0	30.2	171.3	157.2	24.6	181.8
25–29	116.7	37.7	154.4	135.6	31.0	166.6
30–34	92.3	39.3	131.6	107.9	31.5	139.4
35–39	82.0	39.2	121.2	98.2	31.7	129.8
40–44	71.8	37.9	109.7	87.8	30.2	118.0
45–49	60.8	38.3	99.2	75.9	29.7	105.6
50–54	53.6	34.6	88.2	67.9	26.8	94.7
55–59	44.5	27.1	71.6	55.2	20.3	75.5
60–64	38.4	23.2	61.5	51.5	18.4	70.0
65–69	27.7	15.9	43.6	37.3	13.4	50.8
70–74	20.1	9.4	29.5	28.9	7.8	36.7
75–79	12.6	4.4	17.0	17.6	4.3	21.9
80+	8.6	3.6	12.2	14.2	3.6	17.9
Total	1,601.6	392.5	1,994.1	1,748.7	323.8	2,072.5
Percentage	47.8	54.8	49.0	52.2	45.2	51.0

Table 35. Scots-Born by Age and Sex, Scotland and outside Scotland, thousands, 1881. Source: Unpublished figures from the North Atlantic Population Project, which provided complete counts from the population censuses of Scotland, England, Wales, and Canada for 1881 and the 1880 US census. The ages for the Scots-born in Ireland, Australia, and New Zealand for 1881 were estimated by the author. South Africa was omitted because of lack of data.

Ages	Males			Females		
	Scotland	Outside Scotland	Total	Scotland	Outside Scotland	Total
0–4	209.9	5.2	215.1	206.0	5.1	211.2
5–9	223.4	15.1	238.5	220.4	14.6	235.0
10–14	207.5	22.4	229.9	204.2	21.4	225.7
15–19	209.4	27.3	236.7	210.4	25.3	235.7
20–24	192.6	49.4	242.0	204.0	46.7	250.6
25–29	172.8	64.1	236.9	189.4	58.4	247.8
30–34	148.5	62.0	210.5	172.2	61.4	233.6
35–39	129.3	58.0	187.2	156.4	60.9	217.4
40–44	119.6	64.0	183.6	142.6	60.5	203.0
45–49	114.1	65.7	179.8	135.7	58.3	194.1
50–54	110.3	59.0	169.3	125.5	51.5	177.0
55–59	99.5	46.5	146.0	109.3	40.6	149.8
60–64	79.4	37.9	117.3	89.3	33.4	122.7
65–69	59.4	30.2	89.6	72.1	27.7	99.8
70–74	40.6	21.5	62.1	54.3	21.6	75.9
75–79	21.8	13.2	35.0	32.4	13.6	46.0
80+	12.1	8.8	20.9	22.7	10.5	33.2
Total	2,150.1	650.4	2,800.5	2,347.1	611.4	2,958.5
Percentage	47.8	51.5	48.6	52.2	48.5	51.4

Table 36. Scots-Born by Age and Sex, Scotland and outside Scotland, thousands, 1931. Source: The population censuses for Scotland, England and Wales and Canada for 1931, the 1930 US census, and author's estimates from the censuses for Australia (1933), Northern Ireland and the Irish Republic (1926 and 1936), and the 1936 censuses for New Zealand and South Africa.

Bibliography

INTRODUCTION

This is mainly a thematic listing of the various works I used to write this book, not a comprehensive bibliography. Where works are available on the Internet, I have given their location as well as useful Internet sites generally. The listing of a work does not necessarily mean my endorsement; it may merely indicate a work or site that might be of interest. There is a good general guide to the main works on Scottish history up to the early 1980s in Rosalind Mitchison, *A History of Scotland,* 3rd ed. (London: Routledge, 2002), which can be supplemented by the bibliography in Clive H. Lee, *Scotland and the United Kingdom: The Economy and the Union in the Twentieth Century* (Manchester: Manchester University Press, 1995). For secondary works, there is a comprehensive listing in Thomas M. Devine, *To the Ends of the Earth: Scotland's Global Diaspora, 1750–2010* (London: Allen Lane, 2011).

Historical atlases are an especially useful way of coming to grips with history. They are underestimated for their effectiveness to convey information and raise questions. For the pre-1500 period, there is much valuable Scottish material in Angus Mackay and David Ditchburn (eds.), *Atlas of Medieval Europe* (London: Routledge, 1997). G. Whittington and I. D. Whyte (eds.), *An Historical Geography of Scotland* (London and New York: Academic Press, 1983), pays most attention to the pre-1900 era. Ian Barnes, *The Historical Atlas of the Celtic World* (London: Cartographica, 2009), provides an attractive general view of Celtic history in coffee table format with due attention to global migration.

Migration is a meeting ground for a number of academic disciplines, general history, historical demography, economic history, and historical geography, each of which brings a different perspective to a complicated topic. There are good general introductions to the theory of migration in Robert Woods, *Population Analysis in Geography* (London: Longman, 1979), and Huw Jones, *Population Geography,* 2nd ed. (London: Paul Chapman, 1990), a work that uses Scottish examples. Sources for the statistical sources that are the core of this work are set out in sections 15 to 18.

OUTLINE OF THE BIBLIOGRAPHY

The bibliography is set out as follows:

1. Bibliographies and Genealogical Research Guides
2. Scotland: General Surveys and Reference
3. Scotland: Population History and Related Studies
4. Immigration Encyclopedias and Population Histories
5. Robert Wallace and the Population Debate
6. Selected Pre-1830 Scottish Sources
7. Scottish Nationalism and Scotland's Future
8. Economic History
9. British Emigration
10. Scotland: Emigration and Immigration
11. Scottish-Born in Australia and New Zealand
12. Scottish-Born in Canada
13. Scottish-Born in the United States
14. Scottish-Born in Other Countries
15. Statistical Sources: Scotland
16. Statistical Sources: Scottish-Born Outside Scotland
17. Life Tables
18. Population and Related Works

1. BIBLIOGRAPHIES AND GENEALOGICAL RESEARCH GUIDES

Anglo-Scottish Family History Society. *A Dictionary of Scottish Emigrants.* 2 vols. Manchester: Manchester and Lancashire Family History Society, 1988.
Anthony, Adolph. *Collins' Tracing Your Scottish Family History.* London: Collins, 2008.
Beckett, J. D., ed. *A Dictionary of Scottish Emigrants into England and Wales.* Manchester: Anglo-Scottish Family History Society, 1984.
Bibliography of Scotland. Edinburgh, National Library of Scotland, 1988 to date.
Holton, Graham S., and Jack Winch. *Discover Your Scottish Ancestry: Internet and Traditional Sources.* Lanham, MD: Roberts Rinehart, 2004.
Humphery-Smith, Cecil R., ed. *The Phillimore Atlas and Index of Parish Registers.* 3rd ed. Chichester, UK: Phillimore, 2003. Includes maps on the parishes of the Scottish Highlands.
Lawson, Bill, ed. *Register of Emigrants from the Western Isles of Scotland, 1750—1900. Vol. 1, Isle of Harris.* Northton, Isle of Harris: Bill Lawson, 1992.

Mason, Margaret, ed. *Scottish Genealogy: A Digest of Library Sources*. Manchester: Manchester and Lancashire Family History Society, 1985.
Scottish Record Office. *The Scots in Australia: Historical Background, List of Documents, Extracts and Facsimiles*. Edinburgh: Scottish Record Office, 1994.
———. *The Scots in New Zealand: Historical Background, List of Documents, Extracts and Facsimiles*. Edinburgh: Scottish Record Office, 1994.

2. SCOTLAND: GENERAL SURVEYS AND REFERENCE

Buchan, James. *Capital of the Mind: How Edinburgh Changed the World*. London: John Murray, 2003. One of the few works to give any attention to Robert Wallace.
Cairncross, Alec K., ed. *The Scottish Economy: A Statistical Account of Scottish Life by Members of the Staff of Glasgow University*. Cambridge: Cambridge University Press, 1954. This is a wide-ranging account of Scotland's economy and society in about 1950 with much historical material. It has two articles on population and others on health, housing, crime, education, and religion, and it assembles much important information.
Devine, Thomas M., Rosalind Mitchison, et al., eds. *People and Society in Scotland, 1760–1990*. 3 vols. Edinburgh: John Donald in association with the Economic and Social History Society of Scotland, 1988, 1990, and 1992.
Donaldson, Gordon. *Scotland: The Shaping of a Nation*. 3rd ed. Nairn, Scotland: David St John Thomas Publisher, 1993.
Donnachie, Ian, and George Hewitt, eds. *A Companion to Scottish History from the Reformation to the Present*. London: B. T. Batsford, 1989.
Garvie, Christopher. *No Gods and Precious Few Heroes: Scotland, 1914–1980*. London: Arnold, 1981.
Herman, Arthur. *The Scottish Enlightenment: The Scots' Invention of the Modern World*. London: HarperCollins, 2001.
Houston, Robert A., and W. W. Knox, eds. *The New Penguin History of Scotland*. London: Penguin Books, 2001.
Lynch, Michael, ed. *The Early Modern Town in Scotland*. London and Wolfeboro, NH: Croom Helm: 1987.
———, ed. *The Oxford Companion to Scottish History*. Oxford: Oxford University Press, 2001.
———. *Scotland: A New History*. London: Century, 1991.
Marr, Andrew. *The Battle for Scotland*. Harmondsworth, England: Penguin, 1992. An accessible account of the modern Scottish independence movement.
Munro, David, and Bruce Gittings, eds. *Scotland: An Encyclopedia of Places and Landscape*. Glasgow: Collins, 2006.
Ross, David. *Chronology of Scottish History*. New Lanark, Scotland: Geddes & Gosset, 2002.
Smout, T. C. *A Century of the Scottish People, 1830–1950*. London: William Collins Sons, 1986.
———. *A History of the Scottish People, 1560–1830*. 2nd ed. London: Collins, 1970.
Trevor-Roper, H. R. *The Invention of Scotland: Myth and History*. New Haven, CT: Yale University Press, 2008.
Whittington, G., and I. D. Whyte, eds. *An Historical Geography of Scotland*. London and New York: Academic Press, 1983.
Wormald, Jenny ed. *Scotland: A History*. Oxford: Oxford University Press, 2005.

3. SCOTLAND: POPULATION HISTORY AND RELATED STUDIES

Anderson, Michael, and Donald J. Morse. "High Fertility, High Emigration, Low Nuptiality: Adjustment Processes in Scotland's Demographic Experience, 1861–1914." *Population Studies* 47, no. 1 (March 1993): 5–25.

Bowley, A. L., et al. *The Third Winter of Unemployment: The Report of an Enquiry Undertaken in the Autumn of 1922.* London: P. S. King & Son, n. d. [c. 1923]. Contains an important report on unemployment in Glasgow in September 1922 at pp. 188–217.
Boyd, Kenneth M. *Scottish Church Attitudes to Sex, Marriage and the Family, 1850–1914.* Edinburgh: Donald, 1980.
Carstairs, Andrew M. *The Tayside Industrial Population: The Changing Character and Distribution of the Industrial Population in the Tayside Area, 1911–1951.* Dundee: Abertay Historical Society, 1974.
Cooper, Thomas M. "The Number and Distribution of the Population of Medieval Scotland." *Scottish Historical Review* 26 (1947): 2–9.
Crowe, P. R. "The Population of the Scottish Lowlands." *Scottish Geographical Magazine* 40, no. 3 (1927): 147–67.
Davies, G. L. "The Parish of North Uist." *Scottish Geographical Magazine* 72, no. 2 (1956): 65–73. A pioneering case study of population change in the Outer Hebrides.
Dingwall, Helen M. *Late Seventeenth-Century Edinburgh: A Demographic Study.* Aldershot, England: Scolar Press, 1994.
Flinn, Michael, ed., with contributions from Duncan Adamson and Robin Lobban. *Scottish Population History: From the 17th Century to the 1930s.* Cambridge: Cambridge University Press, 1977. A pioneering work mainly concerned with the pre-1939 period.
General Register Office for Scotland. *Scotland's Population—2004: The Registrar General's Annual Review of Demographic Trends, 150th Edition.* Edinburgh: General Register Office for Scotland, 2005. Available online.
Hogan, E. A. "Population Changes, 1861–1951." *Annual Report of the Registrar-General for Scotland,* 1953, pp. 8–95.
Houston, Robert A. *Scottish Literacy and the Scottish Identity: Illiteracy and Society in Scotland and Northern England, 1600–1800.* Cambridge: Cambridge University Press, 1985.
Houston, Robert A., and I. D. Whyte, eds. *Scottish Society, 1500–1800.* Cambridge: Cambridge University Press, 1989.
Jones, Huw R., ed. *Population Change in Contemporary Scotland.* Norwich, England: Geo Books, 1984.
Kyd, James G., ed. *Scottish Population Statistics, including Webster's Analysis of Population, 1755.* Edinburgh: T. and A. Constable, 1952. Reprinted in 1975.
Kyd, John G., et al. *Scotland's Changing Population.* London: Scottish Council of Social Services, 1947.
Lewis, J., and A. Townsend, eds. *The North–South Divide: Regional Change in Britain the 1980s.* London: Paul Chapman, 1989.
Lloyd, O., F. Williams, W. Berry, and C. Florey. *An Atlas of Mortality in Scotland.* London: Croom Helm, 1987.
Lumb, Rosemary. *Migration in the Highlands and Islands of Scotland.* Aberdeen, Scotland: Institute for the Study of Sparsely Populated Areas, University of Aberdeen, 1980.
Macdonald, Donald F. *Scotland's Shifting Population, 1770–1850.* Glasgow: Jackson, Son and Co., 1937. A classic work and the first academic study of the subject. It was reprinted in 1978 by Porcupine Press, Philadelphia.
Migration Watch UK. *The Outlook for Scotland's Population: Does Scotland Need Its Own Immigration Policy?* Briefing Paper 10.10, June 21, 2005. Available online at www.migrationwatchuk.com/publications.asp#9.
Mitchison, Rosalind, and Leah Leneman. *Sexuality and Social Control: Scotland 1660–1780.* Oxford: Basil Blackwell, 1989. Concerned mostly with illegitimacy.
O'Dell, Andrew. "The Population of Scotland, 1755–1931: A General Survey." *Scottish Geographical Magazine* 48, no. 5 (September 1932): 282–90.
Osborne, Richard H. "The Movement of People in Scotland, 1851–1951." *Scottish Studies* 2, part 1 (1958): 1–46.
———. "Scottish Migration Statistics: A Note." *Scottish Geographical Magazine* 72, no. 3 (1956): 153–59.
Pacione, Michael. *Glasgow: The Socio-Spatial Development of the City.* Chichester, NY: John Wiley, 1995.

Redford, Arthur. *Labour Migration in England, 1800–1850.* 2nd and rev. ed. by W. H. Chaloner. Manchester: Manchester University Press, 1964. Contains some Scottish material.

Snodgrass, Catherine P. "Recent Population Changes in Scotland." *Scottish Geographical Magazine* 60, no. 2 (1944): 33–38.

4. IMMIGRATION ENCYCLOPEDIAS AND POPULATION HISTORIES

Anderson, Michael, ed. *British Population History: From the Black Death to the Present Day.* Cambridge: Cambridge University Press, 1996

Cordasco, Francesco, ed. *Dictionary of American Immigration History.* Lanham, MD: Scarecrow Press, 1990.

Haines, Michael R., and Richard H. Steckel, eds. *A Population History of North America.* New York: Cambridge University Press, 2000.

Jupp, James, ed. *The Australian People: An Encyclopedia of the Nation: Its People and Their Origins.* 2nd ed. New York: Cambridge University Press, 2001.

Magocsi, Paul R. M., ed. *Encyclopedia of Canada's Peoples.* Toronto: University of Toronto Press, 1999. The entry on the "Scots" by J. M. Bumstead (pp. 1115–42) is of special importance and value.

Rothenbacher, Franz, ed. *The Societies of Europe: The European Population, 1850–1945.* Houndmills, Basingstoke, England: Palgrave Macmillan, 2002. A detailed statistical handbook of population history with an extensive bibliography; unusually for a work of this kind, Scotland receives separate attention as opposed to simply being included in the "United Kingdom."

Thernstrom, Stephan, Ann Orlov, and Oscar Handlin, eds. *Harvard Encyclopedia of Ethnic Groups.* Cambridge, MA: Harvard University Press, 1980. A pioneer work with much information on the Scots.

Wrigley, E. A., and R. S. Schofield. *The Population History of England, 1541–1871: A Reconstruction.* London: Edward Arnold, 1981.

5. ROBERT WALLACE AND THE POPULATION DEBATE

Glass, David V. *Numbering the People: The Eighteenth-Century Population Controversy and the Development of Census and Vital Statistics in Britain.* Farnborough, England: D. C. Heath, 1973. Contains a number of original documents as well as the origins of the population debate.

Godwin, William. *Enquiry Concerning Political Justice and Its Influence on Modern Morals and Happiness.* Harmondsworth, England: Penguin, 1976. First published in 1798.

Malthus, Robert. *An Essay on the Principle of Population.* Harmondsworth, England: Penguin, 1970. Contains the text of the original essay and the *Summary View of the Principle of Population.* The introduction should be treated with caution.

———. *An Essay on the Principle of Population.* Vol. I, 6th ed. London: John Murray, 1826. Gives Malthus's views on Scotland (pp. 4590 ff.). Available as a Google book.

Price, Richard. *An Essay on the Population of England, from the Revolution to the Present Time.* London: T. Cadell, 1780. Available on microfilm.

Wallace, Robert. *A Dissertation on the Numbers of Mankind, in Ancient and Modern Times.* 2nd and rev. ed. London: Constable, Hunter, Park, and Hunter, 1809. First published in 1753 and reprinted 1969; available as a Google book.

William Godwin. *Of Population: An Enquiry Concerning the Power of Increase in the Numbers of Mankind Being an Answer to Mr. Malthus's Essay on That Subject.* London: Longman, Hurst, Rees, Orme, and Brown, 1820. Can be accessed online chapter by chapter.

Youngson, A. J. "Alexander Webster and His 'Account of the Number of People in Scotland in the Year 1755.'" *Population Studies* 15, no. 2 (November 1961): 198–200.

6. SELECTED PRE-1830 SCOTTISH SOURCES

Cleland, James. *Enumeration of the Inhabitants of the City of Glasgow and County of Lanark for the Government Census of M.DCCC.XXXI*. 2nd ed. Glasgow: J. Smith & Son, 1832. Available in microform.

———. *A Historical Account of Bills of Mortality, and the Probability of Human Life, in Glasgow and Other Large Towns*. Glasgow: E. Khull, 1836. Available in microform.

———. *Statistical Tables Relative to the City of Glasgow*. 3rd ed. Glasgow: J. Lumsden & Son, 1823. Available in microform.

Defoe, Daniel. *A Tour through the Whole Island of Great Britain*. Edited by G. D. H. Cole. London: Peter Davies, 1927. First published in 1727. The second volume of this edition, unlike later expurgated abridgements, which give the impression that Defoe was writing a popular travel guide, includes the complete text to the Scottish section; Defoe's introduction to this section is particularly important.

Forsyth, Robert. *The Beauties of Scotland: Containing a Clear and Full Account of the Agriculture, Commerce, Mines, and Manufactures; Population, Cities, Towns, Villages, &c. of Each County*. Vol. III. Edinburgh: Arch. Constable & Co., and John Brown, 1806. Contains population count of Glasgow and its suburbs for 1802. Available as a Google book.

Sinclair, Sir John. *Analysis of the Statistical Account of Scotland: A General View of the History of That Country and Discussions on Some Important Branches of Political Economy*. Edinburgh: William Tait, 1831. Originally issued in two volumes in 1825–1826, this work is exactly what it says it is. It contains important statistics not published elsewhere (notably an age distribution by persons by ten-year groups for 1811) and an extensive commentary. Available as a Google book.

———. *The Statistical Account of Scotland, Drawn Up from the Communications of the Ministers of the Different Parishes*. 21 vols. Edinburgh: William Creech, 1791–1799. The first series, together with Webster's census, is fundamental for the study of eighteenth-century Scottish demography. A second series was published from 1834 to 1845; both these *Accounts* can be accessed by a modest subscription online at http://edina.ac.uk/stat-acc-scot/access/prices.html.

7. SCOTTISH NATIONALISM AND SCOTLAND'S FUTURE

Bowie, James A. *The Future of Scotland: A Survey of the Present Position, with Some Proposals for Future Policy*. Edinburgh: W. & R. Chambers, 1939.

Brown, J. Gordon, and Robin F. Cook, eds. *Scotland—the Real Divide: Poverty and Deprivation in Scotland*. Edinburgh: Mainstream Pub, 1983.

Devine, Thomas M., ed. *Scotland and the Union, 1707–2007*. Edinburgh: Edinburgh University Press, 2008.

———, ed. *Scotland's Shame? Bigotry and Sectarianism in Modern Scotland*. Edinburgh: Mainstream, 2000.

Finlay, Ian. *Scotland*. London: Oxford University Press, 1945.

Gibb, Andrew D. *Scotland in Eclipse*. London: Humphrey Toulmin, 1930.

———. *Scotland Resurgent*. Stirling: Eneas Mackay, 1950.

Gibb, Andrew. *Glasgow: The Making of a City*. London: Croom Helm, 1983.

MacDiarmid, Hugh. *Albyn: or, Scotland and the Future*. London: Kegan Paul, 1927.

Macdonell, Archibald G. *My Scotland*. Jarrolds: A. G. MacDonell, 1937. Concerned with the Highlands.

MacEwen, Alexander M. *The Thistle and the Rose: Scotland's Problems To-day*. Edinburgh: Oliver and Boyd, 1928.

Maclehose, Alexander, and Sir John Orr. *The Scotland of Our Sons*. London: A. Maclehose, 1937. Concerned with the Highlands.

Murray, George T. *Scotland: The New Future*. Glasgow: Scottish Television; Blackie, 1973.

Pittock, Murray. *The Road to Independence? Scotland since the Sixties.* London: Reaktion, 2008.
Quigley, Hugh. *The Highlands of Scotland.* 4th ed. London: B. T. Batsford, 1949. First published in 1936.
———. *A Plan for the Highlands. Proposals for a Highland Development Board.* London: Methuen, 1936.
Scott, Paul H. *Scotland Resurgent: Comments on the Cultural and Political Revival of Scotland.* Edinburgh: Saltire Society, 2003.
Scottish Council (Development and Industry), Growth Strategy Committee. *A Future for Scotland: A Study of the Key Factors Associated with Growth in Scotland, and Proposals Necessary to Achieve Success in the '80's and Beyond.* Edinburgh: The Council, 1973. Discusses economic conditions in Scotland from 1918 to 1973.
Thomson, George M. *Scotland—That Distressed Area.* Edinburgh: Porpoise Press, 1935.
Underwood, Robert, ed. *The Future of Scotland.* London: Croom Helm for the Nevis Institute, 1977.

8. ECONOMIC HISTORY

Cameron, Alexander D. *The Caledonian Canal.* Lavenham: Dalton, 1972.
Campbell, Roy H. *The Rise and Fall of Scottish Industry, 1709–1939.* Edinburgh: Donald, 1980.
Devine, Thomas M., ed. *Farm Servants and Labour in Lowland Scotland, 1770–1914.* Edinburgh: J. Donald, 1984.
Dow, Alexander C., and Sheila C. Dow, eds. *The History of Scottish Economic Thought.* London: Routledge, 2006.
Hunt, E. H. *Regional Wage Variations in Britain, 1850–1914.* Oxford: Clarendon Press, 1973. Divides Scotland into three broad regions and discusses population change including migration.
Jones, David T., et al. *Rural Scotland during the War.* London: Oxford University Press, 1926.
Knox, William. *Industrial Nation: Work, Culture and Society in Scotland, 1800 to Present.* Edinburgh: Edinburgh University Press, 1999.
Lee, Clive H. *Scotland and the United Kingdom: The Economy and the Union in the Twentieth Century.* Manchester: Manchester University Press, 1995.
Lenman, Bruce. *An Economic History of Modern Scotland, 1660–1976.* London: Batsford, 1977.
Rankin, Keith. "New Zealand's Gross Domestic Product, 1859–1939." *Review of Income and Wealth* 38, no. 1 (1991): 49–69. Available online.
Scott, William R., and J. Cunnison. *The Industries of the Clyde Valley during the War.* Oxford: Clarendon Press, 1924.
Urquhart, M. *Gross Domestic Product, Canada, 1870–1926: The Derivation of Estimates.* Kingston, Ontario: McGill-Queen's University, 1993. Available as a Google book.
Whatley, Christopher A. *The Industrial Revolution in Scotland.* Cambridge: Cambridge University Press, 1997. A general account with a detailed bibliography.
Whyte, Ian D. *Scotland before the Industrial Revolution: An Economic and Social History, c.1050–1750.* London: Longman, 1995.
Williamson, Samuel H. "What Was the U.S. GDP Then?" *Measuring Worth*, August 2013. http://measuringworth.com/usgdp.

9. BRITISH EMIGRATION

Berthoff, Rowland T. *British Immigrants in Industrial America, 1790–1950.* Cambridge, MA: Harvard University Press, 1953. Despite its age, this pioneering study remains of value,

particularly by drawing attention to the importance of return migration. It was reprinted in 1976.
Bridge, Carl, and Kent Fedorowich, eds. *The British World: Diaspora, Culture, and Identity.* London: Frank Cass, 2003.
Erickson, Charlotte J. *Leaving England: Essays on British Emigration in the Nineteenth Century.* Ithaca, NY: Cornell University Press, 1994.
———. "Who Were the English and Scots Emigrants to the United States in the Late Nineteenth Century?" In *Population and Social Change*, edited by D. V. Glass and Roger Revelle, 347–81. London: Edward Arnold, 1972. This chapter contains an analysis of occupations.
McCarthy, Angela, ed. *Personal Narratives of Irish and Scottish Migration, 1921–65: 'For Spirit and Adventure.'* Manchester: Manchester University Press, 2007.
Murdoch, Alexander. *British Emigration, 1603–1914.* Houndmills, Basingstoke, Hampshire: Palgrave Macmillan, 2004.
Richards, Eric. *Britannia's Children: Emigration from England, Scotland, Wales and Ireland since 1600.* London: Hambledon and London, 2004. Excellent general account.
Scotch Church [Manchester] Young Men's Society. *Statistical Report of the Scottish Population of Manchester, Taken in 1837.* Manchester: James Galt, 1838. Available in microform. One of the earliest surveys of an emigrant community.
Thomas, Brinley. *Migration and Economic Growth: A Study of Great Britain and the Atlantic Economy.* 2nd ed. Cambridge: Cambridge University Press, 1973. Contains much useful data on Scottish migration, but the author's claim (p. 356) that there are no age statistics for the Scots in the United States before 1930 is wrong, and the author's source for this statement does not exist; for the correction see the entry for George Arner, section 16. Many of the author's interpretations should be handled with care.

10. SCOTLAND: EMIGRATION AND IMMIGRATION

Adams, Ian H., and Meredyth Somerville. *Cargoes of Despair and Hope: Scottish Emigration to North America 1603–1803.* Edinburgh: John Donald, 1993.
Allison, Hugh G. *Rivers Running Far: The Story of Those Who Went Away.* Kinloss: Librario, 2005.
Birrell, J. Hamilton. "Emigration with Special Reference to Scotland: A Review and A Discussion." *Scottish Geographical Magazine* 46, no. 3 (May 1930): 159–66.
Braber, Ben. *Jews in Glasgow, 1879–1939: Immigration and Integration.* London: Vallentine Mitchell in association with the European Jewish Publications Society, 2007.
Brander, Michael. *The Emigrant Scots.* London: Constable, 1982. Covers the period from 1300 to 1900.
Brock, Jeanette M. *The Mobile Scot: A Study of Emigration and Migration, 1861–1911.* Edinburgh: John Donald, 1999.
Bumstead, J. M. *The People's Clearances: Highland Emigration to British North America, 1770–1815.* Edinburgh: Edinburgh University Press, 1982.
Cage, R. A., ed. *The Scots Abroad: Labour, Capital, Enterprise, 1750–1914.* London: Croom Helm, 1985.
Clark, Helen, Lorraine Dick, and Basabi Fraser. *Peoples of Edinburgh: Our Multicultural City: Personal Recollections, Experiences, and Photographs.* Edinburgh: City of Edinburgh Council, Department of Recreation, Museums and Galleries, 1996.
Craig, David. *On the Crofters' Trail: In Search of the Clearance Highlanders.* London: Cape, 1990.
Devine, Thomas M. *Scotland's Empire and the Shaping of the Americas, 1600–1815.* London: Allen Lane, 2003.
———, ed. *Scottish Emigration and Scottish Society: Proceedings of the Scottish Historical Studies Seminar, University of Strathclyde 1990–91.* Edinburgh: John Donald, 1992.
———. *To the Ends of the Earth: Scotland's Global Diaspora, 1750–2010.* London: Allen Lane, 2011.

Devine, Thomas M., and Willie Orr. *The Great Highland Famine: Hunger, Emigration, and the Scottish Highlands in the Nineteenth Century.* Edinburgh: J. Donald, 1988.

Dobson, David. *Emigrants and Adventurers from Southern Scotland.* St. Andrews: D. Dobson, 1994. Genealogy.

———. *Scottish Emigration to Colonial America, 1607–1785.* Athens: University of Georgia Press, 2004. Originally published in 1994, this an excellent, accessible survey work.

Edward, Mary. *Who Belongs to Glasgow?* Rev. ed. Edinburgh: Luath Press, 2008.

Gray, Malcolm. *Scots on the Move: Scots Migrants, 1750–1914.* Dundee: The Economic and Social History Society of Scotland, 1990.

Handley, James Edmund. *The Irish in Modern Scotland.* Cork: Cork University Press, 1947.

Harper, Marjory. *Adventurers and Exiles: The Great Scottish Exodus.* London: Profile, 2003.

———, ed. *Emigrant Homecomings: The Return Movement of Emigrants, 1600–2000.* Manchester: Manchester University Press, 2005.

———. *Emigration from Scotland between the Wars: Opportunity or Exile?* Manchester: Manchester University Press, 1998. A thorough treatment of the issues, particularly strong on policy.

Hollingsworth, T. H. *Migration: A Study Based on Scottish Experience between 1939 and 1964.* Edinburgh: Oliver & Boyd, 1970. Mainly concerned with internal migration and migration to other parts of the United Kingdom.

Hunter, James. *Scottish Exodus: Travels among a Worldwide Clan.* Edinburgh: Mainstream, 2005.

Imrie, John. *The Scot at Home and Abroad.* Toronto: Imrie, Graham, 1898. Available on microfilm.

Knox, W. W. *Migration: Scotland's Shifting Population, 1840–1940.* A general survey, available at www.scran.ac.uk/scotland/pdf/SP2_7migration.pdf.

Koczy, Leon. *Haste Ye Back to Scotland: An Extended Lecture Given at the Annual Meeting of the Scottish-Polish Society in Edinburgh on the 26th August 1977.* Leon Koczy, 1977.

Lamont, Stewart. *When Scotland Ruled the World: The Story of the Golden Age of Genius, Creativity and Exploration.* London: HarperCollins, 2002. A handy and reliable set of lives of Scottish achievers.

McBride, Terence. *The Experience of Irish Migrants to Glasgow, Scotland, 1863–1891: A New Way of Being Irish.* Lewiston, NY; Lampeter, South West Wales: Edwin Mellen Press, 2006.

McIntosh, Ian. *English People in Scotland: An Invisible Minority.* Lewiston, NY; Lampeter, South West Wales: Edwin Mellen Press, 2008.

McLeod, Mona. *Leaving Scotland.* Edinburgh: National Museums of Scotland, 1996.

Ó Catháin, Máirtín. *Irish Republicanism in Scotland, 1858–1916.* Dublin: Irish Academic Press, 2007.

Perceval-Maxwell, M. *The Scottish Migration to Ulster in the Reign of James I.* London: Routledge & Kegan Paul, 1973.

Richardson, Ralph. "Italian Emigration to Scotland." *Scottish Geographical Magazine* 29 (November 1913): 581–85.

Scottish Association of Family History Societies. *European Immigration into Scotland: Proceedings of the 4th Annual Conference of the Scottish AssocICtion of Family History Societies, September 12th 1992.* Glasgow: Glasgow & West of Scotland Family History Society, 1993.

Simpson, Grant G., ed. *The Scottish Soldier Abroad, 1247–1967.* Edinburgh: John Donald, 1992.

Smout, T. C., Ned C. Landsman, and Thomas M. Divine. "Scottish Emigration in the Seventeenth and Eighteenth Centuries." In *Europeans on the Move: Studies on European Migration, 1500–1800,* edited by Nicholas Canny, 76–112. Oxford: Clarendon Press, 1994. The best general account available with a detailed bibliography at pp. 289–95.

Watson, Murray. *Being English in Scotland.* Edinburgh: Edinburgh University Press, 2003.

Wright, Robert E. *The Economics of New Immigration to Scotland.* Edinburgh: David Hume Institute, 2008.

11. SCOTTISH-BORN IN AUSTRALIA AND NEW ZEALAND

Brooking, Tom, and Jennie Coleman, eds. *The Heather and the Fern: Scottish Migration and New Zealand Settlement.* Dunedin, New Zealand: University of Otago Press, 2003.
Butterworth, Susan. *Chips off the Auld Rock: Shetlanders in New Zealand.* Wellington: Shetland Society of Wellington, 1997.
Foden, Frank. *Connections: Orkney and Australia.* Kirkwall, Orkney, UK: Herald, 1992.
Frost, Lucy. *Abandoned Women: Scottish Convicts Exiled beyond the Seas.* Sydney: Allen & Unwin, 2012. A study of women and their children sent to Tasmania in 1838.
Hall, Mary B., compiler. *The Largs Australians.* Largs: Largs & District Historical Society, 1995.
Lucas, David. *The Welsh, Irish, Scots and English in Australia: A Demographic Profile with Statistical Appendix.* Canberra: Australian Institute of Multicultural Affairs, 1987.
Macmillan, David S. *Scotland and Australia, 1788–1850: Emigration, Commerce and Investment.* Oxford: Clarendon Press, 1967.
McCarthy, Angela. *Scottishness and Irishness in New Zealand since 1840.* Manchester: Manchester University Press, 2011.
Pearce, G. L. *The Scots of New Zealand.* Collins: Auckland, 1976.
Phillips, Jock, and Terry Hearn. *Settlers: New Zealand Immigrants from England, Ireland and Scotland, 1800–1945.* Auckland: Auckland University Press, 2008. An expanded version of this work is available at www.nzhistory.net.nz/culture/home-away-from-home/sources.
Prentis, Malcolm D. *The Scots in Australia: A Study of New South Wales, Victoria and Queensland, 1788–1900.* Sydney: Sydney University Press, 1983.
Watson, Don. *Caledonia Australia: Scottish Highlanders on the Frontier of Australia.* Sydney: Collins, 1984.

12. SCOTTISH-BORN IN CANADA

Calder, Jenni. *Scots in Canada.* Edinburgh: Luath Press, 2003.
Campey, Lucille H. *The Scottish Pioneers of Upper Canada, 1784–1855.* Toronto: Natural Heritage Books, 2005.
———. *An Unstoppable Force: The Scottish Exodus to Canada.* Toronto: Dundurn, 2008.
———. *With Axe and Bible: The Scottish Pioneers of New Brunswick, 1784–1874.* Toronto: Natural Heritage Books, 2007.
Galbraith, John Kenneth. *The Scotch.* Baltimore, MD: Penguin Books, 1964. A perceptive memoir of the Scottish community on Lake Erie set mainly in the 1920s.
Harper, Marjory, and Michael E. Vance, eds. *Myth, Migration, and the Making of Memory: Scotia and Nova Scotia, c.1700–1990.* Halifax, Nova Scotia: Fernwood, 1999.
MacDonell, Margaret. *The Emigrant Experience: Songs of Highland Emigrants in North America.* Toronto: University of Toronto Press, 1982. www.electricscotland.com/history/canada/scot/index.htm.
Mackay, Donald. *Scotland Farewell: The People of the Hector.* Edinburgh: Birlinn, 2006. Originally published in 1980s by McGraw-Hill Ryerson, this work deals with the Scottish settlement of Nova Scotia from 1763 to 1876.
McLean, Marianne. *The People of Glengarry: Highlanders in Transition, 1745–1820.* Montreal: McGill-Queens University Press, 1991.
Messamore, Barbara J., ed. *Canadian Migration Patterns from Britain and North America.* Ottawa: University of Ottawa Press, 2004.
Norton, Wayne R. *Help Us to a Better Land: Crofter Colonies in the Prairie West.* Regina, Saskatchewan: Canadian Plains Research Center, University of Regina, 1994.

13. SCOTTISH-BORN IN THE UNITED STATES

Bailyn, Bernard. *Voyagers to the West: A Passage in the Peopling of America on the Eve of the Revolution.* New York: Knopf, 1986.
Fischer, David Hackett. *Albion's Seed: Four British Folkways in America.* New York: Oxford University Press, 1989.
Fitzgerald, Patrick, and Steve Ickringill, eds. *Atlantic Crossroads: Historical Connections between Scotland, Ulster, and North America.* Newtownards, County Down, Northern Ireland: Colourpoint, 2001.
Glazier, Ira A., ed. *Emigration from the United Kingdom to America: Lists of Passengers Arriving at U.S. Ports.* Lanham, MD: Scarecrow Press, 2006 to date. A detailed listing of British immigrants to the United States who arrived in New York that is planned to cover the period between 1870 and 1897. By late 2014, eighteen volumes have been published for arrivals from 1870 to 1881.
Landsman, Ned C., ed. *Nation and Province in the First British Empire: Scotland and the Americas, 1600–1800.* Lewisburg, PA: Bucknell University Press in association with the Eighteenth-Century Scottish Studies Society, 2001.
Leyburn, James G. *The Scotch-Irish: A Social History.* Chapel Hill: University of North Carolina Press, 1962. Despite its age and subsequent research, this is a study that contains much valuable information based on primary sources.
Millett, Stephen M. *The Scottish Settlers of America: the 17th and 18th Centuries.* Baltimore, MD: Clearfield, 1999.
Murdoch, Alexander. *Scotland and America, c.1600–c.1800.* New York: Palgrave Macmillan, 2010.
Newton, Michael S. *We're Indians Sure Enough: The Legacy of the Scottish Highlanders in the United States.* Saorsa Media, 2001.
Van Vugt, William E. *British Buckeyes: The English, Scots, and Welsh in Ohio, 1700–1900.* Kent, OH: Kent State University Press, 2006.

14. SCOTTISH-BORN IN OTHER COUNTRIES

Dobson, David. *Scots in Poland, Russia and the Baltic States: 1550–1850.* Baltimore, MD: Clearfield, 2000.
Drummond, Barb. *Losing El Dorado: Scots in Latin America.* Bristol: Barb Drummond, 2008. A nineteenth-century study.
Karras, Alan L. *Sojourners in the Sun: Scottish Migrants in Jamaica and the Chesapeake, 1740–1800.* Ithaca: Cornell University Press, 1992.
MacKenzie, John M., and Nigel R. Dalziel. *The Scots in South Africa: Ethnicity, Identity, Gender, and Race, 1772–1914.* Manchester: Manchester University Press, 2007.
McCrae, Alister. *Scots in Burma: Golden Times in a Golden Land.* Edinburgh: Kiscadale, 1990.
Stewart, Iain A. D., ed. *From Caledonia to the Pampas: Two Accounts by Early Scottish Emigrants to the Argentine.* East Linton, East Lothian, UK: Tuckwell Press, 2000.

15. STATISTICAL SOURCES: SCOTLAND

Note: The main site for official Scottish statistics is www.gro-scotland.gov.uk.

Adam, D. T. "Life-Table for Scotland, Based on the Census Enumerations of 1891 and 1901, and on the Recorded Deaths for the Decennium 1891–1900." *Journal of the Royal Statistical Society* 67, no. 3 (September 1904): 448–78.

Bateman, John. *The Great Landowners of Great Britain and Ireland.* 4th ed. London: Harrison, 1883. Reprinted with an introduction by David Spring, Leicester University Press, 1971. Lists the main land owners for every Scottish county by name, size, and income.

Carrier, N. H., and J. R. Jeffery. *External Migration: A Study of the Available Statistics, 1815–1950.* General Register Office, Studies on Medical and Population Subjects no. 6. London: Her Majesty's Stationery Office, 1953. A primary source for British emigration, although hard to obtain, its main Scottish figures were summarized in Michael Flinn's study.

Great Britain, Office of Population Censuses and Surveys. *International Migration: Migrants Entering or Leaving the United Kingdom.* 1974 to date.

Lee, Clive H. *British Regional Employment Statistics, 1841–1971.* Cambridge: Cambridge University Press, 1979. This remarkable work includes industry and occupational data for eight Scottish regions.

Registrar General for Scotland. *Annual Reports,* 1855 to date. The primary published source for Scotland along with the population census that the registrar general conducted for Scotland from 1861. For the pre-1920 period, there are two types of annual reports, a summary and a detailed version. Both types of reports up to 1919 are available from www.histpop.org.

Scottish Executive. *Scottish Economic Report.* Edinburgh: Stationery Office, 2000 to date.

Scottish Office. *Scottish Economic Bulletin.* Edinburgh: Stationery Office, 1971–1999.

Scottish Statistical Office. *Digest of Scottish Statistics.* Edinburgh: Scottish Statistical Office, 1953–1971. Originally issued by the Scottish Home Department.

———. *Scottish Abstract of Statistics.* London: Her Majesty's Stationery Office, 1971–1998.

16. STATISTICAL SOURCES: SCOTTISH-BORN OUTSIDE SCOTLAND

16.0. General

Ferenczi, Imre, and Walter F. Willcox. *International Migrations: Volume I—Statistics.* New York: National Bureau of Economic Research, 1929. Although there is no Scottish section, this work contains occasional Scottish figures of great value; notably, it conveniently lists Scottish disembarkations in Canada from 1829 to 1880 on p. 360. It is a gold mine of historical data, and sources and can be downloaded for particular nationalities from www.nber.org/books/fere29-1.

16.1 Australia

The two main statistical sources for the Scots in Australia are the census of population and the vital statistics publications. Printed reports for both collections are available as pdf files from 1911.

The catalogue for the Australian Bureau of Statistics website is listed at www.abs.gov.au/websitedbs/D3310114.nsf/4a256353001af3ed4b2562bb00121564/1c25c0499720503fca25757100019873f!OpenDocument.

The pre-1911 censuses for the Australian colonies can be accessed at http://hccda.ada.edu.au.

After the 1961 census, most of the detailed information for the Scots was no longer published, and obtaining it has become an expensive undertaking, raising the value of the following sources:

Hugo, Graeme. *Atlas of the Australian People—1996 Census: National Overview.* Adelaide, South Australia: University of Adelaide, Department of Geographical and Environmental Studies, 1999.

Hugo, Graeme, and Chris Maher. *Atlas of the Australian People—1991 Census: National Overview.* Canberra, Australian Capital Territory: Bureau of Immigration, Multicultural and Population Research, 1995.

Lucas, David. *The Welsh, Irish, Scots and English in Australia: A Demographic Profile with Statistical Appendix.* Canberra, Australian Capital Territory: Australian Institute of Multicultural Affairs, 1987.

16.2 Canada

Canada. Population Census. A listing of the tables in the Canadian census, but not their contents, can be accessed at http://datalib.chass.utoronto.ca/major/censusag.htm.

Canada, Department of Manpower and Immigration/Employment and Immigration Canada. *Immigration Statistics.* Ottawa, 1966–1992; continued as Canada, Minister of Public Works and Government. *Citizenship and Immigration Statistics.* Ottawa, 1993–1996. Total arrivals and departure statistics for the Scots and other nationalities from 1901 were published in the *Canada Year Book.*

Individual records can be searched for the censuses conducted before 1921 as follows:

1871:

First General Census of Canada, 1871. www.bac-lac.gc.ca/eng/census/1871/Pages/1871.aspx. Note: Volume 4 of the printed version of the census includes the all the birthplaces collected by previous censuses, mainly from 1842, but there are a few pre-1800 figures, too.

1881:

Second General Census of Canada, 1881. www.bac-lac.gc.ca/eng/census/1881/Pages/1881.aspx. This database can be searched by name and keyword (e.g. Scotland).

1891:

Third General Census of Canada, 1891, www.bac-lac.gc.ca/eng/census/1891/Pages/1891.aspx

1901:

Fourth General Census of Canada, 1901. www.bac-lac.gc.ca/eng/census/1901/Pages/1901.aspx. This was the first Canadian census to contain length of residence data.

1911:

Canada, Dominion Bureau of Statistics. *Vital Statistics.* Ottawa: Dominion Bureau of Statistics. The issues for 1921 to 1950 contain statistics on Scottish-born deaths in cities and towns with ten thousand or more people and marriages as well as children born to Scottish-born parents. The geographical coverage was limited before 1925.

Fifth General Census of Canada, 1911. www.bac-lac.gc.ca/eng/census/1911/Pages/1911.aspx. The manuscript records for individuals by area are available as downloadable pdf files. The records can also searched by name at http://automatedgenealogy.com/census11.

16.3 New Zealand

The population census (1858 to date) is the primary statistical source for Scots in New Zealand. The various vital statistics publications included deaths by age for the Scots from 1909 to 1978. Apart from the *Official Year Books of New Zealand* (which are available online), other government publications of value for studying the Scots are:

New Zealand Census and Statistics Department. *Statistical Report on Population and Building.* Wellington: Census and Statistics Department, 1933–1934 to 1953–1954. This publication was renamed *Report on the Population, Migration and Building Statistics of New Zealand* from 1954 to 1955.

New Zealand Census and Statistics Office. *Statistical Report on the External Migration of the Dominion of New Zealand.* Wellington: W. A. G. Skinner, Government Printer, 1922–1932. Contains the most detailed figures on Scottish migration for any country for the 1920s.

New Zealand, Parliament, House of Representatives. *Appendix to the Journals of the House of Representatives.* The migration reports in this voluminous work are the primary source for assisted migrants, including Scots, from 1871 to 1892.

16.4 South Africa

Scots were recorded in the national population census from 1904 to 1961, but the 1921 and 1926 censuses are of special importance because of their length of residence figures for the Scots and the age by sex by length of residence tables for the "white" outside-born in 1926. Arrival and departures for the Scots from 1913 to 1956 were published in the *Official Year Books of South Africa.*

16.5 United States

The main statistical sources for the U.S. Scots are: (1) the population census, 1850 to date, which can be accessed at www.census.gov/prod/www/decennial.html, and (2) *The Statistical Abstract of the United States*, 1878 to date, and the 1976 version of *Historical Statistics of the United States.*

Arrival statistics for the Scots from 1825 to 1975 by decade are also available in Stephan Thernstrom, ed., *Harvard Encyclopedia of Ethnic Groups.* Cambridge, MA: Harvard University Press, 1980, 1047–49.

Although interest in detailed information for Western European migrants was much reduced after the 1930 census, there is important information in the 1980 census on length of residence and citizenship (section B: "Regions," tables 312 and 313), which can be supplemented by the works of Susan J. Lapham for the 1990 census listed below. Other important official works with statistics on the Scots are:

Arner, George B. L. *Age of the Foreign-Born White Population by Country of Birth.* Washington, DC: U.S. Department of Commerce, Bureau of the Census, U.S. Government Printing Office, 1933. One of a number of supplementary reports to the 1930 U.S. census, this outstanding publication contains comprehensive age statistics by sex for the Scots and other nationalities from the 1910 census, figures that were not published at the time, as well as a sample of twelve states from the 1930 census. It is available online at www.census.gov/prod/www/decennial.html.

Gibson, Campbell J., and Emily Lennon. *Historical Census Statistics on the Foreign-Born Population of the United States: 1850–1990.* Population Division Working Paper no. 29. Washington, DC: U.S. Bureau of the Census, 1999. Available online at www.census.gov/population/www/documentation/twps0029/twps0029.html.

Lapham, Susan J. *1990 Census of Population: Ancestry of the Population in the United States.* Washington, DC: U.S. Department of Commerce, Economic and Census Administration, Bureau of the Census, 1993.

Lapham, Susan J., and Patricia A. Montgomery. *1990 Census of Population: Detailed Ancestry Groups for States.* Washington, DC: U.S. Department of Commerce, Economic and Census Administration, Bureau of the Census, 1992.

Truesdell, Leon E. *Nativity and Parentage of the White Population: General Characteristics, Country of Origin, and Mother Tongue.* Washington, DC: U.S. Government Printing Office, 1943. A supplement to the 1940 census, this publication includes the Scots-born, and it is available online at www.census.gov/prod/www/decennial.html.

———. *Special Report on Foreign-Born White Families by Country of Birth of Head.* Washington, DC: U.S. Department of Commerce, Bureau of the Census, U.S. Government Printing Office, 1933. A supplement to volume 6 of the 1930 census, this publication contains a large amount of information on the Scots-born, and it is available online at www.census.gov/prod/www/decennial.html.

17. LIFE TABLES

General

Much of this work was based on life tables that are easy to find from official sites for the present but much less so for the past. For pre-1860 populations, Ansley J. Coale and Paul Demeny, *Regional Model Life Tables and Stable Populations,* 2nd ed. (New York: Academic Press, 1983), is fundamental. This is the ultimate book on the subject and a must-have work for serious students. Previously hard to obtain, or available only as battered, expensive second-hand copies, it was reprinted in 2014 using a larger font size. It is also available online. There are two ways to match its model life tables to a population:

1. If the age structure is known (e.g., Scotland, 1821), and
2. If the ages by year of deaths are known (e.g., from parish registers).

If either ages or ages by year of death are accurately known, this work will provide a suite of verifiable figures including:

- Birth rate,
- Death rate,
- Infant mortality,

- Average age, and
- Births to population for those aged 15 to 44.

In addition to the United Nations, *Demographic Year Books* (available online), there is a handy selection of historical life tables in Samuel H. Preston, *Mortality Patterns in National Populations with Special Reference to Recorded Causes of Death* (New York: Academic Press, 1976), which is available as a Google book.

Australia

Official life tables were first published in the 1911 census and covered the 1880s, 1890s, and 1900s and have been prepared for each subsequent census. The Australian Bureau of Statistics has also published annual life tables since the 1970s.

For the pre-1880 period, I have used the following:

- 1861–1881: Coale and Demeny's Model West Tables, level 13
- Pre-1861: Coale and Demeny's Model West Tables, level 12

This allocation was based on the following:

Burridge, A. F. "On the Rates of Mortality in Australia." *Journal of the Institute of Actuaries and Assurance Magazine* 24 (April 1884): 352–53. Covers 1870–1881.

Pell, M. B. "On the Rates of Mortality in New South Wales and the Construction of Mortality Tables." *Journal of the Institute of Actuaries and Assurance Magazine* 21 (January 1879): 276–81. Covers 1860–1875.

Canada

The University of Montreal has made a full set of official Canadian life tables since 1831 available at www.prdh.umontreal.ca/BDLC/data/pdfs/CAN.pdf.

New Zealand

The most convenient source for historical life tables for New Zealand from 1881 to 1964 is Samuel H. Preston, *Mortality Patterns in National Populations with Special Reference to Recorded Causes of Death* (New York: Academic Press, 1976). For the pre-1881 period, I have used the same life tables as for Australia.

Scotland

Although official life tables are available for Scotland from the 1860s to the present, they are constructed in different ways and are of varying accuracy. To get around these problems and to ensure consistency and accuracy, I have prepared my own tables from 1860 to 2012 using figures from the *Annual Reports of the Registrar-General for Scotland* and an online template constructed by the Office for National Statistics based on the method devised by Chin L. Chiang, even though there are few differences between these tables and the official ones since about 1960. This template, which produced superior results for the pre-1940 era, can be downloaded from www.ons.gov.uk/ons/search/index.html?pageSize=50&newquery=ONS+Template+Life+table.

As the pre-1931 life tables may still be of interest, here are their locations:

The *Detailed Annual Reports of the Registrar General for Scotland* contain earlier life tables; see 1903, pp. xciii–xcix (1860–1900), and the supplement for 1877 (pp. liv–lxiii), which sets out the first full official life table by Dr. William Robertson based on the 1871 census. These reports can be accessed from the histpop website.

Dunlop, James C. "The Expectation of Life in Scotland in the Year 1911." *Transactions of the Faculty of Actuaries* 70 (1915): 357–78.

———. "Scottish Life Tables, 1921." *Transactions of the Faculty of Actuaries* 10, part 1, no. 92 (1924): 1–22.

South Africa

The first official life tables for South Africa were prepared for 1920–1922 (United Nations, *Demographic Year Book*, 1953, pp. 304–5). As they show that mortality in South Africa was much closer to England and Wales than for Australasia, I used the official life tables for England and Wales for the earlier years as published in Samuel H. Preston, *Mortality Patterns in National Populations with Special Reference to Recorded Causes of Death* (New York: Academic Press, 1976).

United States

The older life tables for the United States are now obsolete and have been replaced by the following collections:

Bell, Felicitie C., and Michael L. Miller. *Life Tables for the United States Social Security Area, 1900–2010, Actuarial Study No. 20*. Social Security Administration; Office of the Chief Actuary, SSA Publication No. 11–11536, 2005. This work can be downloaded from www.ssa.gov/oact/NOTES/pdf_studies/study120.pdf.

Hacker, J. David. "Decennial Life Tables for the White Population of the United States, 1790–1900." *Historical Methods* 43, no. 3 (April–June 2010): 45–79. Available online at www.ncbi.nlm.nih.gov/pmc/articles/PMC2885717.

18. POPULATION AND RELATED WORKS

Cipolla, Carlo M. *The Economic History of World Population.* 7th ed. Harmondsworth, England: Penguin, 1978. A masterly work of compression, scholarship, and style.

Coale, Ansley J., and Susan C. Watkins, eds. *The Decline of Fertility in Europe.* Princeton, NJ: Princeton University Press, 1986. Based on regional information for Western European countries, including Scotland.

Jones, Huw. *Population Geography.* 2nd ed. London: Paul Chapman, 1990. This work has some Scottish examples.

Lamb, H. H. *Climate, History and the Modern World.* London: Methuen, 1982.

McEvedy, Colin, and Richard Jones. *Atlas of World Population History.* Harmondsworth, England: Penguin, 1978.

Siegel, Jacob S., and David A. Swanson, eds. *The Methods and Materials of Demography.* 2nd ed. San Diego, CA: Elsevier Academic Press, 2004. The standard work on demography, this is a one-volume revised abridgement of a work originally published in two volumes by the U.S. government printer in 1972. The older work is much more detailed, has an international perspective, and, despite its age, is indispensable for serious students interested in population sources and problems other than those of the United States; thankfully, it is available as a Google book.

Woods, Robert. *Population Analysis in Geography.* London: Longman, 1979.

Index

Aberdeen, 11, 15, 19–20, 29
aborigines, Australian, 13, 14
agricultural employment, 45, 47–48, 104
American Civil War, 80
American Declaration of Independence, Scottish signatories to, 61
American War of Independence, 59, 60
Anderson, Michael and Donald J. Morse, 38
Antonine Wall, 13
army, 31, 32, 45, 55, 59–60, 61, 75
Australia, 47–48, 67, 68, 103, 116–117

Bailyn, Bernard, 56, 59
Baptists, 88, 92
Bateman, John, 44
Belfast, 47, 53
Bell, Alexander Graham, 66
Berthoff, Rowland, 82
Bible, supremacy of, 16
birth rate. *See* fertility
Black Death, 30
Black Watch, 75
Boer Wars, 97, 98
British Columbia, 84, 92
British North America. *See* Canada
Brown, Robert and Janet, 86
Burns, Robert, 24, 45
Butlin, Noel G., 29

Caesar, Julius, 13

Cairncross, Alec K., 2, 112
California, 92, 100, 115
Campbell, A. D., 112
Canada, 61, 62, 67, 68, 79–80, 90, 114
Carlyle, Thomas, 4
Carnegie, Andrew, 66
Carrier, N. H. and J. R. Jeffry, 2, 63
Catholics, 19, 37, 50, 88, 91, 108
childbirth, 31, 32
citizenship (US), 93, 115
clearances. *See* evictions, forced
Cleland, James, 33–34
Coale, Ansley J. and Paul Demeny, 10
Cockrone, Maggie, 101
construction employment, 52
convicts, 100
Cooper, Thomas M. Lord, 2, 27
Crowe, P. R., 2
Cumberland, Duke of, 14
Cumberland, Richard, 17

Dale, David, 11, 43
Darnley, Lord Henry, 29
David I, 15
Davies, G. L., 60
death rate. *See* mortality
Defoe, Daniel, 13, 46, 58
Detroit, 70
Devine, Thomas M., 4, 43, 55–56
diaspora, misuse of, 79
Diodorus of Sicily, 13

distressed regions, Britain, 51
divorce, Scotland, 38
Dobson, David, 4, 58
Docherty, Thomas H., 46, 99, 116, 121
domestic servants, 39, 49, 77, 87
Donald II, 15
Donaldson, Gordon, 3
Duncan, Rev. Dr. Alexander, 59
Dundas, William P. Dundas, 35
Dundee, 20, 53

economy, Scottish, 43–53
Edinburgh, 2, 13, 15, 16, 20, 32, 33, 40–41, 43, 46, 62, 66, 77, 117
England, 9, 14, 15, 16, 18, 20, 22, 23, 24, 26, 27–28, 29, 31, 35, 38, 39, 43, 45, 46, 48, 49, 50, 51, 52, 53, 55, 58, 59, 60, 61, 61–62, 64, 65, 66, 68, 69, 70, 71, 72, 73–78, 89, 91, 94, 106, 107, 111, 112, 113–114, 114, 116, 118, 119
Enlightenment, Scottish, 16, 27, 117
Erickson, Charlotte J., 3
evictions, forced, 12
exodus, misuse of, 79
expatriates, Scottish, 61–62, 72

family history, 5–7
family reconstruction, 9
family size, 41
famine, 15, 16, 21, 30, 67, 102, 118
farmers, 45, 47, 56, 84, 85, 86–87, 94, 98, 103, 105
fertility, 31, 38, 41, 106, 107–108, 118
Flinn, Michael, 3, 30, 32
Frederick the Great, 21
future, of Scotland, 70

Galbraith, John Kenneth, 86, 87, 92, 95
Gauguin, Paul, 7
Gay, John D., 76
geography, effect on Scotland, 13–15
Gibb, Andrew D., 70
Glasgow, 2, 11, 20, 23, 28–29, 32, 33–34, 36, 37, 43, 46, 47, 58, 62, 67, 77, 78
Godwin, William, 25
gold rushes, 98, 100–101
Gray, Jane, 110
Great Glen, 14

Harper, Marjory, 4
health, 55, 77, 104, 105, 109
Hebrides, 14, 60
Henry, Louis, 9
Herman, Arthur, 56, 61
Hicks, Neville, 106
Highlands, problems of definition, 11
Hill, Jessie, 6
Hill, William and Janet Young, 5–6
Hogan, Edmund A., 2, 11, 112
home ownership (US), 94
household size, 40
household structure, 89–90, 94
housing, 5, 35, 46, 52, 53, 70
Hume, David, 18
Hunt, E. H., 43

infant mortality, 31, 34
internal migration. *See* migration, internal
Ireland, 1, 44, 51, 56, 70
Irish migration, 2, 36, 37, 49–51, 67, 73, 80

Jamison, John, 5
Jews, 37, 88, 91
John of Fordun, 14
Johnson, Samuel Dr., 14, 59, 73, 117
journeys, analysis of, 63–64, 65
Jupp, James, 99

King David's sin, 16
Knibbs, George, 99
Knox, John, 37
Kyd, James G., 2

labor force, Scotland, 47, 52, 113
land hunger, as a reason for of emigration, 45, 67
land ownership, Scottish, 44
Landsman, Ned C., 4, 55–56
Lee, Clive, 43
length of residence, importance of, 10, 63, 64, 82–83, 95, 98, 114, 115
Leser, C. E. V., 112
letters, received in Scotland, 52, 60
Leyburn, James G., 57
life expectancy, 20, 30, 31, 41
life tables, 9
Lipsius, Justus, 17
literacy, 16, 104

lodgers, 91
London, 66, 70, 73, 74, 75, 76
Loyalists, 79

MacDiarmid, Hugh, 70
Macdonald, Donald F., 2, 70
MacEwen, Alexander M., 70
MacKenzie, John M. and Nigel R. Dalziel, 98
Mackie, John D., 2
MacKillop, Mother Mary, 108
Macniven, Duncan, 3
Macquarie, Lachlan, 60, 61
Malthus, Rev. Thomas R., 24–27
Manchester, 1837 survey, 74
Manitoba, 44, 79, 84, 101
manufacturing employment, 23, 27, 34, 41, 43, 45, 47, 49, 50, 53, 56, 61, 76, 77, 86–87, 111
marriage, 23, 28, 38–40, 78, 88, 106
marriage, in-marriage and out-marriage, 74, 78, 89, 107
Martin, Martin, 14
Maryland, 43
Mattingly, Harold, 5
Mayhew, Henry, 75
McEvedy, Colin and Richard Jones, 5
Medieval Warm Period, 15
Meikle, James, 46, 78
Melbourne, 100, 103
Melville, Andrew, 19
Methodists, 37, 88
migration, cost of, 56, 66, 71
migration, government-assisted, 102, 116
migration, internal, 62–63
migration, nature of, 7–8
migration, regional, 69, 77, 92
migration, results, 33, 71
migration, return, 65, 82–83, 94, 101–102
migration, seasonal, 2, 11, 70, 73, 81, 82, 94, 119
migration, theories of, 7–9, 55
mining employment, 48, 50, 52, 53, 68, 76, 77
Mitchison, Rosalind, 3, 43
modelling, of populations, 9–10
Mormons, 38
mortality, 3, 10, 21, 24, 26, 27, 28, 30–31, 32–33, 33–34, 39, 41, 55, 72, 109, 112

Morris, Ian, 26
Munch, Edvard, 46
Muret, Jean-Louis, 26

names, Scottish, 35–36, 81, 87
names, samples of, 64–65
National Party of Scotland, 71
nationalism, modern Scottish, 71
New Inverness (modern Darien), 58
New Jersey, 61, 84, 89, 115
New South Wales, 39, 48, 61, 99, 101, 103, 104, 106, 107, 108
New York State, 81, 115
New York City, 58, 70
New Zealand, 47, 68, 104, 105, 116–117
North and South Carolina, 59, 60, 85
North Atlantic Population Project, xiii, 80
North Uist, parish of, 60
Northern Ireland, 49, 50, 51, 53, 69, 94, 118
Norway, 1, 10, 14, 15, 67
Nova Scotia, 56, 61, 79

O'Dell, Andrew, 2
Oglethorpe, General James, 62
Ontario, 66, 80, 84, 86, 87, 90, 92, 100
Orwell, George, 12
Osborne, Richard H., 2, 62
Owen, Robert, 43

parish registers, 23–24, 28
Parry, M. L., 30
Perth, 19
Philadelphia, 56
Phillips, Jock and Terry Hearn, 99
physicians and surgeons, 71
Picts, 15
pipers, 60, 75
Pittsburgh, 66
population debate, 16–18, 23
population history, 3, 4–5
ports, arrivals and departures, 51, 63–64, 65, 82, 98, 100, 103
Prague, 120
Presbyterian Church, 19, 31, 37, 76, 108
Price, Rev. Richard, 18

railroads, 46, 50, 84
Redford, Arthur, 1

religion, 37–38, 88
remittances, 60, 71, 83
Richardson, Ralph, 109
Rickman, John, 23–24
Roman Catholics. *See* Catholics
Rugby, England, 78

Sage, William, 101
Samuels, Jacob and Sarah, 91
Saskatchewan, 84, 86, 101
Schörner, Field Marshal Friedrich, 120
Scotch Church Young Men's Society, 74
Scotch-Irish, 56–58, 61, 72, 79
Scoti, 15
Scots, reputation of, 1, 9
Scottish ancestry, 89, 120
Scottish co-operative movement, 49
Scottish Co-operative Wholesale Society, 112
Scottish history, study of, 2–4
Scottish Poor Law Act (1845), 67
secretary of state for Scotland, 44
Selkirk, Earl of, 44, 79
services, employment in, 47, 49
Seven Years War, 59
Shetlands, 14
shipbuilding, 47, 52, 53
Sinclair, Sir John, 14, 21–22
smallpox, 29, 31
Smith, Adam, 27, 35, 49
Smith, John, 35
Smout, T. C., 3, 4, 55–56
Snodgrass, Catherine P., 2, 70–71
Stewart, Charles Edward, 31
Strathclyde, 40, 69, 77, 113
St Andrews, 2, 6, 46, 99, 116
Sweden, 10, 16, 20–21

Switzerland, 16, 26, 30
Sydney, 70, 99, 100, 103, 110, 116

Templeman, Thomas, 27
tenancy, 94
Thirty Years War, 55
tobacco, 43, 56
Toronto, 70, 91, 103
Trevor-Roper, Hugh, 71
tuberculosis, 46

Ulster, 55–58, 72
United States, 3, 115
Urbanization, 38, 45, 45–46, 68, 70, 76, 84–85, 98, 101, 103, 117

Victoria, 103, 106, 116
Virginia, 43, 58
Vossius, Isaac, 17

wages, 49, 67, 72, 79, 83, 112
Wakefield, Edward Gibbon, 102
Wales, 23, 47, 53, 113
Wallace, Robert, 14, 16–18
war brides, 115
Webster, Alexander, 19, 57, 59
Whiston, William, 17
White, Ian, 3
Wickens, Charles, 99
Wilkie, Rev David, 20
widowhood, 6, 19, 21, 39, 46, 89
Winnipeg, 44
women, 32–33, 59–60
World War I, 53
World War II, 14
Willmott, Peter and Michael Young, 36

About the Author

James C. Docherty was born in Gosford, New South Wales, in 1949. He is a second-generation Australian; both of his parents were born in Scotland, his father in St. Andrews and his mother in Milngavie, north of Glasgow. He graduated from the University of Newcastle, New South Wales, with the University Medal in History in 1972 and went on to gain a master's and a doctorate in history from the Australian National University. Between 1978 and 2004 he was an Australian federal government employee in various departments. He was an Honorary Research Associate with the National Centre for Australian Studies at Monash University from 1990 to 1996.

His publications include *Selected Social Statistics of New South Wales, 1861–1976* (1982); *Newcastle: The Making of an Australian City* (1983); and "English Settlement in Newcastle and the Hunter Valley" in James Jupp (ed.), *The Australian People: An Encyclopedia of the Nation, Its People and Their Origins* (1988). He was an editorial consultant and contributor to *Australians: Historical Statistics* (1987); contributed the entries on Australian history, politics, industrial relations, and institutions in David Crystal (ed.), *The Cambridge Encyclopedia* (1990); and was an editor and contributor to *Workplace Bargaining in the International Context* (1993). He is the author of three historical dictionaries with Scarecrow Press: *Historical Dictionary of Australia* (1992, 1999, 2007), *Historical Dictionary of Socialism* (1997), and *Historical Dictionary of Organized Labor* (1996, 2004). He became interested in Scottish population history and migration while researching his family history.

www.ingramcontent.com/pod-product-compliance
Lightning Source LLC
Chambersburg PA
CBHW021849300426
44115CB00005B/87